MORALITY AND METAPHYSICS

In this book, Charles Larmore develops an account of morality, freedom, and reason that rejects the naturalistic metaphysics shaping much of modern thought. Reason, Larmore argues, is responsiveness to reasons, and reasons themselves are essentially normative in character, consisting in the way that physical and psychological facts – facts about the world of nature – count in favor of possibilities of thought and action that we can take up. Moral judgments are true or false in virtue of the moral reasons there are. We need therefore a more comprehensive metaphysics that recognizes a normative dimension to reality as well. Though taking its point of departure in the analysis of moral judgment, this book branches widely into related topics such as freedom and the causal order of the world, textual interpretation, the nature of the self, self-knowledge, and the concept of duties to ourselves.

CHARLES LARMORE is W. Duncan MacMillan Family Professor in the Humanities at Brown University. He is the author of thirteen books, including *The Morals of Modernity* (Cambridge University Press, 1996), *Les pratiques du moi* (2004), *The Autonomy of Morality* (Cambridge University Press, 2008), *Das Selbst in seinem Verhältnis zu sich und zu anderen* (2017), and *What Is Political Philosophy?* (2020).

MORALITY AND METAPHYSICS

CHARLES LARMORE

Brown University

Shaftesbury Road, Cambridge CB2 8EA, United Kingdom

One Liberty Plaza, 20th Floor, New York, NY 10006, USA

477 Williamstown Road, Port Melbourne, VIC 3207, Australia

314–321, 3rd Floor, Plot 3, Splendor Forum, Jasola District Centre, New Delhi – 110025, India

103 Penang Road, #05–06/07, Visioncrest Commercial, Singapore 238467

Cambridge University Press is part of Cambridge University Press & Assessment, a department of the University of Cambridge.

We share the University's mission to contribute to society through the pursuit of education, learning and research at the highest international levels of excellence.

www.cambridge.org
Information on this title: www.cambridge.org/9781108459273

DOI: 10.1017/9781108691321

First published 2021
First paperback edition 2023

A catalogue record for this publication is available from the British Library

ISBN 978-1-108-47234-0 Hardback
ISBN 978-1-108-45927-3 Paperback

Contents

Acknowledgments

I would like to thank my editor at Cambridge University Press, Hilary Gaskin, for her advice and support during the preparation of this volume. I also thank my acute copyeditor, Alex Kats, who saved me from a number of serious mistakes. Two anonymous readers for the Press gave me invaluable comments and suggestions. I am indebted as well to the many colleagues and audiences who have commented on various versions of these essays over the years.

All previously published essays in this volume have been substantially revised and expanded. They have also been modified so as to form a coherent book. I am grateful to the original publications and publishers for their permission to reuse the material here.

Chapter 1, originally published in *Social Philosophy & Policy* 27(2), 2010, 1–28. © 2010 Cambridge University Press. Also published in E. F. Paul et al. (eds.), *Moral Obligation*, Cambridge University Press, 2010. © 2010 Cambridge University Press. Reprinted with permission.

Chapter 2, originally published as "Réflexions sur l'idée de devoirs moraux envers soi-même" in Claude Romano (ed.), *Du moi à l'authenticité. La Philosophie de Charles Larmore*, Éditions Mimésis, 2017, 13–34. Translated by the author. © 2017 Éditions Mimésis. Reprinted with permission.

Chapter 3, originally published as "Zur Ethik des Lesens" in *Deutsche Zeitschrift für Philosophie* 63(3), 2015, 427–447. Translated by the author. © 2015 De Gruyter. Reprinted with permission.

Chapter 4, originally published in *European Journal of Political Theory* 12(2), 2013, 205–216. © 2013 Sage Publications. Reprinted with permission.

Chapter 5, originally published in *International Yearbook of German Idealism* IX, 2011, 3–21. © 2011 De Gruyter. Reprinted with permission.

Chapter 6, Sections 6.1–6.4 originally published as "Morals and Metaphysics" in *European Journal of Philosophy* 21(4), 2013, 665–675. © 2013 John Wiley & Sons. Reprinted with permission.

Chapter 7, originally published as "Die Bedingungen menschlicher Freiheit" in *Konzepte 1: Praktische Identität*, 2015, 109–148. Translated by the author. © 2015 Klostermann Verlag. Reprinted with permission.

Chapter 8, originally published as "Selbstwissen und Selbstfestlegung" in *Deutsche Zeitschrift für Philosophie* 63(4), 2015, 686–704. Translated by the author. © 2015 De Gruyter. Reprinted with permission.

Introduction

Of the two concepts in the title of this book, the first, morality, is probably one the reader and I understand somewhat similarly – though various chapters will analyze and extend the concept in novel ways. However, the same is not true of the other concept, namely, metaphysics. So I must explain what I mean by the term as well as by the connection between metaphysics and morality that runs as a guiding thread through these chapters originally written over the past ten years.

I.1 Metaphysics

Many of the leading movements of philosophy in the previous century defined themselves to an important extent by the way they eschewed or rejected what they called "metaphysics." Husserl's phenomenology aimed to lay bare the essential structures of experience and consciousness without taking a position on "metaphysical" disputes about the ultimate nature of reality. Heidegger regarded the entire Western "metaphysical" tradition as propelled by a pervasive forgetfulness of the primordial question of Being. Wittgenstein and members of the Vienna Circle maintained, despite otherwise striking changes of view, the conviction that "metaphysical" propositions are meaningless, an abuse of language. From the start, the Frankfurt School believed that "metaphysics" must be a thing of the past, so that even when Habermas exchanged Adorno and Horkheimer's lament about the hegemony of instrumental thought for his more optimistic theory of communicative reason, he enrolled it under the banner of "post-metaphysical" thinking. I have been putting the term "metaphysics" within quotation marks since these different figures did not understand the same thing by the word. Nor was their understanding of the kinds of philosophical thought they labeled "metaphysical" particularly well informed or accurate.

Admittedly, in the second half of the century, the situation began to change. Rejecting the supposed dichotomy between conceptual and empirical truths, Quine argued for "a blurring of the supposed boundary between speculative metaphysics and natural science." Strawson approvingly termed "descriptive metaphysics" the analysis of our basic conceptual scheme for dealing with the world, as opposed to the dubious efforts of "revisionary metaphysics" to modify or replace that scheme.[1] Yet these two well-known rehabilitations of the idea were less than satisfactory. Instead of being continuous with empirical science, ought not metaphysics to be understood as a more reflective enterprise, concerned with determining the fundamental features of reality as a whole, including those that must exist if the sciences themselves are to count as giving us knowledge of the world? This question is all the more pertinent given that Quine's own "naturalism," his conviction that the sciences provide the measure of what exists, is not a conclusion of the sciences themselves, but instead a philosophical – indeed, metaphysical – thesis. And why, we may also ask, should metaphysics be engaged, as Strawson urged, in describing our basic conceptual scheme instead of, more forthrightly, the structure of reality itself? For if the latter, then validating some parts of our existing modes of understanding may well go hand in hand with revising other parts.

Today, metaphysics flourishes in far less reserved forms. Indeed, one could say that the last fifty years have been a great period of metaphysical theorizing, at least in the Anglophone world. (Large swathes of French and German philosophy continue to labor under Heideggerian or Habermasian proscriptions.) Yet even now, there remains in many quarters a certain distrust of metaphysics. When discussing one topic or another, many philosophers often declare that they do not want to get "too metaphysical." I need, therefore, to clarify what I mean by "metaphysics" in holding as I do, and without any reluctance, that metaphysics should play an indispensable role in our understanding of the nature of morality.

According to an old story, the term "metaphysics" began life as an editorial makeshift. In compiling his edition of Aristotle's works in the first century BC, Andronicus of Rhodes needed a title, it is said, for the various treatises he intended to include after (*meta*) the physical works. It was merely fortuitous that these treatises happened to deal with questions concerning an underlying structure of reality (involving such notions as substance, being, first principles, ultimate causes, and God) that makes possible the study of physical nature, questions that came to epitomize the

[1] W. V. O. Quine, "Two Dogmas of Empiricism," in *From a Logical Point of View* (Cambridge, MA: Harvard University Press, 1953), 20; P. F. Strawson, *Individuals: An Essay in Descriptive Metaphysics* (London: Methuen, 1959), 9–11.

later concept of metaphysics. This story is almost certainly false. Ample evidence shows that the expression "*ta meta ta physika*" had long been current in the Peripatetic school, and that Andronicus placed those treatises after the books on physics because he, like others, believed their treatment of the ontologically more fundamental questions – questions that Aristotle himself assigned to "first philosophy" (*prōtē philosophia*) – had to proceed in the light of an understanding of physical phenomena, which are more directly accessible.[2] From the start, therefore, metaphysics has meant – to put the idea broadly – inquiry into the ultimate structure of reality, aiming to tie together all the various dimensions of our experience into a unified conception of the way things basically are and hang together. It must draw, to be sure, on our knowledge of the natural world. But it aims to provide a deeper and more comprehensive account of all that can be said to exist. Such is the definition I follow in this book, without, of course, necessarily endorsing any specific Aristotelian doctrines.

One may still wonder why metaphysics in this sense, going beyond what the sciences can tell us about the world, should prove indispensable or whether it is even possible. So let me turn to those aspects of morality that, as I maintain in the following chapters, we cannot fully comprehend without pursuing ontological questions that go beyond the domain of the empirical sciences. The need for metaphysical thinking, at least in these regards, should then become plain.

I.2 Morality

The part of morality that is my principal concern has to do with the nature of moral judgments. A perennial question has been whether claims about what is good and right are simply the expression of certain attitudes of approval or disapproval, as Hume maintained, or whether they also purport to describe moral facts that obtain independently of our attitudes, and, if so, what such moral facts can be like in virtue of which of these judgments are true or false. Beginning in Chapter 1, but throughout the rest of the book as well, I argue that a "realist" approach is correct. Our moral judgments do indeed aim, by their very nature, to get it right about the moral facts there are. "Expressivist" theories, by contrast, fail to do justice to essential features of our moral thinking. One can, for instance, always ask about whatever may be the attitudes of approval or disapproval

[2] See, for instance, Hans Reiner, "Die Entstehung und ursprüngliche Bedeutung des Namens Metaphysik," *Zeitschrift für philosophische Forschung* 8(2), 1954, 210–237.

expressed by moral judgments whether they are, in the case at hand, morally appropriate or not.

What then are these moral facts like? There is nothing wrong in saying that "generosity is a virtue" is true because there really exists the virtue of generosity. But in what does generosity being a virtue consist? In general, I hold, moral qualities can be analyzed in terms of impersonal reasons, valid in abstraction from one's own interests and affections, to concern oneself with the good of others. "Generosity is a virtue" is true in virtue of there existing impersonal reasons to give unstintingly of one's time, attention, and resources to those who are in particular need. Explaining in Chapter 1 the nature of this moral point of view, I go on in the two subsequent chapters to explore two areas in which it proves, perhaps unexpectedly, to be applicable. Not only are there impersonal reasons to concern oneself with one's own good, leading to what may be called duties to oneself, but our moral relation to others carries over to our reading of texts, giving rise to what may properly be called an ethics of reading. Yet to return to the matter at hand: Moral claims do not express solely attitudes of approval or disapproval. They also convey moral beliefs, and the facts that make these beliefs true or false are facts about the reasons there are to concern ourselves with the good of others independently of how this may affect our own good.

Some philosophers will no doubt object that moral judgments cannot be statements about what we believe to be moral facts since beliefs, in and of themselves, cannot move us to act, having no effect on our will except in conjunction with relevant desires, whereas moral judgments are inherently action-guiding: to judge that generosity is a virtue is to be moved, all else being equal, to act generously when the situation calls for it. Now, as I explain in a number of chapters,[3] belief as such is not in fact motivationally inert. A belief is a disposition, and a disposition not merely to affirm, when asked, the thing believed, but to think and act in accord with the presumed truth of what we believe. Belief, in the phrase of C. S. Peirce, is a rule for action.[4] However, there is more. If moral judgments are basically engaged in referring to a certain kind of impersonal reason, then there is a further respect in which they are far from motivationally inert, at least to the extent that we are rational. Reason, as I argue throughout this book, is our capacity of being responsive to reasons. Insofar as we are

[3] See Section 1.3 in Chapter 1, Section 6.3 in Chapter 6, Section 7.7 in Chapter 7, and Section 8.3 in Chapter 8.

[4] C. S. Peirce, "How to Make Our Ideas Clear," in *Selected Writings* (New York: Dover, 1958), p. 121.

rational, recognizing that we have a reason to do something is therefore sufficient to move us to act accordingly in the absence of any countervailing reasons. It is not as though, having perceived a reason to act in a certain way, we must still decide whether we should heed it. Someone who fails to do what they see reason to do is being less than completely rational. Beliefs about reasons are inherently motivating, in virtue of their very object.

I.3 Reason

Reason, I have just said, consists in being responsive to reasons. For though not all our judgments are about reasons, all of them – moral or otherwise – are, or at least intend to be, responsive to reasons. Responsiveness is the crucial point. Several chapters in this book (particularly Chapters 1, 5, and 6) are devoted to exposing the errors in different versions – expressivist once again, but also Kantian – of the contrary and widespread view that in the end we ourselves determine what may count as reasons for thought or action. Expressivists hold that to think one has a reason to do something is not at bottom to claim that such a reason exists, but instead to express one's endorsement of a rule permitting or requiring the doing of that thing. This kind of analysis, however, cannot make sense of the objectivity of reasons, that is, of the fact that they would remain valid even if one happened not to endorse complying with them. For thinking that the reason one has is objectively valid cannot consist, as expressivists tend to reply, in endorsing a higher-order rule requiring endorsement of the first rule, since this only pushes back the difficulty. Merely accepting such a higher-order rule cannot render the reason objectively binding. Instead, there would have to be a reason to accept that rule. And this shows precisely why reasons cannot be explained in terms of the endorsement of rules. The endorsement of rules, if it is other than arbitrary, rests on what one takes to be good reasons to endorse them.

Kantian conceptions of the nature of reasons involve a similar mistake. For Kant, as for the many who have followed his lead, facts in the world acquire the status of reasons for thinking this or doing that in the light of principles our reason gives itself in order to determine what things may then serve to justify various beliefs or actions on our part. Reason, in the Kantian phrase, is "autonomous," self-legislating. But again, when we do indeed impose principles of thought and action on ourselves, there must seem to us to be reasons for imposing them. The explanation is therefore circular. It is also ill-conceived from the start. For the extent to which the principles we abide by are ones we have given ourselves is quite limited. Most principles, and certainly those that are most fundamental for our conduct, are instead principles whose antecedent validity we must simply acknowledge. Consider an example. Knowing my tendency to work such long hours that I end up becoming irritable and rude, I may make it a principle of never working for more than six hours a day. Certainly, I would not be bound by this principle if I had not imposed it on myself. But I have done so because I recognize the authority of a deeper principle that is not of my own making, namely, the duty of trying not to hurt other people's feelings. Principles that are self-legislated make up only a small, circumscribed part of the principles we accept. Kant declared that reason must regard itself as the author (*Urheberin*) of its principles since if it were to receive direction from any other quarter (*anderwärts her*), it would then be subject to alien influences (*fremden Einflüssen*).[5] Yet principles and reasons[6] of which reason is not the author are scarcely alien influences to which it is then subject. They are the very means of its exercise. Without them, reason would be directionless.

The difficulty does not disappear if the notion of the autonomy of reason is reformulated, as it sometimes is today, to mean that we are the authors of such elementary principles as avoiding contradictions and willing the necessary means to given ends in that they are "constitutive" – that is, essential to the possibility – of whatever we may coherently think or do. For it is *heeding* them that is constitutive in this sense. We fail to be intelligibly thinking or acting at all if we fail to acknowledge their authority for all our thought and action. Reason cannot be a law unto itself. It guides our conduct only through being responsive to reasons that exist independently of our attitudes of approval, independently of our endorsement of rules, and independently of our ideas of the reasons we have, ideas that may be true or false. This is so whether we are considering the reason of an individual or the reason embodied in the social practices of a community. In important regards, I remain an old-style rationalist, immune to the allures of both Hume and Kant.

Though the failure of both expressivist and Kantian accounts of the nature of reasons seems to me obvious, there remains the question of why the view that we ourselves determine what may count as reasons is

[5] Kant, Immanuel, *Grundlegung zur Metaphysik der Sitten*, Akademie-Ausgabe (Berlin: Reimer, 1900-), IV, 448.

[6] Principles I understand to be rules designating standing reasons of thought or action that generally outweigh competing considerations.

nonetheless so prevalent. I believe the answer is also evident. Modern philosophy, like modern thought in general, has tended to suppose that all that can be said really to exist are facts about the world of nature, that is, the physical and psychological facts that make up in principle the domain of the empirical sciences. This naturalistic picture of the world leaves no room for reasons as also forming part of reality. For reasons are not themselves physical or psychological in character, but instead normative. Reasons indicate what we *ought* to think or do, all else being equal. More specifically, they consist in the way that physical and psychological facts *count in favor* of possibilities of thought and action we can take up, "counting in favor" consisting, in turn, in the normative relation of justification. The naturalist worldview, so pervasive as often to be more a habit of mind than an explicit doctrine, has therefore led many to believe that being a reason is a status that we confer on facts in the world, instead of a feature of the way things are. But as I have been suggesting – and as I argue systematically in several chapters of this book – that is an untenable position.

Generally, naturalism regards itself as being down to earth, empirical and science-minded, committed to avoiding obscure and needless speculation. In philosophy these days, it is all the rage. One seeks to naturalize this (epistemology) or naturalize that (the mind). Naturalism prides itself on not being metaphysical. Yet it is all the same a metaphysics, at least in the original sense of the term I explained earlier. It advances an account of the ultimate structure of reality and it does so by going beyond the deliverances of the empirical sciences themselves, since it is not and cannot be any conclusion of theirs that all that really exists is what they investigate. Such a claim is a philosophical thesis. If, then, reason is a matter of responsiveness to reasons and if reasons must thus be understood as a dimension of reality itself, naturalism has to be rejected and an alternative metaphysics devised. This is what I set out to do in Chapters 1, 4, 6, and especially 7. Needless to say, I trust, the alternative to naturalism I propose is not any kind of "supernaturalism." God has no place in my conception of what there is. I shall instead speak often of a "platonism" of reasons, since reasons resemble Plato's Forms in constituting a third dimension of reality, neither physical nor psychological in nature. They are not identical with either the empirical facts that give rise to them or with what may happen to be our beliefs about them.

It should now be clearer than it may have been at the start why metaphysics is both a coherent and inescapable enterprise. Thought that is at all reflective about its preconditions and purposes is bound to involve a metaphysics, even if unacknowledged. I have presented this ontology of reasons – as I do in the body of the book – as a result of reflecting on the nature of moral judgment. Whence my book's title. However, it is a line of thought with broad implications, and these too I explore in the chapters that follow.

I.4 Freedom

One implication has to do with what it is for us to be free beings. The Kantian ideal of autonomy represents an influential conception of the basis of our freedom: we are free beings insofar as we are able ourselves, individually or collectively, to determine what bearing things and events in the world should have for our conduct. I have just explained why this conception makes no sense. Yet precisely the grounds on which I reject the ideal of autonomy point the way to a better account of the nature of human freedom. We are free, as I argue in Chapter 7, to the extent that we think and act in accord with an understanding of the reasons that justify what we are doing. Freedom rests on reason, properly conceived. For what is compulsion, the opposite of freedom, if not being caused to think or act by factors either external or internal (such as addictions or obsessions) that prevent us from heeding what we can see good reason to do? Consider the difference between jumping out of someone's way and being pushed aside.

This view of freedom tallies with what I said about the very nature of reasons, which consist in the way that facts in the world count in favor of possibilities of thought and action we can take up. We are not the only beings with possibilities. Just about anything could be other than it is. But we are beings that, unlike, say, rocks and trees, can take up or choose possibilities they have. This is what makes us free beings. Yet we take up these possibilities in response to the reasons we see as counting in their favor. Depending on how accurate our understanding of the relevant reasons may be, we therefore are generally more or less free in what we think or do. Freedom is a matter of degree. This means, I contend (Chapter 7, Section 7.5), that the classic moral principle of "*ought* implies *can*" should in fact be discarded, though without, I would add, compromising the *ought*. One may be unable to see the reasons for acting as one should without it being any less true that one is then acting wrongly. Freedom is also, as that chapter argues as well, compatible with its being part of the causal order of the world. For not only do the facts that give us the reasons for which we think or act still constitute causes of what we do. Our very understanding of these reasons, be it ever so faultless, is shaped causally by our experience and character. The conception of freedom I present is one that is both rationalist and compatibilist.

I.5 The Self

Another implication concerns the nature of the self. It seems axiomatic that each of us is a self in virtue of an underlying relation we have to ourselves in all that we think and do. The key question has to do with how this basic self-relation is to be conceived. Taking up this topic in Chapters 2 and 7, I pursue it at length in Chapter 8. To summarize the theory I develop there, let me begin by recalling what I have already said about belief. A belief, I remarked, is a disposition to think and act in accord with the presumed truth of what is believed. Such a disposition therefore entails being responsive to the reasons for thought and action the belief's being true would give us. So too, we cannot come to believe something without thinking it to be true, and this means without supposing we see some reason to think it true. (Try to believe that the number of hairs on the top of Caesar's bald head was seven!) In both its formation and its function, belief essentially involves, therefore, guiding ourselves by reasons, and precisely this self-relation – *guiding oneself by reasons* – constitutes, I argue, the basic relation to ourselves that makes each of us a self. For the same kind of analysis applies to desires. Any desire represents its object as something desirable and thus as something there are reasons to have or to pursue. (Try to imagine desiring someone's company without finding it attractive in the slightest regard! It's not as though you could find it attractive simply because you desired it.) Plus, any desire inclines us, unless we ignore or repress it, to think and act as the apparent desirability of its object gives us reason to do.

So it is with all other "intentional," object-directed mental states or events, such as emotions and feelings – you cannot love or feel angry without loving or feeling angry at someone or something – since, taking shape in response to the reasons their object appears to provide for their arising, they in turn shape our behavior through what they indicate we have reason to think and do. You cannot get angry at a person except for some apparent provocation, and your anger no doubt points you to ways of getting back.[7]

[7] Sensations, such as an experience of redness or a feeling of pain, are not intentional and so do not involve a responsiveness to reasons. As a result, beings whose mental life consists solely in sensations (earthworms?) must lack selves. But by the same token, my view is that we are not the only beings

As should be plain, reason conceived as responsiveness to reasons is not, in my view, one mental faculty among others, opposed, for instance, to desire as on many typical models of the mind. It is rather the foundation of all the operations of the mind, since beliefs, desires, emotions, and feelings are defined by how, if in characteristically different ways, they are shaped and oriented by what we regard as reasons. They prove more or less rational to the extent that these reasons actually exist and happen to be relevant. Just as reason lies at the heart of our freedom, so it also is essential to being a self. In responding to reasons, we align ourselves on their import for our conduct. This is the basic way of relating to ourselves by which we are selves at all. It explains why we count as responsible for what we think and do. We are selves, however, only in relation as well to a normative order of reasons of which we are not the author and thus to the physical and psychological facts on which they depend. Traditional ideas of the "interiority" of the self are mistaken. Such, then, is the "metaphysics of the self" I advance, showing how being a self fits into the structure of reality as a whole.

What I have been calling the self has often been termed by much of modern philosophy the "subject," and the account I have been summarizing indeed aims at explaining the nature of subjectivity. I prefer the term "self" because it brings out clearly that subjectivity consists in a pervasive relatedness to ourselves in everything we think and do. Modern philosophy has also generally supposed that the relation we as a self or subject must bear to ourselves is one of self-awareness. Such a conception, however, is very different from the one outlined here. It leads, in fact, either to paradox if this self-awareness is understood as a relation of reflection – all knowledge involves a distinction between knower and known, so that the self on this view would have to exist prior to its awareness of itself – or to mystery if the self-awareness is equated with an intimate, pre-reflective kind of self-acquaintance that excludes all distinction between subject and object. These well-known problems disappear when the relation to ourselves that makes each of us a self or subject is conceived as consisting in guiding ourselves by what we see as reasons. I would add that the conception based on self-awareness tends naturally to suggest that the self or subject can be conscious of itself prior to any consciousness of the

with selves, since the higher animals, too, have beliefs and desires. They too are responsive to reasons, though their reason is considerably more limited and less flexible than ours. See, for instance, Section 1.1 in Chapter 1 and Section 7.7 in Chapter 7.

world. The previous paragraph has already mentioned why my conception rejects this notion of subjectivity as an "inner" realm.

Moreover, one of its significant consequences, as I argue at length in Chapter 8, is that reflection, in which we take up the perspective of another on ourselves, provides (along with the actual insights of others) our only means of acquiring knowledge of our own minds. Contrary to a common idea, there is no such thing as self-knowledge of an essentially first-person kind. First-person utterances such as "I believe tomorrow will be a bad day" or "I would like to have a drink," which it makes little sense for others to challenge as false, are not infallible statements about the character of our own thinking. They are not claims to knowledge at all, but instead avowals, in which, like Martin Luther's "Here I stand, I can do no other," we express, not report, the state of mind we are currently in. This analysis squares with the familiar experience that others can often perceive what is in our mind better than we can, though generally we know a lot more about ourselves than others do, since we tend to find ourselves endlessly fascinating.

The reader should now be able to see why, in my view, accepting that moral judgments are not simply expressions of attitude or of principles we have given ourselves should impel us to reject the reigning naturalism of our day and embrace a more complex picture of the world. It is a metaphysics that recognizes that reasons, irreducibly normative in character, also form part of the structure of reality. As I have suggested and explain further in this book, this metaphysics has important implications for our understanding of such key concepts as freedom, subjectivity, and reason itself, all concepts whose significance extends well beyond the domain of morality itself. Starting out from reflection on the nature of moral judgments, I have thus gone on to develop a general metaphysics. I do not deny that there are other connections between morality and metaphysics or that other lines of thought besides this one can lead to the kind of "platonistic" position I have espoused. But it is the route I have followed in these essays.

I.6 Philosophy

My thinking in this book has been governed throughout by two general philosophical commitments I have long held. The first is a rejection of theoretical quietism. Some philosophers regard philosophical problems as more to be dissolved than solved, as resting on confusions that, once dispelled, will leave our understanding of the world and of ourselves in other respects pretty much like what it has always been. The aim of philosophy, they believe, is not the construction of theories. I could not disagree more. Certainly confusions are rife in philosophy. But confusions are dispelled by a better account of the subject matter, and this account then needs to be followed through to its ultimate implications. This is what quietists, or otherwise bold philosophers in their quietistic moments, do not do. They content themselves with halfway measures or with formulae designed to cut off further reflection. Thus, they may well agree that judgments about what reasons we have can be true or false, that it makes sense to say we know we have a reason to think this or to do that. Yet they then hedge on whether reasons should be said really to exist, claiming – I discuss such cases in this book – that statements about reasons enjoy an "objectivity without objects," that reasons exist but not in an "ontological" sense, or that existence is, properly speaking, not a matter of being part of the totality of all that is, but is instead always relative to a specific domain of discourse. They may reject naturalism as incapable of doing justice to the normative dimension of our experience, yet they advance no alternative vision of the world in its place. This is a failing. As I will insist a number of times, only a metaphysics can replace a metaphysics. Philosophy, as an enterprise of systematic, unrelenting reflection, must aim to see things whole, in their essential interconnections, and for what they really are, independently of what may happen to be our conceptions of them.

The second commitment, though not incompatible with the first, does rub a bit against it. It is the recognition that philosophy is subject to what I call *a law of the conservation of trouble* (Chapter 6, Section 6.4). Philosophical problems tend to be both fundamental in nature, their implications ramifying through many areas of our experience, and remarkably cohesive, our judgment about how well any specific aspect has been handled turning on our conception of the problem as a whole. The solution that looks convincing when certain aspects are deemed crucial can thus look doubtful or even wrong-headed when the problem is approached from a different angle, where different considerations are paramount. This is why philosophical problems prove so difficult. They resist being broken down, as in the sciences, into manageable questions resolvable to everyone's satisfaction and deeper issues that can be left for a later time. Only a comprehensive solution will do, yet none is likely to tie everything together neatly. Reasonable disagreement is to be expected. The best we can do in any philosophical controversy, I believe, is to weigh together the pros and cons and judge where on balance the stronger reasons lie.

This conviction has been particularly in my mind as I have sought in many of these essays to lay bare the defects of the naturalistic worldview and to develop a different metaphysical perspective that takes seriously the reality of reasons. For once we accept that reasons too exist, yet without being reducible to physical or psychological facts, a significant difficulty arises. It has to do with a phenomenon I have not so far mentioned in this introduction. In many cases – when, for instance, we are deliberating about what we ought to think or do – it is important to suppose that we can be moved, not just by our ideas of the relevant reasons, but also by the reasons themselves. That is precisely our aim in deliberating. Indeed, the possibility of rationality, of being responsive to reasons, depends on it, since our beliefs about reasons may always be false, after all. Moreover, when our ideas of the reasons we have are true, they count as knowledge only if our having them is due to these very reasons. But the question is, how can reasons, if they are of an essentially normative character, act on the mind? How can reasons be causes? For on the usual understanding of causality, cause and effect are appropriately situated in space and time. Reasons, however, being normative in character, have no spatial location.

Naturalistic conceptions of reasons (to the extent they are coherent, which I doubt) will have, of course, no trouble explaining how reasons, as they understand them, can be causes. Meanwhile, other philosophers who reject such conceptions, as I do, have not ventured any solutions to the problem, in part because they have not even acknowledged the phenomenon that gives rise to it, but also because of their failure to see the need for an alternative comprehensive conception of the world. So I have felt somewhat alone. Still, the prospects for the sort of anti-naturalist metaphysics I have sketched do not appear to me to be hopeless. Section 6.8 in Chapter 6 and Section 7.6 in Chapter 7 propose an account of how reasons, not just ideas of reasons, can be causes. Its essential thrust is that reasons can act as causes by riding piggyback, as it were, on the empirical (physical and psychological) facts on which they depend, when these facts also shape what we think or do. I do not pretend that this account answers every doubt one may have. But it is a start. And philosophical reflection, as the law of the conservation of trouble implies, has no natural end.

I hope, therefore, that the reader will not mistake for dogmatism the forthright way I have argued for my own views and rejected those of others. In philosophy, nothing is to be gained by being coy. Only when one states clearly where one stands is criticism likely to be fruitful and reflection itself further advanced. I have tried to make as explicit as possible where I think the balance of reasons lies. That has meant indicating what I also think are the most serious difficulties my views face.[8]

[8] The commitment I pursue in the present book to developing a comprehensive view of mind and world and to rejecting every form of philosophical quietism should be distinguished from the special reasons a liberal political philosophy has to set aside comprehensive conceptions of the good life in determining what should be the fundamental principles of political association. On the latter, see my book, What is Political Philosophy? (Princeton: Princeton University Press, 2020), Chapter 3, §1.

PART I

The Structure and Scope of the Moral Point of View

CHAPTER 1

Reflection and Morality

1.1 Our Humanity

Morality is what makes us human. One meaning of this common saying is plain enough. Refraining from injury to others, keeping our word, and helping those in need constitute the elementary decencies of society. If most of us did not observe these practices most of the time, or at least give one another the impression of doing so, no one would have the security to pursue a flourishing life. Not even a life of basic dignity would be possible if we found ourselves continually at the mercy of aggression, treachery, and indifference. Morality makes us human by providing rules of mutual respect without which there can be neither social cooperation nor individual achievement.

However, another meaning suggests itself as well. It has to do, not with morality's function, but with its source. Other animals are like us in being able to show deference and feel affection, even to the point of sacrificing themselves for those whom they love. But if by "morality" is meant – as I shall mean in this chapter – looking beyond our own concerns and allegiances in order to give equal attention to the good of others, considered just as such, then morality lies beyond their ken. Does not then our very ability to think morally in this sense point to a peculiarly human power of self-transcendence, a power that we alone among the animals have of regarding ourselves from the outside as but one among others and that finds in morality, if not its only, then certainly its most striking expression? This question engages our attention far less than it should. When people, philosophers included, wonder about the nature of morality, they tend to focus on what reasons there may be to be moral, what acting morally entails, or in what sense, if any, moral judgments count as true or false. These are important issues. But often the taken-for-granted deserves the greatest scrutiny. That we should be able at all to view the world impersonally, recognizing the independent and equal standing of others, involves an overcoming of self that is no less remarkable for having become largely second nature.

Among philosophers, Immanuel Kant was one of the few, and certainly the most famous, to argue directly that morality is, in this sense, what makes us human. "Duty! Sublime and mighty name, what is an origin worthy of you?" Only a freedom, he replied, that "elevates man above himself as a part of the world of sense ... a freedom and independence from the mechanism of all of nature."[1] Our moral consciousness, according to Kant, testifies to the freedom we alone have to rise above all that experience has made of us, so that we may act in accord with demands we understand as binding on us independently of our given interests and desires. I believe, like many, that Kant was on the track of an essential truth. But, like many too, I do not believe that the source of morality can be anything so extravagant (if morality itself is not to be an illusion) as a freedom unshaped by the course of experience. Freedom, in any form we can conceive, depends not only on external conditions proving conducive to our ends but also on our having acquired, through training and effort, the abilities necessary for exercising control over ourselves and the world.[2] After all, we have to learn how to think morally, which means developing a sense of social expectations as well as the self-discipline needed to distinguish the good of others from our own as well as from what we might wish their good would be.

Thus, Kant's intuition needs to be brought down to earth. One proposal might be that the capacity for self-transcendence to which morality gives expression consists in our nature as normative beings, responsive not merely to the causal impress of the environment but to the authority of reasons as well. To see that we have a reason to think or act in a certain way is to see that we ought to do so, all other things being equal, and heeding an "ought" – as is clear with the moral "ought" – means holding ourselves to a demand we regard as binding upon us. Why is not this kind of subordination of self the self-transcendence at issue?

Certainly morality is not possible except for beings that can respond to reasons. Yet the "ought" is not limited to the moral realm, any more than it is true that the only reasons for action we have are moral in character. Indeed, the subordination of self involved in the recognition of reasons as

[1] Immanuel Kant, *Kritik der praktischen Vernunft (Critique of Practical Reason)* (1788), Akademie-Ausgabe (Berlin: Reimer, 1900–), vol. V, 86–87.

[2] In Chapter 7 ("The Conditions of Human Freedom"), Sections 7.3–7.5, I develop in greater detail this critique of Kant's conception of freedom.

such falls importantly short of the way that morality asks us to look beyond ourselves.

Suppose, for instance, that we are pursuing some interest of our own or the good of someone we hold dear and doing so because that interest or that person matters to us. The reasons we then perceive to act one way rather than another are ones we would have to agree that anyone similarly disposed would also have in such circumstances. All reasons are *universal,* binding on one person only if binding on all who, having the same interests and similar allegiances, happen to find themselves in the same conditions. That is what it is for reasons to be binding and why responding to reasons means holding ourselves responsible to the authority of an "ought," distinct from our individual will. Nonetheless, this subordination of self is not the self-transcendence that morality demands. For the reasons in question only apply to us insofar as we happen to care about those ends. Their authority, though real, remains conditional.

Imagine, however, that we think we have reason to help someone simply because that person is in distress. Perhaps it is someone whom we also hold dear, but we are attending, not to the love we feel, but only to the person's suffering. Reasons of this sort are not just universal, as all reasons are. They are *impersonal* as well, applying to us in abstraction from our own interests and affections.[3] Or, more exactly, their applicability does not depend on any such factors insofar as these factors are identified as ours, since it is possible to have an impersonal reason to satisfy a desire of ours if the desire is understood solely as one belonging to a person like any other. (I may have, for instance, an impersonal reason to advance the welfare of a certain group, just because its needs are deserving of my attention, even when I happen to be one member among others of that group). In short, impersonal reasons derive from the way things are in and of themselves, that is, in the cases mentioned, from people's actual condition, irrespective of how they may figure in our own concerns. Now it is just this impersonal element that constitutes the hallmark of moral reasons for action. Helping others is moral in character insofar as we are motivated by their being in need, whether or not we feel any particular affection for

[3] Impersonal reasons are what Thomas Nagel, in *The Possibility of Altruism* (Princeton: Princeton University Press, 1970), chapter 10, called "objective" reasons, whose "defining predicate" contains no free, unbound, occurrence of the variable referring to the agent whose reasons they are. (If I jump out of the way of an oncoming truck because that will preserve my life – and not just someone's life, that "someone" happening to be me – then my reason will count as "subjective," not "objective" or impersonal.) I prefer my terminology, since reasons that are not impersonal are, in my view, nonetheless real.

them. Thus, acknowledging the force of reasons is not by itself sufficient for us to be able to look beyond ourselves in the way that morality requires. Nor is it, incidentally, a distinctively human capacity. Many of the higher animals also have, or can be trained to have, a sense of how they ought to behave. They too can respond to reasons, as is shown, for instance, by how they pick up on cues in their environment in order to pursue better ways of getting what they want. Yet moral thinking, the grasping of impersonal reasons, remains beyond their reach.

This last point suggests the direction of a more promising approach. Though other animals can respond to reasons, they appear significantly limited in their ability to reflect about what they ought to do, that is, to evaluate and weigh the reasons they see, or think they see, to favor one option or another. They cannot, in particular, engage in the kind of impersonal reflection of which we are capable, standing back so as to regard ourselves from the outside, as though we were just one among many, in order to figure out what anyone in the circumstances really ought to think or do.[4] Why is it not then our capacity for impersonal reflection that makes morality a distinctive expression of our humanity? Are we not better able to consider others as persons in their own right, apart from the personal concerns that ordinarily color our perception of the world, the more reflective distance we achieve toward ourselves? Of course, as the last question implies, reflection need not always be impersonal. Sometimes we reflect by asking ourselves what someone close to us would think about our situation. This is precisely the sort of reflection of which other animals too are capable, as when my dog Hardy, who loves sticks, comes upon a stick on one of our walks, but pauses and looks to me to hear whether he should "bring the stick" or "leave it." However, in the fact that reflection can be more or less distanced lies a strength of the approach I propose. For now the freedom that is integral to morality becomes intelligible. It is the ability to overcome, by taking up an impersonal point of view, the hold that an absorption in our own affairs naturally exercises over our thinking. This ability allows us to grasp the intrinsic value in the good of others. Yet it also, as I explain in Section 1.2, grows out of the less impartial ways we have of standing back from ourselves. Impersonal reflection is a creature of experience and so a more sensible answer than Kant's to the question of what constitutes our peculiar power of self-transcendence.

[4] This capacity for impersonal reflection is what Helmuth Plessner, in his great book, *Die Stufen des Organischen und der Mensch* (1928), analyzed as the essential feature of "excentricity" (*Exzentrizität*) that distinguishes us from the other animals.

Morality is not, of course, the only example of impersonal reflection (any more than it could be the only example of the nonempirical freedom that Kant postulated). When we reflect upon what we should believe about a certain matter and ask not what we are inclined to suppose or what our friends or community would conclude, but rather what the facts themselves require, we are reflecting impersonally. For our target then consists in impersonal reasons for belief – reasons (in parallel to impersonal reasons for action) that we grasp as binding on us independently of our desires and loyalties in virtue of being based on what is true about the subject matter itself. Morality, however, provides a privileged illustration of our capacity for impersonal reflection. For what could be a more conspicuous expression of our ability to stand back from our own attachments, as though we were merely one person among many, than to consider other people's good as of equal moment with ours, particularly when doing so is to our personal disadvantage?

In this chapter, I examine more deeply the way reflection serves as the source of our moral thinking. How is it that by viewing ourselves from without we can learn to see others as having an equal claim on our attention? Reflection, as I have said, need not always assume an impersonal form. What, then, is involved in its coming to exhibit the sort of self-transcendence that morality demands? Obviously, the place to begin is the nature of reflection itself.

As may already be apparent and will become plainer as I proceed, reflecting about what to believe does not, to my mind, differ substantially from reflecting about how to act – except, of course, in subject matter. Grand distinctions are often made between theoretical and practical reason, particularly in the Kantian tradition. But they are largely overdrawn. (In this regard too, as in many others, the rationalism I espouse departs radically from Kant's.) Reason is best understood as the ability to respond to reasons, be they reasons for belief or for action, and the point of reflection, as I shall explain, is to consider explicitly what we have reason to think or do in regard to some problem that has disrupted our settled routines. Though the relation between reflection and morality is my ultimate concern, Sections 1.2 and 1.3 will therefore look at the nature of reflection along quite general lines. I will not be losing sight, however, of what is involved in reflecting about how to act. It is precisely this comprehensive approach that reveals the true character of such reflection, the common structure and function it shares with reflection about what to think and believe. Both aim essentially at a knowledge of the reasons there are. This general account will guide the more specific analysis of moral thinking to which I then return in Sections 1.4 and 1.5. There my concern will be to show how our capacity for impersonal reflection shapes the makeup of the moral point of view, its preconditions and implications. Because this capacity sets us off so dramatically from all the other animals, morality can indeed be said to form a signal expression of our humanity.

1.2 The Nature of Reflection

It is characteristic of the human condition that we often fail to be at one with ourselves. Sometimes we feel torn between competing commitments. Or no sooner do we make some decision of moment than we recall our doubts about whether a different option might not be better. To deliberate honestly is to risk having a mind divided, for our inner conflicts seldom amount to mere confusions, vanishing in the wake of a more careful scrutiny. Usually, they mirror the real complexity of our situation, the multiplicity of demands that rightly exercise a hold on our attention. Even when we conclude that we have good reason to take one path rather than another, we leave behind something of ourselves in the possibilities we reject.

Yet conflicts of this sort are not the only or the deepest way in which we fail to coincide with ourselves. Even more fundamental is our continual alternation between doing and reflecting. We move back and forth between two standpoints, the view from within and the view from without. Because each of us has a life that is ours alone to live, we naturally approach the world in the light of the interests and allegiances that happen to be ours. So long as everything goes its customary way, we think and act from within our own perspective. Yet frequently we are moved to reflect on our thought and action – not for the pure pleasure of doing so, but because some problem has emerged that puts into question the way we have been proceeding. We may no longer be clear about the sort of person we are or, far more often, about what we should believe or do with regard to some other matter. Reflection is a response to a problem. It is the attempt to reestablish a fit between expectation and reality.

Reflecting also means, however, ceasing to live our lives from within, in order to look at ourselves from without. To be sure, we stand back so as to examine the particular difficulty that has arisen. But even if it is something quite circumscribed (some particular trait or activity of ours and not the shape of our life as a whole), and even if it concerns something distinct from us (the real character of someone else or the confusing nature of some natural or social phenomenon), it is still ourselves, and not merely the difficulty, that we regard from the outside. As a response to a problem that has disturbed our routine, reflection is always a turning back upon ourselves, since it aims to figure out what *we* are to do about the difficulty before us. At the same time, it requires us to look at ourselves *from without,* since reflecting on what we ought to do means making ourselves and our situation into an object of inquiry, seeking to discover what solution we have reason in the circumstances to adopt. When we simply respond to reasons, without reflecting, we do not take this sort of detour. We do not make ourselves into an object in order to get at what we should do. We just see what we should do and act accordingly, as when we are driving and come to a stop sign (or so I hope). But deliberating about what reasons we may have is a different matter. That is the essence of reflection, and it requires us to make ourselves into an object of our thinking, to regard ourselves from without, though not necessarily, as will become clear, from an impersonal distance.[5]

Reflection, therefore, always involves self-distancing. This fact, incidentally, points to an important truth about the pursuit of self-knowledge. Reflection need not have self-knowledge as its aim, of course, since often we reflect in order to discover what we should do or what we should believe about other matters in the world. When we do seek to know ourselves better, it is because some conflict has appeared between our existing conception of what we are like and the behavior of ours we observe, the thoughts and desires we notice, or the unsettling remarks that others have made about us. And since we then handle this sort of problem by regarding ourselves as an object of scrutiny, we need to examine who we are as we would anyone else we were trying to understand, namely by collecting evidence and drawing inferences. Here as elsewhere, we must guard against substituting how we would like things to be for what an unprejudiced view shows them to be. Our knowledge of ourselves is thus built up in the same empirical, trial-and-error way as our knowledge of others. We have no more immediate, privileged access to the makeup of our own minds, which is why others can sometimes know us better than we do ourselves. I will return to this subject in greater detail in Chapter 8.

In general, whatever the subject, there are two distinct dimensions along which we objectify ourselves when we reflect. First, in order to get hold of

[5] In my book *Les pratiques du moi* (Paris: Presses Universitaires de France, 2004; English translation: *The Practices of the Self*, Chicago: University of Chicago Press, 2010), chapter 3, I discuss at greater length the general nature of reflection. For more on simply responding to reasons, without reflection, see Chapter 7, Section 7.8. And for a distinction between cognitive reflection, the object of discussion here, and what I call practical reflection, see Chapter 8, Section 8.5.

the problem we have encountered, we must adopt toward our own person the same sort of observational stance we occupy toward others when, living our lives from within, we regard their thoughts and feelings as among the elements of our environment. We look at ourselves as someone with a certain problem to solve and we study its ins and outs with more or less care. But, second, we cannot determine what we, as such a person, ought to do in response except from a standpoint of evaluation that consists, not in everything we happen to believe and want, but in the standards and assumptions we think ought to govern our decision. This is as much as to say that, in deliberating about how we are to proceed, we examine ourselves through the eyes of someone we imagine as embodying just such an evaluative standpoint. In effect, we ask what such a person would conclude that we should do. The two kinds of self-distancing are quite distinct: in the one, we try to describe ourselves (along with the problem we face) as we are; in the other, we figure out what we are to do. It is in the way they work together that reflection functions as it does. To reflect is not simply to contemplate our own person, as though gazing at our reflection in a mirror, which is what the first kind of self-distancing alone would entail. We turn our attention toward ourselves in order to overcome some obstacle that has disrupted our relation to the world or to ourselves.

Despite these differences between living our lives from within and reflecting on them from without, it would obviously be wrong to suppose that reflection stands opposed to life or that it constitutes a luxury we might choose to forgo. Nothing could be more perverse than to think with Rousseau that "the state of reflection is a state contrary to nature and a man who meditates is a depraved animal."[6] We become the persons we are through the problems we confront. There is no end to the need for standing back, and we live as much outside ourselves, thinking about what we should do, as within the various activities we in fact pursue. Indeed, little in the way we see the world around us fails to show the mark of what we have learned by reflecting. That is why a concern for others, though it has its roots in reflection, can form an important part of our everyday lives. Internalizing what we have learned, we can come to act straightaway with an eye to the well-being of those – family, friends, and associates – about whom we care enough to have considered how they feel. Similarly, we can incorporate into our dealings with others moral principles we have

[6] Rousseau, *Discours sur l'origine et les fondements de l'inégalité parmi les hommes* (*Œuvres complètes* III, Paris: Gallimard, 1964, 138): "Si elle [la Nature] nous a destinés à être sains, j'ose presque assurer que l'état de réflexion est un état contre Nature et que l'homme qui médite est un animal dépravé."

acquired by reflecting impartially on how one should, in general, treat one's fellow man. What I am calling the view from within is not essentially self-interested.

Nonetheless, the business of living easily keeps us in the pull of our own orbit. This we often discover if we happen to reflect anew. For reflection knows no inherent limits. It allows us to make out the ways in which the very habits of mind we have acquired by reflecting still remain tied to the particularities of our life. Thus, we recognize, on taking a broader view, that our various loyalties and loves are likely to matter little to others with their own lives to live, their own ties and causes. Even the moral principles we espouse may begin to appear a bit parochial or biased once we consider the extent to which they have been shaped by culture or class.

As I have previously remarked, reflection can proceed from more than one type of standpoint of evaluation. It need not aim at being impersonal – that is, at judging how we ought to think or act irrespective of our own interests and attachments. We may, for instance, base our evaluation of the options before us on what we imagine some individual (real or fictional) whom we hold dear would do in our place, or would want us to do. Philosophers tend to neglect this mode of reflection, perhaps because they believe themselves to be above it, but they are certainly wrong to do so. All of us lean from time to time on various exemplars, internalized heroes and idols, to figure out how we ought to think and act. Moreover, modeling ourselves on others is not in itself a vice, as though the proper course were always to think on our own. Everything depends on the worth of the models to which we appeal. Though it is often simple chance, or some special allure, that has led them to represent for us a kind of person we would like to be, this too is not necessarily deplorable. We may not have the time or the means to check their reliability. And even when we do, some trait of theirs may later prove exemplary in ways we could not anticipate when first confirming their appropriateness.

So little is identifying with others always to be avoided that it plays an essential role in our coming to grasp the impersonal point of view.[7] The capacity for reflection does not spring full-blown from anyone's head. It develops over time. In early life, reflection upon who we are and what we should do consists, quite naturally, in imagining what those who are close

[7] Cf. the accounts in Adam Smith, *The Theory of Moral Sentiments* (1759, 1790; Indianapolis, IN: Liberty Classics, 1976), part III, chapters 2–3, as well as George Herbert Mead, *Mind, Self, and Society* (Chicago: University of Chicago Press, 1934), part III. For an analysis of the strengths and weaknesses of Smith's account, see my article, "The Visible Hand," in *The New Republic*, October 18, 1999, 42–45.

to us would say. As our horizons broaden and we discover that parents and friends disagree, we find ourselves impelled to devise more abstract angles of evaluation: thus, we come to examine ourselves by the standards of some larger community to which we feel bound. But the same factors tend to push us beyond that perspective as well. And thus we may eventually fashion the idea of a fully informed and perfectly rational standpoint, transcending the limitations in the attitudes of particular individuals and societies – though, even then, identification is not at an end, since commonly we do so by looking in our own culture for exemplars of such a standpoint to take as our models. Only through this sort of process do we learn what it is to hold ourselves accountable to an impersonal standard of thought and action. Only in this way can we come to grasp the specifically moral point of view, which is to see in another's good, separately from our own interests and attachments, a reason for action on our part. And because we arrive at the moral point of view by working over less impersonal forms of reflection as well as by often identifying with those we take to be its paradigms, there are bound to be disagreements about what, more precisely, the moral viewpoint consists in – a point to which I shall return in Section 1.5.

Nonetheless, whether we assume the outlook of some other individual or reflect instead from an impersonal standpoint, certain elements remain constant. One is that reflection aims, in response to a problem, at determining what we have reason to think or do. Reasons, as I have pointed out, are universal in character: if they are binding on us, then they are binding on all who find themselves in conditions similar to those that make them applicable to us. It follows that even when we reflect, not impersonally, but by identifying with the more particular standpoint of someone we esteem, our conclusions are still ones we must assume that anyone like us ought to endorse in such a situation. That is not an awkward implication. For would we adopt that standpoint if we did not presume it to be attuned to how people should really behave who have interests like those that impel us to take it up? If I pattern my wardrobe on what some movie star wears, I am assuming that person knows how people who want to be "cool" ought to dress.

Another constant is that, in reflecting, we have to rely on our current understanding of the world. We cannot regard ourselves from without except by continuing to think, at least in part, from within the perspective we presently occupy. Precisely because reflection is the response to a problem, it is always situated: only in the light of our existing views can we so much as identify the problem before us, and we cannot hope to handle it except by drawing upon the relevant information at our disposal. When we reflect by imagining what someone important to us would say, we make use (for example) of what we understand to be that person's characteristic habits of mind. So too, when we consider impersonally what we ought to think or do, we base our reasoning on the knowledge we have acquired, not only of the matter before us, but also, more broadly, of how belief should be proportioned to evidence or of how people are to be treated fairly. The impersonal point of view is not the view from nowhere. It always bears the mark of our time and place.

And yet, I must add, its claim to being impersonal does not thereby show itself to be a sham. Our access to reality as it is in itself is always mediated through the contingencies of history. This is not the place to enter into a discussion of epistemological questions, but the general position to which I am alluding is easily summarized.[8] Impersonal reasons, I have said, are reasons that stem solely from facts outside of us, uncolored by our own interests and attachments. Though reflecting on what impersonal reasons we have certainly entails appealing to our existing conception of those facts, our conclusions are still valid precisely to the extent that the beliefs on which we then rely, for all their rootedness in the prior course of our experience, constitute knowledge of the matter at hand. To be sure, we may be wrong about the reliability of these beliefs. But that just means that our ideas concerning what impersonal reasons we have are always revisable, which is neither surprising nor ruinous. Impersonal reflection is, after all, an achievement, and, consequently, it is the subject of constant scrutiny for lingering traces of bias or distortion.

At this point, however, there arise some crucial questions. Does reflection, impersonal or not, really aim at truth? Is it an organ of knowledge, and if so, what can it provide knowledge *of*? These questions would appear to admit of a ready answer. We reflect in order to be better able to discern how we ought to think or act in the given circumstances, and that seems clearly to count as an object of knowledge. For it is something of which we begin by feeling ignorant and seek, by reflecting, to gain a correct grasp. What we ought to do is tantamount to what there is reason for us to do. So reflection, in essence, aims at knowledge of reasons for belief and action.

Such a conception results from taking literally the way we ordinarily talk about reflection, and in my view it should be no cause for alarm. But many disagree. In their eyes, it entails an untenable metaphysics and is, in any

[8] For a closer discussion, see my book, *The Autonomy of Morality* (Cambridge: Cambridge University Press, 2008), chapter 1, "History and Truth."

case, untrue to the nature of reflection. To suppose that reflection's relation to reasons is one of knowledge means not only attributing to the world a domain of irreducibly normative fact but also imagining that knowledge by itself could ever move us to action as reflection manifestly does. Belief by itself seems motivationally inert and able to lead us to act only in conjunction with some additional, conative element of the mind, such as a desire or a commitment. Reflection, it is thus claimed, is a practical rather than a theoretical enterprise: when we reflect on what we have reason to do, our purpose is to settle how we want to live, not to discover some fact about the world. To this set of claims I now turn.

1.3 Reflection and Knowledge

Reasons for belief and action are essentially normative in character.[9] What we have reason to do is what we *ought* to do, all else being equal. There is no explaining what is meant by reasons except by appeal to this or similar ways of speaking. Reasons cannot therefore be equated with any features of the natural world, physical or psychological, even though they certainly depend on the natural facts being as they are. That is why many philosophers balk at allowing that reasons can properly count as objects of knowledge. If knowledge is of what is the case independently of our coming to hold a view about it, then supposing that reasons figure among the things we can know entails that the world, as the totality of what is the case, must include normative facts about how we ought to think and act. Such a view runs counter to the *naturalism* that forms the reigning philosophical orthodoxy of our day. All that really exists, it is said, belongs to the domain of the natural sciences, the realm of physical fact or of psychological fact too, if the latter is not further reducible to the physical. As should be plain, I reject this naturalistic world picture. Further explanation can be found in Chapters 5 and 6. Here, however, my aim is to clarify the character of reasons and to explain why we should conceive of reflection as a way of acquiring knowledge about them.

Consider then, first, why it is that a reason cannot consist in a physical state of affairs. We sometimes say that the rain, or the fact that it is raining, is a reason to take an umbrella when leaving the house. Philosophers themselves have said this sort of thing.[10] But it is really a bit of shorthand.

[9] In Chapter 6, Sections 6.4–6.5, I return to this topic in further detail.

[10] Two recent examples are Benjamin Kiesewetter, *The Normativity of Rationality* (Oxford: Oxford University Press, 2017), 6: "Normative reasons are, at least typically, ordinary facts (or true

Strictly speaking, my reason to take an umbrella is not the rain itself, but rather a certain relation that the rain bears to my possibilities of action. After all, I could agree that it is raining yet dispute that there is a reason to take an umbrella. One can say, if one likes, that being a reason is a property of the fact, a property that some might then dispute it actually possesses. Yet since the property is a relational property, this just means that being a reason is essentially a relation – the relation of justifying or *counting in favor of* – that an empirical fact (that it is raining) stands in to one of my possibilities of action (taking an umbrella). I shall therefore generally talk of an empirical fact not as being a reason but as giving or providing a reason to do (or to believe) this or that. Now this relation of counting-in-favor-of is not a physical quality of the rain or a physical relation the rain stands in to some other empirical fact. It is *normative* in character. "The rain is (or gives me) a reason to take an umbrella" means the same as "Given the rain, I *ought* to take an umbrella." To be sure, other things may count in favor of not taking one, of wearing a hat instead, or of just getting wet. As a rule, reasons are in themselves *pro tanto,* as are the *oughts* to which they correspond. Only if they are not outweighed by contrary considerations do they indicate what we overall have reason or ought to do. But whether *pro tanto* or decisive, reasons, being of a normative character, cannot be identical with the physical facts that may give rise to them.

So too, the reason people have to believe this or to do that is not the same as any psychological state in which they find themselves. In particular, it is not, contrary to a common view, a combination of belief and desire.[11] My reason to take an umbrella, some would say, consists in my belief that it is raining conjoined with my desire to keep dry. But that cannot be right. It may be true that I would not have such a reason unless I wanted to stay dry, so that in this respect the reason is indeed conditional, binding only insofar as I have that desire. (Though it can also make perfect sense to say that I ought, for the sake of my health, to take an umbrella against the rain whether I want to keep dry or not.) Even so, the reason does not consist in the desire as such, but rather in the fact that the

propositions) such as the fact that you have promised to attend a meeting, or the fact that some treatment will provide the cure for a disease"; and Errol Lord, *The Importance of Being Rational* (Oxford: Oxford University Press, 2018), 7: "Objective normative reasons are facts that count in favor of various reactions . . . The fact that it is going to rain in the city I'm traveling to next week is a reason for me to intend to bring an umbrella."

11 The classic statement of such a doctrine is Donald Davidson, "Actions, Reasons, and Causes" (1963), reprinted in Davidson, *Essays on Actions and Events* (Oxford: Oxford University Press, 1980), 3–19.

desire counts in favor of taking an umbrella. After all, I might have the desire and still have no reason to take one, if, for example, the rain – unbeknown to me – has ceased. Moreover, what makes it true that the desire favors that action is not my belief that it is raining, as though the reason were constituted by that belief conjoined appropriately with the desire. The reason to take an umbrella depends in no way on my believing that it is raining. It is the fact that it is raining that gives rise to the reason. If you learned that the weather had just improved, you would inform me that I really have no reason to fetch my umbrella, even though I still believe it is raining. In short, a reason is the possible object of a belief and not itself a mental state of any sort, since we can be wrong about the reasons we really have.

"Internal" reasons, as Bernard Williams famously defined them, are reasons we would come to grasp were we to deliberate soundly on the basis of our existing beliefs and desires.[12] According to him, they are the only sorts of reasons we can rightly be said to have. I do not think this thesis is correct, if only because reasons may be at a given time inaccessible through deliberation and yet come to be understood by other routes, namely by training, in which the importance of certain possibilities is inculcated in us by others through discipline and reward. This is the only way we can learn, when very young, to appreciate the most basic kinds of reasons (the reason to go to school, for instance), and heeding such reasons is often the precondition for deliberating well about what else to believe or do. But in any case, "internal" reasons as Williams conceived them are not – contrary to what the term may suggest – anything "in" the mind. When we conclude that our present convictions give us a reason to believe this or to act thus, we do not suppose we have discovered a fact about our own thinking, but rather about what we should do. For the reason does not derive from our having those convictions, but from what those convictions are about. That is after all the object of our deliberation.

Recognizing that the reasons we *have* cannot consist in anything psychological, some have nonetheless supposed that the reasons that *move* us must belong to the mind. How else could it be said that reasons can cause us to act? Whence a common distinction between "normative" reasons, which serve to justify an action, and "motivating" reasons, which are

[12] Williams, "Internal and External Reasons," in *Moral Luck* (Cambridge: Cambridge University Press, 1981), 101–113, and, for the clarification that such reasons are those accessible by a "sound deliberative route," his later essay "Internal Reasons and the Obscurity of Blame," in *Making Sense of Humanity* (Cambridge: Cambridge University Press, 1995), 35–45 (35).

invoked to explain it.[13] Yet there are not in reality two different kinds of reasons. Talking about reasons as though they were motivating states in the mind is also a bit of shorthand. Strictly speaking, the reference is to our view of the reasons we have, since in such cases only this attitude of ours, not the actual existence of those reasons, is thought relevant to the sort of explanation being sought. But the reasons we believe there to be are the reasons that appear to us to justify what we do. So-called motivational reasons, understood as psychological states moving us to act, are therefore no more than our conception of the normative reasons we have. Moreover, sometimes there actually being such reasons, and not just our thinking they exist, does play an explanatory role – as when it turns out that we did the right thing for in fact the right reason. In such cases, reasons themselves lead us to act, via our correct ideas of them.[14]

It is, then, their essentially normative character that precludes identifying reasons with any physical or psychological facts. As a consequence, they can have no place in the world itself as naturalistically conceived. This implication, as I have said, has led to one main line of argument by which many philosophers deny, either implicitly or as a matter of doctrine, that reflection about what we ought to think or do can rightly count as a mode of knowledge. Conclusions about the reasons we have are not, it is held, really descriptive in intent, but serve instead only to embody or announce our commitments for dealing with the world around us. After all – and this is meant to be a corroborating argument – knowledge alone cannot move us to act, as reflection is geared to do. The judgments we make about what we ought to think or do are practical, not theoretical, in nature.

It is a sign of how thoroughly modern philosophy has absorbed the naturalistic worldview that the otherwise rival schools of Hume and of Kant, which today occupy so much of the terrain, are each impelled to embrace this view of reflection. Expressivists in the Humean tradition construe judgments of the form "A has a reason R to do X," not as aiming to describe correctly the reasons A has, but as expressing our endorsement of A doing X. More specifically, such judgments are held to express, for instance, our acceptance of a norm that permits or requires A to do X in the given circumstances.[15] Reflection is seen as charged with making clear to ourselves what norms we want in this sense to endorse, or what the

[13] See, for example, Michael Smith, *The Moral Problem* (Oxford: Blackwell, 1994), 94ff.

[14] How reasons can be causes is a difficult philosophical problem to which I turn in Chapters 6 (Section 6.8) and 7.

[15] This is the analysis given by Allan Gibbard in *Wise Choices, Apt Feelings* (Cambridge, MA: Harvard University Press, 1990).

norms we do endorse entail in a given situation. Kantians may differ from Humeans in their eagerness to deduce necessary constraints governing the sorts of rules we can in this way coherently make our own – constraints that supposedly amount, for instance, to the basic features of morality. But they agree that reasons cannot form part of reality itself. What we have reason to think or do is determined by principles of thought and action that we impose upon ourselves. Only through our own "autonomy" – that is, self-legislation – can the value-neutral facts of experience acquire significance for our conduct. "The ethics of autonomy," Christine Korsgaard declares in a Kantian spirit, "is the only one consistent with the metaphysics of the modern world."[16] Allan Gibbard, a leading expressivist, is equally explicit about his naturalistic approach to the nature of reasons:

> On the Platonistic picture, among the facts of the world are facts of what is rational and what is not . . . If this is what anyone seriously believes, then I simply want to debunk it. Nothing in a plausible, naturalistic picture of our place in the universe requires these non-natural facts.[17]

Since writing these words, he has come to allow, in accord with a "quasi-realism" he now shares with Simon Blackburn,[18] that judgments about reasons may count as true or false, but only because he now accepts a minimalist conception of truth according to which to assert a proposition as true amounts to no more than just to assert that proposition. He continues to deny that they purport to describe the way things are really, that reasons for belief or action obtain independently of our attitudes toward them.[19] Both Gibbard and Korsgaard are consequently at one in holding that reasons are something we introduce into the world from without, coloring the neutral face of nature with normative distinctions of our own devising.

[16] Korsgaard, *The Sources of Normativity* (Cambridge: Cambridge University Press, 1996), p. 5. I examine her views at greater length in Chapter 5, Section 5.5.

[17] Gibbard, *Wise Choices, Apt Feelings*, p. 154. I take up the question of platonism below (Section 1.4).

[18] Blackburn, *Ruling Passions* (Oxford: Clarendon Press, 2001).

[19] The quasi-realist account appears in Gibbard, *Thinking How to Live* (Cambridge, MA: Harvard University Press, 2003); see particularly 18–19, 182. Normative judgments are conceived fundamentally as expressing attitudes of endorsement rather than describing reasons for belief or action (9–10, 112), but since asserting an endorsement is held to be equivalent to asserting it as true, they supposedly function as though they also expressed beliefs (181, 189–191). The commitment to a naturalistic conception of what ultimately exists therefore remains (xi, 194), as well as the explicit scorn for "Platonism" (182n). As to whether the quasi-realist conception can succeed in capturing all the way normative judgments function, see note 25 later in this chapter.

As Korsgaard's statement rightly indicates, this widespread view of reasons and reflection is indeed driven by metaphysical assumptions. For naturalism, one should remember, is not a conclusion of the modern natural sciences themselves, which make no claim about encompassing all that can count as real. Global assertions of this kind are instead the province of metaphysics, which, as I explained in the Introduction, is that part of philosophy concerned with laying out the ultimate structure of reality. There is nothing wrong with the enterprise of metaphysics as such. But I object when metaphysical views – that is, views about what fundamental sorts of things can be said to exist and about what existence itself means – are simply assumed rather than critically examined, particularly if they contradict essential aspects of our everyday self-understanding. That is the case here. The notion of reasons espoused, explicitly or tacitly, by expressivists and Kantians alike can make no sense of what it is to reflect or even to reason.

Expressivists often focus on morality alone, even though their task is to explain the nature of normative judgment as a whole. It may perhaps seem plausible that moral judgments do no more than express a certain kind of approval or disapproval of their object, given the ease with which some people can persuade themselves that moral distinctions are ultimately of our own creation. But expressivism looks far less palatable when stated in its properly universal form. Can we honestly believe that the canons by which we judge that a scientific theory is true – its fit with experimental data, its coherence with existing doctrine, its performance on severe tests – have only the authority we bestow on them? If we hold that there is good reason to adhere to these principles inasmuch as they are objectively valid, are we only expressing our endorsement of a norm to the effect that everyone (ourselves included) ought to abide by them whether one happens to want to or not?[20] Does our endorsing such a norm explain what it is to regard those principles as valid? If we were not constrained by an allegiance to naturalism, we would surely suppose that the order of explanation is the other way around. It is the perceived validity of the principles that accounts for why we think anyone ought to adhere to them and to endorse a norm to this effect. And if our perception is correct, then it is their validity itself that ultimately explains why we have endorsed that norm, just as it is the actual existence of a chair in the corner that explains why we perceive one there and walk over in order to sit down. This is the

[20] This is Gibbard's account of what we mean in asserting that principles of thought and action are not merely ones we accept but are objectively valid. See *Wise Choices, Apt Feelings*, 164–166.

way we would ordinarily understand the matter unless we had an antecedent commitment to a naturalistic metaphysics.

Now denying that we reflect in order to discover something we do not yet know – namely, what there is reason to think or do in the given circumstances – renders the process of reflection unrecognizable. In fact, the underlying refusal to countenance the reality of reasons distorts the very nature of reason, as we can observe if we look at the parallel Kantian notion of autonomy. Kantians think of reason as self-legislating, as giving itself principles of conduct, intellectual and practical, in the light of which alone facts in the world can acquire the status of being reasons to think and act in certain ways.[21] But reason, like any faculty of mind, is to be defined in terms of the activity that is its characteristic exercise. What then could be more obvious than that *reason* is the faculty of *reasoning?* And how else can the activity of reasoning be understood except in terms of its being responsive to *reasons?* The most straightforward account of the nature of reason presumes, therefore, that reasons are a reality we discover, not an artifact of our ways of thinking. To be sure, we do sometimes impose rules on ourselves whose authority is, to this extent, of our own making. But we do so precisely because there appear to be reasons that warrant this step. If I give myself a rule never to borrow, it is in virtue of both knowing how prone I am to borrow more than I can pay back and accepting the antecedent authority of the principle that debts are to be repaid. Autonomy makes no sense as a global account of the nature of reasons. (I return to this critique of the idea of autonomy in Chapter 5).

Yet what of the counterargument that figuring out what reasons we have, which typically leads us to act one way or another, cannot consist in simply discovering some further facts about the way things are? Beliefs purport to represent the facts as they are, but beliefs alone, so it is held, cannot move us to act. Thus, when we conclude that we have reason to act in a particular way, we are not reporting a discovery, but rather expressing our confidence that the conduct in question satisfies or promotes our existing needs, interests, or commitments: "the word 'reason' refers to a

[21] Such is the way Korsgaard defines her "procedural moral realism," in contrast to a "substantive" realism that regards reasons as a reality to which our reasoning responds (Korsgaard, *The Sources of Normativity,* 36). I caution that the sense of "autonomy" in question is the one for which Kant coined the term and which concerns our relation to the reasons for which we think and act. It is not the sense that has to do with our relation to other people, as when it is said that autonomous agents decide matters for themselves instead of being impelled by custom or coercion. Autonomy in this latter sense is not my concern here. On these different senses of autonomy, see Chapter 5.

kind of reflective success."[22] Reasons, it is said, are the outcome of reflection when carried out well, not a reality to which reflection responds: what we have reason to think or do is what we can coherently endorse as we put our thinking in order.

This line of argument is a mainstay of both the Kantian and Humean traditions. Yet for all its popularity, it is rather poor. First, recall (from Section 1.1) the obvious fact that people (and other animals too) often act for reasons without reflecting. A further, more telling objection is that endorsing some option on the basis of our existing convictions depends on supposing that they justify this decision, that is, that they give us reason to endorse the option. Reasons cannot simply be the output of reflective success, since success in reflecting consists precisely in how well we respond to the reasons there are.

However, the underlying error lies deeper still. It is a flawed conception of belief. Conclusions about reasons certainly serve to guide our conduct. Yet this does not mean that they cannot have the character of beliefs. For belief by itself is not in fact motivationally inert. Clearly our beliefs are able on their own, in response to relevant evidence, to move us to draw certain inferences. Why are they then not similarly able, in response to particular circumstances, to move us to act in certain ways?

Consider what it is, in general, to believe this or that. A belief is not a feeling (say, the particular vivacity with which an idea stands before the mind, as Hume supposed), nor is it the act of assenting to some proposition. It is a disposition, and one intimately connected with both the presumed truth of what is believed (since to believe that *p* means to believe that *p* is true) and with the behavior of the person whose belief it is (since we attribute beliefs to people in order to explain what they do). To believe that *p* is to be disposed to think and act in accord with the presumed truth of *p*. A person who has said she believes that the cat is on the mat yet walks across the mat as though nothing were there will not normally be held to believe what she has said she believes. To be sure, the specific things a belief disposes someone to do depend on other elements in their outlook, just as it is true that one sometimes fails to heed a belief one has. So the person in question may have her reasons for ignoring the cat or may be tramping across the mat out of inadvertence. But if she believes the cat is there, then she will be moved, all other things being equal, to comport herself compatibly with what, in her view, the truth of that belief implies. Beliefs do not merely represent the way things are or consist in holding

[22] Korsgaard, *The Sources of Normativity*, 93.

certain facts to be true. They are at once descriptive and prescriptive. Being disposed to draw appropriate inferences from what we believe is an inherent part of believing. In other words, beliefs are commitments in their own right, commitments to think and act in accord with the presumed truth of what is believed.[23]

Thus, reflection can very well aim at discovering what we have reason to do at the same time as it guides us in how to live. Its goal is to arrive at correct beliefs about the reasons we have, beliefs that themselves, like all beliefs, commit us to conducting ourselves accordingly. Reflection is inseparably both theoretical and practical.

1.4 The Reality of Reasons

So far, I have been arguing that reflection can be an organ of knowledge and that its domain can consist in reasons of an essentially normative character, existing independently of our conceptions of them. But I have yet to explain just what sort of reality is constituted by the reasons for thought and action that are the objects of reflection. Here I will be somewhat brief, since I take up this topic in more detail in Chapters 6 and 7.

If reasons form part of the fabric of reality, they are not, to be sure, some sort of independent entities, hovering alongside the more down-to-earth things we see and touch. As I have already suggested, reasons consist in a certain *relation* – the relation of *counting in favor of* – that features of the natural world, the physical and psychological facts making it up, bear to our possibilities of thought and action. This is a normative relation, and so reasons cannot be equated with anything in nature. Yet, being relational, they manifestly depend on the existence of what they relate, and that means they depend on the natural (physical and psychological) facts being as they are, as well as on our having (a further psychological fact) certain possibilities of thought and action that we can take up. Reasons exist only because beings like us, which are in this sense intelligent and free (thus the higher animals as well), do so too.[24] It would certainly be bizarre to think otherwise. It does not follow, however, that we are the authors of the reasons there are, that they amount to the significance we bestow upon those facts. That one thing counts in favor of another is a relation

[23] I return to the nature of belief in Chapter 8, Section 8.3.

[24] Rocks and trees have possibilities too, but not possibilities they can choose to take up. That is why it makes no sense to say they have reasons. See Chapter 7, Section 7.7.

(a normative relation) that we discover, that we can be right or wrong about, not one we institute ourselves. Relations are no less real than the things they relate when they enjoy this sort of independence from our beliefs about their existence and nature. Reasons, then, too, form part of the world, understood broadly as the totality of what exists.

This conception can be called "platonistic" in that it holds that reasons, like Plato's Forms, constitute an intrinsically normative order of reality, neither physical nor psychological in character. But it is not an extravagant kind of platonism. It does not suppose that reasons dwell in some platonic heaven, unsullied by the vicissitudes of the world here below. On the contrary, it follows closely our ordinary sense of what reasons are. When we suppose, as we ordinarily do, that how we ought to think and act is a matter of how the facts bear on the options before us, what we mean, in effect, is that reasons for belief and action are both *relational* and *real*. And when we conclude, in particular, that we have an impersonal reason to do something, what we mean is that the facts by themselves, apart from our own interests and attachments, count in favor of that option. Theories that reduce reasons to an expression of our commitments have to devise formulas to mimic these ways of talking without taking them literally, and it is not surprising that the simulation never quite succeeds.[25]

Not only do reasons not exist independently of the natural world or of us in particular; they also do not exist independently of one another. Reasons bear various logical and evidential connections to one another, normally in virtue of what they happen to be reasons for. Sometimes, for instance, the reason we have to do one thing is contingent on our having a reason to do another, as when, thinking we have reason to believe the noise behind the bushes is a wild boar, we conclude that we have reason to climb up a nearby tree. And sometimes the reason to do a certain thing derives from the way a far broader and standing reason – in other words, a principle, governing how we ought in general to comport ourselves – bears

[25] Gibbard, for instance, claims that to say we have a reason to do X independently of our interests and attachments is to mean we accept both a norm requiring us to do X and a (higher-order) norm requiring us to accept that norm whether we want to or not (Gibbard, *Wise Choices, Apt Feelings*, 168–170). Now, is our supposed acceptance of this higher-order norm a brute fact, a mere decision, or is the norm instead one we ought or have reason to accept? Only the latter will allow this analysis to keep pace with what is meant by an impersonal reason to do X. And yet Gibbard must analyze this alternative, in turn, as our acceptance of a still higher-order norm requiring us to accept the first higher-order norm whether we want to or not. The Gibbardian theory is constantly chasing after the idea of impersonality without ever catching up.

on the particular circumstances at hand.[26] Thus, the reason to save some of our monthly income derives from our having reason to be prudent and to think about our long-term good.

What, then, about the relation between moral reasons and the other sorts of considerations or reasons that can move us to act? It has often been thought, both in everyday life and in moral philosophy, that acting morally needs to be shown to be ultimately in the agent's own best interest. The idea goes back to Glaucon's appeal to Socrates at the beginning of Book II of Plato's *Republic* (357b): "Prove to us that it is better in every way to be just rather than unjust." Only if the reason to concern ourselves with another's good can be derived from the presumably more basic reason we have to pursue our own good can morality really be authoritative for our conduct. The philosophical proofs have taken many different forms, depending on how both the agent's good and practical rationality have been conceived. Plato had Socrates respond to the challenge by arguing that "justice" or morality alone ensures the harmony of the soul to which we each ultimately aspire. The more common version in our own day follows the lead of Thomas Hobbes, arguing that the adoption of principles of mutual restraint and cooperation is the most efficient means for each individual to satisfy his own interests over the long run, whatever they may be, given the essentials of the human condition.

This is not the place to evaluate in detail these various attempts to show how we may reason ourselves into the moral point of view from a standpoint located outside it and presumed to be more basic.[27] Let me observe here, not only that they all fail (for that should be well known), but that they fail in two distinct ways. They do not succeed in explaining how the moral "ought" derives from the "ought" of individual prudence, duly enlightened. Even more importantly, the very understanding of morality on which they rely is typically defective, since it is slanted to fit the extra-moral starting point they invoke.

Consider the Hobbesian approach, as developed in our time by a great many writers. It conceives of morality as a set of rules for social cooperation, founded upon mutual advantage. The limits these rules place on the pursuit of our own ends are held to maximize our good in the long run through the interactions they permit with others, provided that others,

[26] I discuss further the relation between reasons and principles in *What Is Political Philosophy?* (Princeton: Princeton University Press, 2020), chapter 1, §7.

[27] See my book *The Autonomy of Morality*, chapter 5, §§1–6. There I examine, among other attempts, David Gauthier's version of the Hobbesian argument; a summary of my objections appears in the next two paragraphs.

too, comply with these restraints. Yet such a view excludes from the domain of moral concern two groups of people whom it is the business of morality to move us to treat better than we would otherwise be inclined to do: those unlikely to come into frequent contact with us and thus ever to contribute to our good, and those with neither the power nor the ability to enhance or jeopardize our interests in any way, however often we may cross their path. Morality conceived as a cooperative scheme for mutual benefit fails to embody so fundamental a norm as the respect we owe to *strangers* and to *the weak*. This is not, moreover, a failure to account for some marginal phenomena, to be remedied by further refining the theory. For surely it belongs to the very core of our moral thinking that we are to show equal respect to those who, through circumstance or misfortune, may never be in a position to benefit us in return. Indeed, we act toward the powerful and the useful in a moral and not merely prudent fashion, when we behave as we would even if they lacked those assets that make them of interest to our own endeavors. We aim then to treat them too with the respect they deserve as human beings, not with the sort of circumspection we exercise in dealing with the various natural forces for good and ill in our environment. (I return to this theme in Chapter 3, Section 3.5).

The Hobbesian version of morality reflects the notion of the rational agent, concerned to pursue one's own interests as efficiently as possible, that Hobbesians take as their point of departure for showing how we can reason ourselves into morality. That is why it is so distorted. For if, as I have assumed from the outset (and will explain more thoroughly in Section 1.5), the moral point of view consists in seeing in another's good, considered just as such, a reason for action on our part, then how could it ever come within reach of a person whose reasoning focuses essentially on satisfying their own interests? Let these interests be other-directed as well as self-directed; it does not matter. There is all the difference in the world between respecting or fostering another's good because one has among one's interests a particular attachment to that person and doing so simply because that person's good is in question. It is the latter, the impersonally motivated act, that embodies the properly moral attitude. Every attempt to bring the moral point of view within the orbit of the rational pursuit of one's own concerns is bound to erase its most distinctive feature, which is the concern we conceive for another's good just because it is his or hers. We cannot, then, reason ourselves into an appreciation of what it is to act morally, beginning from some location outside the moral point of view. Morality has to speak for itself. It constitutes a class of reasons for action that is *sui generis*, unintelligible in terms of any supposedly more primitive class of reasons. This idea ought not to be disturbing, though it does have important philosophical consequences.

To understand why it does not make a mystery of moral thinking, consider the case of prudence – precisely the form of reasoning in which many philosophers (and no doubt others too) feel a hankering to ground morality. How would we go about changing the mind of someone who perceives no reason to be prudent, no reason to take into account, in deciding what to do, the desires and interests he will predictably have later even if they are not his at the moment? We might have some luck by exposing the erroneous assumptions that keep him perhaps from recognizing the value of prudence (such as the notion that reasons for action can be but the expression of one's given desires). But if negative arguments of this sort do not work, what else can we do? There can be no prospect of reasoning him into an acceptance of prudential reasons by appealing to some deeper set of motivations he could be presumed to possess. What could such an argument look like? That it is in his interest to be prudent? That is hopelessly circular. The fact is that prudence is just like morality: it constitutes a class of *sui generis* reasons for action, underivable from any more basic sorts of considerations.

Herein lies an important philosophical lesson, not just about morality but about reflection in general. If, I have just said, we are to move the person who has been stubbornly refusing to listen to the voice of prudence, we can only urge something like: "Think about what you will surely want one year from now. Don't you see that you ought to act accordingly?" In the end, people just have to acknowledge that there exist reasons of prudence. There is no way they can be led to reason themselves from some external standpoint into a sense of the value of prudence. So, too, with morality. We simply have to see in another's good, considered in itself, a reason for action on our part. Reflection does not always proceed, then, by inferring some reasons from others with which are already familiar. It also includes the power of acknowledging the force of reasons that speak for themselves. Such is the kind of reflection that deep shifts in our thinking typically require.

This conclusion may seem to contradict my earlier insistence (Section 1.2) that our capacity for reflection develops as we mature. But that is not so. When we are young, as I noted, reflecting means taking up the standpoint (or what we imagine to be the standpoint) of those to whom we feel close, judging ourselves and our possibilities accordingly. As our horizons broaden and we encounter conflicts among our various loyalties, we are moved to work out less parochial standards of evaluation. Thus, we develop an ability to reflect impersonally on what we ought to believe and do. Yet though this process takes place step by step, it does not consist in grasping how our various interests and attachments, along with the desire to handle the tensions among them, point us to reasons for belief and action that are impersonal in character. The capacity of reflection is one thing; its objects are another. We may learn to stand back from our individual commitments so as to view the world as it is in itself. But this achievement by itself leaves open what reasons, if any, we then discover about how we are to think and act. To see what reasons there are, we must actually reflect. After all, when we realize that our own good does not, absolutely speaking, matter more than the good of others, we might perhaps conclude that therefore neither theirs nor ours matter at all. Being impartial has been known more than once to produce indifference.

Some will contend that if we are not to remain indifferent, we must care about how people in general fare. This is true. Yet the ready appeal to feelings does little to illuminate the matter. For why would we care if not that we see some reason to do so? The point at issue is precisely how we come to discern such a reason. It is not, I have argued, by determining what in the long run or in the deepest sense will serve our own good. If there is a reason to care about the good of others, taken in itself, it has to be one that speaks for itself when we view the world impersonally. Yet it is also true that impersonal reflection must look in the right place. We need, in particular, to focus not on the thought that ultimately no one's good matters much at all but on the undeniable fact that each person's good matters enormously from his or her own perspective. It is not that we can then deduce from this fact that their good should be an object of concern for anyone. No psychological fact can simply entail a normative reason. However, this fact is what gives us a reason to care about their good just because it is theirs. It is what counts in favor of our caring about their good.

1.5 The Moral Point of View

Such then are the basic features of reflection, its modalities and aims. We reflect in order to figure out what we ought to think or do in response to a problem that has disrupted our usual ways of dealing with the world. To find a solution, we stand back from how we have gone on before, looking at ourselves from the outside and appraising our options from a standpoint we consider authoritative for the problem at hand. The object now before our mind is what we have reason to think or do, and the reasons we seek to discover are by definition *universal:* if they are valid for us, then they are valid for all under similar circumstances. They are, in addition, *impersonal* if they are reasons we can grasp as binding on us independently of our own interests and attachments.

With this framework in place, it is time to return to the main theme. We are moral beings, I have said, because of the remarkable power of self-transcendence that reflection makes possible when it becomes impersonal. We can learn how to stand back from our own concerns so as to be able to see in another's good, considered just as such, a reason for action on our part. The preceding analysis has shown what is involved in reflection taking on an impersonal form. But much more needs to be said about the role that impersonal reflection plays in our moral thinking.

I have said little, for instance, to explain what sort of being this "other" is whose good appears from the moral point of view as an intrinsic object of concern. Is it any human being as such, or is it more broadly all living beings, animals and even plants included, that may be thought to possess a good? How widely does our moral responsibility extend? I have been assuming that it encompasses every human being, and that is the assumption in all that follows. But I do not assume that our moral concern must stop at the boundaries of humanity. As to how far it should extend, I have no systematic answer, and I believe moreover that we should not be in a rush to devise one. Uncertainty about the scope of our moral responsibility seems to me in keeping with the present intellectual situation. For plainly those traditional answers will not do that equate the objects of moral concern with beings who are themselves able to take up the moral point of view. Such is the approach adopted whenever one conceives of morality as a set of rules for social cooperation (as in the Hobbesian tradition) or as a system of reciprocal claims rational agents make upon one another (as in the Kantian tradition). And this approach fails because it cannot even attribute to all human beings a moral standing in their own right – not to infants, not to the mentally disabled, not to the doddering elderly, which with the advances of modern medicine we all have a good chance of becoming. At best, it can award such people only a derivative status, dependent on what is owed to their morally functioning trustees. Surely, then, the domain of moral concern must extend beyond the domain of moral agents, and how far it reaches is a question at the frontiers of moral thinking today.[28]

[28] Cf. Martha Nussbaum, *The Frontiers of Justice* (Cambridge, MA: Harvard University Press, 2006).

What I do want to discuss in some detail is the relation itself between impersonal reflection and morality. On several different scores, one might in fact dispute whether so intimate a connection exists between the two as I have been asserting. Does the essence of the moral point of view really consist in recognizing that the good of another, purely by virtue of being a person's good, is of equal moment with our own?

It will help to review the position I have taken. There is, I have observed, more than one basis on which we can see in another's good a reason for us to act in some way, to refrain from doing what might otherwise prove attractive or even to do what we can to help her to achieve her good. We may, for instance, hope that thereby the person, or others happening to witness our behavior, will treat us well in return. Or we may feel a special bond of affection for the person – a relative, friend, or coreligionist perhaps – and on this basis put her good at the center of our attention. Finally, however, we may act so as to respect or foster another's good without an eye to our own interests and attachments but simply because someone's well-being is at stake. The person may not be anyone we know or suppose we will ever meet again, or she may be an individual to whom we do have some particular tie but whose situation and needs we are considering apart from that bond. In either case, the reason we then recognize to care about the other's good is impersonal in character, and this sort of thinking – such has been my refrain – constitutes the heart of the moral point of view. It can become a matter of habit, and that is quite desirable. Yet not only do we acquire this sort of concern for others by learning to reflect impersonally, but we need continually to reflect anew, exercising the same capacity of distancing ourselves from our own interests and attachments to survey the possibilities before us, if we are to monitor and refine our moral outlook on the world.

Now one might immediately object that this conception of morality is a highly contentious one. Does not its insistence on impersonality and the need to stand back from our own concerns signal an allegiance, for all my rejection (Section 1.3) of the idea of autonomy, to the rigoristic distinction between duty and inclination typical of Kantian ethics? In large part, this objection is a misunderstanding. I have so far said little about moral feelings such as sympathy, but my aim has not been to deny their importance when we take an intrinsic interest in another person's good. Contrary to Kant, moral character does not show through most when one does what is right despite "being cold in temperament and indifferent to the sufferings of others,"[29] since there is nothing much left for moral character to be, given that sort of insensibility. Our thinking about right and wrong takes shape through experience in the way I sketched earlier (Section 1.2). We handle the conflicts between our various allegiances by learning to consider others from a wider perspective, and this process involves a generalization of the ability to care about how another fares that we first acquire in our relations to those who are close to us. But it is crucial to understand rightly the role feelings play in this process. To sympathize with the pain or joy of others, at least insofar as morality is concerned, is not to feel their pain or joy ourselves, as though by a sort of contagion; it is to feel sadness *at* their suffering, delight *at* their happiness, a second-order feeling in which we express our sense that they have *reason* to feel as they do. Sympathy consists in being moved by the good of others. It thus remains narrower than it might otherwise be, so long as it is shaped by our own interests and attachments. Feelings come to have a moral role precisely to the extent that they take us out of ourselves, and for this to be so, they must become indeed impersonal.

Nothing, then, in the conception of morality on which I have been leaning appears peculiarly Kantian. In fact, if I had to cite a single source of inspiration, it would not be Kant, but rather Scripture – though I hasten to add that my agenda is strictly secular. In both the Hebrew Bible and the New Testament, we meet the precept, "Love thy neighbor as thyself."[30] It contains, I believe, a profound insight into the true character of moral thinking. All of us by nature love ourselves, caring immensely whether our desires are satisfied and whether our lives go as we would like. Obviously, this self-love often stands in the way of our caring about others as we morally should. Yet it also offers a paradigm of what a concern for others would be like if we were to look beyond our own sphere – beyond, that is, our individual interests as well as the interests of those who matter to us because of their special connection to ourselves. For the conspicuous feature of self-love is not so much its magnitude as its immediacy. The concern we feel for our own good is not channeled through other considerations: we do not care about how our own lives go because we are someone to whom we feel particularly close, or because we hope that we

[29] Immanuel Kant, *Grundlegung der Metaphysik der Sitten (Groundwork of the Metaphysics of Morals)* (1785), Akademie-Ausgabe (Berlin: Reimer, 1900–), vol. IV, 398–399.

[30] Leviticus 19:18; Matthew 19:19, 22:39; Mark 12:31. Note that this precept is quite different from the Golden Rule of doing unto others as we would have them do unto us (Matthew 7:12), at least when the latter is understood as a norm of reciprocity, for then it ties our treatment of others to what would be conducive to our own interests.

will secure from ourselves some benefit in return. Each of us cares quite simply because "it's me!" Suppose, then, we cared about another's good in the same direct, unmediated way, solely because it is his or her good. That would be, in the Biblical phrase, to "love thy neighbor as thyself," or, in the more analytic language I have used, to see in another's good, considered just as such, a reason for action on our part. Such, I claim, is the core of morality.

Two other features of this conception should also be noted, again to avoid misunderstanding. The first is that it does not assume that the demands of morality are supremely authoritative. To see in another's good a claim on our attention no less direct than the claim made by our own does involve regarding these claims as in this respect essentially equal, differing only in the importance and urgency of what is at stake. And the moral point of view does entail seeing oneself as but one person among others. Yet it does not follow that the morally best action must always be the one that, all things considered, we have most reason to do. We become moral beings by learning to recognize in another's good, considered as such, a reason for action on our part. But that means that we must, in given situations, weigh such reasons against the other sorts of reasons we perceive, reasons that may favor our own interests or attachments. There is, I believe, no general principle that can plausibly inform us how to handle every such case, certainly none that can convince us that morality has to override all other concerns. Morality requires us to look at our lives from without, but we must also live our lives from within. Philosophers in the Kantian tradition have often tried to show that morality possesses supreme authority, but as a rule they have proceeded by supposing that reason must give itself its own principles of action, arguing then that the fundamental conditions under which it can coherently do so amount to the self-legislation of basic moral norms. If instead, as I have argued (Section 1.3), reason consists essentially in a responsiveness to reasons, then there can be no such *a priori* guarantee that the claims of morality must prove paramount. We have to consider the particularities of the situation at hand.

Thus, to invoke an example made famous by Bernard Williams, if we can rescue from imminent death only one of two people and one happens to be our spouse, it would appear to be "one thought too many" were we to rush toward our spouse, not solely out of love, but also with the idea that it is morally permissible in such a situation to favor the people we love or even (as a utilitarian might hold) that devotion to loved ones is commonly the best means for each individual to maximize the general good.[31] In cases such as this, requiring an impersonal justification for our response, of the sort provided by morality, is worse than superfluous. It casts considerable doubt on the genuineness of our love. Morality need not always be our ultimate standpoint of evaluation. Sometimes other things rightly matter a lot more. Only the moralistic believe that being moral means always putting morality first.[32]

A second misunderstanding would be to suppose that if the moral point of view consists in seeing everyone's good as of equal moment, acting morally must therefore amount to acting so as to bring about the most good overall. That is not so. Nothing inherently favors this sort of "consequentialist" position. On the contrary, the moral point of view is in itself mute about how exactly we are to advance the good of others and adjudicate the competing claims they may make on our attention. Principles of moral reasoning need to be introduced to make the moral point of view operational.

One principle is aggregative: giving equal consideration to each person's good can be taken to mean that we should consider each person impartially as we determine what will most increase the total good of all. That is precisely the consequentialist approach. But it is wrong to think, like many philosophers, that if we have a concern for other people's good generally, then wanting to bring about as much of it as possible is the only step that makes sense.[33] We could instead resolve to respect each person's good as precious in its own right. Another principle is thus distributive: if each

[31] Bernard Williams, "Persons, Character, and Morality," in Williams, *Moral Luck*, 17–19. In this essay, Williams appears, however, to wrongly suppose that a conception of morality as impersonal must require that moral considerations be always supreme. In other writings, he made further objections to such a conception – for instance, that the idea of categorically binding obligations must entail something like Kant's outlandish, nonempirical notion of freedom – with which I also do not agree. See my book, *The Morals of Modernity* (Cambridge: Cambridge University Press, 1996), 57f, as well as Chapter 7, Section 7.5, in which I show that there are more flexible ways of conceiving the relation between "ought" and "can." In general, I think Williams went wrong in identifying so closely an impersonal conception of morality with Kant's particular variant.

[32] In an earlier work, *Patterns of Moral Complexity* (Cambridge: Cambridge University Press, 1987), 79ff, 132ff, I took a different approach. The idea was to conceive of how we think we should act toward others on the basis of our attachments and affections as a matter of "particularistic obligations," falling under a basic principle of morality I called "partiality." I now think this was a mistake. It is certainly possible to regard things this way. (For more detail, see Chapter 2, Section 2.3). But our feelings of friendship for another can, and often should, move us by themselves to concern ourselves with her good, without the idea that we have an obligation to treat our friends well.

[33] A recent example of this view is Katarzyna de Lazari-Radek and Peter Singer, *The Point of View of the Universe: Sidgwick and Contemporary Ethics* (Oxford: Oxford University Press, 2014), esp. chapter 5.

person's good is to be treated equally – at least in ways that protect and foster their very ability to have and pursue a conception of their good – then it ought not to be compromised or sacrificed even for the sake of ensuring a greater good for others. This is the underlying rationale of so-called deontological theories, which define what we owe to a given person, the treatment we should (as in keeping a promise) and should never (as in doing violence) accord that person, without regard to how we could otherwise act so as to benefit others or to what others might do in response to our action.

It is clear that these two ways of thinking are not the same and can lead to very different judgments about what to do. But it is also clear that sometimes the one and sometimes the other seems the natural approach to take. When a great number of people may be affected and their needs are particularly urgent, satisfying the needs of as many as possible – in other words, bringing about the most good overall – easily looks like the path to adopt. But when that is not the case, or when helping the many entails doing significant harm to some, respecting the integrity of the individual tends to square better with our conscience. Sometimes, of course, we find ourselves unsure about whether, in the given situation, the one or the other stance is more appropriate. I do not believe that we should try to settle, once and for all, which of these two basic principles of moral reasoning, consequentialist or deontological, defines the single correct theory of morality. Each of them is a plausible interpretation of what the moral point of view means in practice. That is why it can so often appear right, depending on the situation, to base our actions on the one instead of on the other. We do better, then, to recognize their common validity as well as their capacity to conflict.[34]

Both the consequentialist and deontological principles have, then, their basis in the impersonal perspective in which each person's good presents itself as constituting an equal reason for concern on our part. It is not that they can be derived from that perspective or that their content can be explicated in terms of that perspective alone. But they presuppose it and are not fully intelligible without it. If, with Henry Sidgwick, we choose to think of the impersonal standpoint of morality as taking up "the point of

[34] In *Patterns of Moral Complexity*, chapter 6, I called this phenomenon the "heterogeneity" of morality. That term now seems to me misleading, since the idea is not that morality has a plurality of ultimate, divergent sources. The two principles are best understood as competing interpretations of the same root idea.

view of the universe,"[35] then, contrary to Sidgwick himself, the point of view of the universe turns out, when we seek to make sense of it, to be a bit untidy.

1.6 Impersonality and Intersubjectivity

One last and important objection to the conception of morality I have been outlining needs to be confronted. In his book, *The Second-Person Standpoint,* Stephen Darwall has argued that moral reasons for action are founded in basic relations of mutual accountability in which we all stand to one another and thus that the moral point of view is "intersubjective" rather than "impersonal."[36] Here is his favorite example to illustrate the thesis. If someone steps on your foot, you might assert that he ought to get off for two different reasons – either because he is in a position to stop the pain you are undergoing, or because he has no business treating you in such a fashion. The one reason is impersonal or "agent-neutral," since a third party would have the same reason to remove that person's foot so as to end the pain if she were able to do so. The other reason is "second-personal" or "agent-relative," since it is one that the perpetrator alone can be said to have in this situation, a reason he has because of the relations of mutual accountability in which he stands with regard to you and others. Moral obligations, Darwall argues, rest essentially on reasons of this second, intersubjective sort.

Such reasons certainly exist. Moreover, in a strict sense (narrower than what has become common usage), the term "moral obligation" refers, not to the whole of what we ought morally to do, but solely to what we owe to others in virtue of the kind of relation in which we stand to them that gives them a corresponding right to demand that we act in the appropriate way, such that if we fail to do so, we have not simply done wrong, but have wronged them.[37] A clear example is the obligation to keep our promises, in contrast, say, to the fact that we ought to give to charity, which is not something we owe to the poor or something they have a right to demand.

[35] Sidgwick, *The Methods of Ethics* (7th ed., 1907; Indianapolis: Hackett, 1981), 382: "the good of any one individual is of no more importance, from the point of view (if I may say so) of the Universe, than the good of any other."

[36] Stephen Darwall, *The Second-Person Standpoint* (Cambridge, MA: Harvard University Press, 2006), 8, 60, 102.

[37] For illuminating remarks on this strict sense of moral obligation, see the essay by H. L. A. Hart, "Are There Any Natural Rights?" *Philosophical Review* 64, no. 2 (April 1955), 175–191. I say more about this strict sense of obligation in the next chapter.

Yet is it not therefore plain that at least part of morality has nothing to do with agent-relative reasons? For surely giving to the poor, like rescuing someone in danger or indeed relieving someone's pain, figures among the things we ought morally to do and constitutes, in an appropriately broad sense, a "moral obligation," even though such duties are ours for the same (agent-neutral) reason that anyone has to aid those who happen to be in distress. Imagine, for instance, that a person is in pain, not because of being treated negligently by someone else, but as a result of some natural disaster. People in a position to help ought morally to do so, despite the fact that the person has not been wronged by anyone. Darwall's theory appears to offer no place for obligations of this sort.[38]

Furthermore, in that part of morality where agent-relative reasons do play an essential role, their validity depends on a deeper set of reasons that come into focus only within an impersonal point of view. Take again the case where someone steps on your foot. Only because it is an act that can cause pain – an ill that, as such, anyone has reason to put an end to – can you claim that that person owes it to you not to do such a thing and that you have a right to complain if he does. The agent-relative reason he has not to treat you in such a way rests on the agent-neutral consideration that pain is something to be prevented or stopped when it occurs. True, the person owes it to you to avoid stepping on your foot even if the act does not happen to cause you any pain, since doing so – or at least keeping his foot planted there – expresses a lack of respect for your person. But it shows disrespect because it is an act that might well have caused pain, or that shows disregard for that possibility.

The same is true in the case of promising. Only because there is an impersonal reason to value the benefits that people derive from being able to trust one another does the practice of promise-keeping acquire the authority it has, and do we thus have the agent-relative reason to keep our promises to those to whom they are made. After all, do we not

[38] Darwall distinguishes between our "obligation to" someone having a correlative right and "obligation simpliciter" or "obligation period." (See Stephen Darwall, "Reply to Korsgaard, Wallace, and Watson," *Ethics* 118, no. 1 [October 2007]: 52–69, at 60–63.) But what he means by the latter notion is the authority belonging to members of the moral community in general (and not just to those to whom we owe certain duties) to demand that we honor our rights-entailing obligations – an authority entitling them to claim, if we fail, that we have done wrong (simpliciter) even if we have not wronged them specifically. Thus, this point does not imply, nor is it meant to imply, that there exist obligations based in agent-neutral reasons. Darwall also broaches the idea that an agent-neutral concern with the welfare of others might be housed within an agent-relative conception of morality, but without really explaining how such a derivation would go (Darwall, *The Second-Person Standpoint,* 95, 130).

conclude that we should break a promise to a person if keeping it would do him or others a far greater harm, judged impersonally, than our breach of trust would cause him or them? It may well be true that this harm must consist not merely in some lessening of their potential happiness but in our failing to honor a weightier duty we have to them (say, to avoid telling them a wicked lie or causing them bodily pain), if it is to license our breaking the promise.[39] But how are we to determine that in the circumstances the other duty takes precedence if not by considering impartially the good of all those involved?

All in all, the kinds of respect we owe to one another depend on these relations of mutual accountability serving what is each person's good, considered impersonally. I do not mean that such relations have a claim on us because they tend to bring about the most good overall, for, again, the impersonal standpoint is not in itself consequentialist, any more than it is in itself deontological. The point is, rather, that only if each person's good is understood to be of equal moment does it become intelligible what is at stake in the kinds of respect we owe to others and why we owe such respect to anyone who happens to stand in certain basic relations to us. Darwall's account of mutual accountability is essentially a reconstruction of the deontological outlook.[40] All the more reason, it seems to me, to recognize that morality, even where it displays this "intersubjective" character, draws upon an underlying impersonal point of view.

We are, therefore, moral beings because we can stand back from our individual concerns and determine by reference to the world itself, peopled by others no less real than ourselves, what we have reason to think and do. It is not, to be sure, in morality alone that we exercise this power of impersonal reflection. We do so, too, whenever we set about to weigh the evidence for some belief without regard for what we would like to be true or for what common opinion would say. Yet nowhere does this self-transcendence show forth more vividly than when we turn our attention from our own happiness to that of others generally, taking the same direct interest in their good – just because it is theirs – as we naturally harbor for our own good.

This ability to stand outside ourselves is our most distinctive trait as human beings. It sets us off from the other animals. It shapes our greatest

[39] W. D. Ross, *The Right and the Good* (Oxford: Oxford University Press, 1930), 18.

[40] I should also observe that Darwall's account attributes an intrinsic moral standing only to those able to make moral claims of others, a view of the sort I criticized at the beginning of Section 1.5. For Darwall's own reflections on this score, see *The Second-Person Standpoint*, 28–29.

and noblest achievements. Clearly, not everything that is valuable in our lives originates from this standpoint. The love we feel for particular individuals does not derive from an impersonal consideration of their merits (as though we found them to be the most deserving of our affection). Its sources are instead the bonds of family, the transports of passion, the blossoming of chance encounters. Nonetheless, our love would not be a truly human love if it did not contain a sense of how small and fleeting an affair it is in the larger scheme of things. Our humanity consists in this mix of attachment and distance, the devotion to our own sphere combined with the realization that it makes up but one life among many others in the world.

We cannot then understand the kind of beings we are except in terms of the capacity for self-transcendence to which our moral thinking so vividly attests. Some philosophers have held that morality is a poor guide to self-understanding on the grounds that it generally disguises the narrower, more elementary motivations on which it actually draws, and never more so than when it presents itself as impersonal in character.[41] This mistrust is too hasty. Theories of the human condition, such as the one just mentioned, claim to base themselves on the facts, asking us to evaluate their truth by taking up toward our own person the same distanced attitude we assume toward the rest of mankind. That we can occupy an impersonal point of view ought consequently not to be in doubt, and the only question is whether, from such a vantage point, we can also see reason to care about another's good, simply because it is his or hers, in the same way that we see an immediate reason to care about our own. There can be no *a priori* way of answering this question, in fact no other way – as I emphasized earlier (Section 1.4) – than to go ahead and reflect, to see what we find. In the end, only conscience can tell whether morality is what it claims to be.

[41] The great champion of this view was, of course, Friedrich Nietzsche, followed more recently by Bernard Williams. See, in particular, Williams, "Nietzsche's Minimalist Moral Psychology," in his *Making Sense of Humanity*, 65–76.

CHAPTER 2

The Idea of Duties to Oneself

The preceding account of the relation between impersonal reflection and morality leads me to take up in this chapter a particularly difficult question in moral philosophy. It is a question that I believe is far more difficult than commonly supposed. Do we have moral obligations to ourselves? Are there things we owe to ourselves from a moral point of view, actions that we are morally obligated to do or not to do in our own regard – such as to develop our talents or to avoid abasing ourselves before other people – just as we are commonly held to have obligations with regard to others? Or does the notion of duties to oneself lack all meaning given that the aim of morality is precisely to correct, in the name of the good of others, the exorbitant attention we ordinarily and so spontaneously accord to ourselves?

In my opinion, the answer is by no means obvious. I am even tempted to say that it ought not to be so, that it is a question in the face of which we should feel drawn in two contrary directions, since in the end it reflects a tension inherent in our nature – a tension I explored in the preceding chapter – between the tendency to live our lives from within and the capacity to look at ourselves, impersonally, from the outside. The function of morality, as I indicated there, is to overcome, in the name of an impersonal point of view, the special attention we naturally give to ourselves. As a result, morality does not appear to have a place for the idea of duties to oneself. Yet insofar as this impersonal point of view requires us to consider ourselves as merely one individual among others, we appear nonetheless obligated to treat ourselves too as an object of our moral concern, and this means we need to take into account, in order to determine what we morally owe ourselves, the special sort of relation we bear to our own person.

Such is, so to speak, the "dialectic" I intend to analyze. After first surveying a number of reasons for thinking that the idea of duties to oneself ought to be rejected, I will then present reasons for embracing the opposite view. This is the position to which I am more strongly inclined, without, however, being able to escape a certain feeling of unease. In defending the concept of duties to oneself I will therefore be advancing not so much theses as hypotheses.

2.1 Problems of Coherence

On the negative side, the most powerful argument seems to me the one I already mentioned: the notion of moral duties to ourselves makes no sense precisely since the function of morality is to have us look beyond ourselves in order to make the good of others our concern. But this argument is not the only one that has been advanced. There have been others, more specific in character, that are far from negligible. Examining them will enable us not only to assess the difficulties with which the idea is faced but also to get a better sense of what would be the nature of such duties, if they can really be said to exist.

Two of the most frequent arguments were laid out in a short but classic article by Marcus Singer more than fifty years ago.[1] If (1) an individual A is subject to an obligation with regard to B, then B can release him from it if she so chooses, but no one, Singer claimed, can release himself from an obligation. Thus, the notion of a duty to oneself is essentially contradictory. Moreover, if (2) the individual A has an obligation with regard to B, then B possesses a corresponding right with regard to A, a right to demand that B comply with this obligation. But it makes no sense, Singer claims, to suppose that someone can have a right with regard to himself.

Before I proceed further and examine these two arguments, I want to pause and make a remark about terminology. I have been using the terms "duty" and "obligation" interchangeably, and in ordinary usage they have indeed become nearly synonymous. Traditionally, however, duties and obligations were distinguished. Though both were held to be moral requirements, obligations, in contrast to duties, were defined as those that are voluntarily incurred.[2] We have an obligation to keep the promises we make, but we have a duty to respect the bodily integrity of others, whatever we may choose to do. So too, if it makes sense to speak of things we owe morally to ourselves, keeping a promise we have made to ourselves would count as an obligation, whereas refusing to abase ourselves before

[1] Marcus Singer, "On Duties to Oneself," *Ethics* 69 (1959), 202–205. See also his reply to critics, "Duties and Duties to Oneself," *Ethics* 73 (1963), 133–142.

[2] See H. L. A. Hart, "Are There Any Natural Rights?" *Philosophical Review* 64, no. 2 (April 1955), 175–191, and John Rawls, *A Theory of Justice* (Cambridge, MA: Harvard University Press, 1971), §18. See also footnote 37 in the preceding chapter.

others would be a duty. This distinction between "obligations" and "duties" is certainly useful. But given contemporary usage, the two terms are likely to be equated unless the distinction is repeatedly emphasized. So I too will usually continue to treat them as synonyms. The exceptions are occasions (as in Section 2.2) when there is a special reason to underscore that distinction. I want to signal, however, that in the remainder of this section I will be considering as examples only what would be strictly called "obligations" to oneself.

Let us then examine argument (1). Is there not a logical problem in the thought that there are things one owes to oneself? How, for example, can one be under the obligation to keep a promise one has made to oneself? For if, as this argument notes, it is the same person who makes the promise as receives it, how can that person really stand under an obligation to keep the promise, the recipient of a promise being always at liberty to cancel any promise that has been made to him? An individual who supposedly made himself a promise could release himself from it whenever he might choose. The situation would not seem to be different with any other sort of obligation to oneself we might imagine, so long as it is a matter of obligations that one has acquired by one's voluntary action, like those having to do with promises. As a rule, obligations of this sort can at any moment be cancelled by the person to whom they are owed, if he or she chooses. That is because – to return to the distinction I mentioned previously – obligations, as opposed to duties, are voluntarily incurred. (The duty to respect the bodily integrity of others is not a constraint from which they may release us).

And yet, we make ourselves promises all the time. We promise ourselves that we will eat better in the future, that we will drink less wine and run longer distances, that we will read *War and Peace* one more time before we die. Can we really be laboring under a massive confusion? Are we not instead relying on our fundamental capacity of looking at ourselves from the outside, a capacity we exercise in this case by dividing ourselves into two in order to treat ourselves as enough of another person to be able to make ourselves a promise? As will become apparent, this same capacity enables us, as I showed at some length in the previous chapter, to take up the moral point of view, and in this chapter I not only return to this fact (Section 2.3) but suggest as well that it plays a part in justifying the very concept of duties to oneself. But to focus on the present case: if we promise ourselves to act in a certain way, it is because we believe the reasons we see for this course of action are so important that we are justified, in order to motivate ourselves all the more, in adding to them the reason there would be to keep such a promise. Since we thus suppose we have good reasons to make ourselves the promise, we cannot in fact believe we are free to cancel it at our pleasure. This is evident in the sort of reproach we make to ourselves if we then end up failing to act as we should. We scold ourselves for having ignored the reasons that were so strong for doing the action as to justify us in promising ourselves to do it. "How could I have been so distracted as not to remember the promise I made myself to visit my aged grandmother!"

To be sure, we can in certain circumstances abandon a promise we have made to ourselves without having cause to regret doing so. But there is an enormous difference between this kind of situation and simply breaking or forgetting such a promise. For when we cancel it instead of failing to heed it, this is because we have changed our mind and concluded that there are not really sufficient reasons for us to make it, the object of the promise not being in the end so important. In such a case, we feel no regret, since we have nothing to reproach ourselves for. In advancing as an obvious principle that no one can free himself from an obligation, Singer failed to take into account the difference between these two sorts of cases.[3] As a result, this principle and, hence, argument (1), which is constructed on its basis, are not sound. In order for it to make sense to say that we can assume obligations toward ourselves, we must certainly not be free to release ourselves from them simply because we no longer wish to comply with them. But the situations in which we are in fact entitled to free ourselves from them, namely when we realize that we do not after all have good reasons to take them up, point precisely to the conditions under which we do have such duties to ourselves.

It is important to note, however, a significant difference in this regard between a promise made to someone else and a promise made to ourselves. When we have promised something to another person, this person is free to annul the promise simply if she pleases, whereas in the case of a promise made to ourselves, we do not enjoy this kind of freedom. We are not entitled to release ourselves from the promise at will but need to have concluded that the reasons for making ourselves the promise are not after all valid. Although Singer's argument (1) is not sound, it remains no less true that these two kinds of promise are not symmetrical. The reason is not

[3] See Singer, "On Duties to Oneself," 202: "It is essential to the nature of an obligation that no one can release himself from an obligation by not wishing to perform it or by deciding not to perform it, or indeed in any other way whatsoever." This is the sole justification he gives of the supposed principle.

difficult to discern. Even if it is necessary to distinguish in any promise we make to ourselves our two roles of promisor and promisee, it is always we ourselves, not two distinct individuals, who fill these two roles, and the reasons we have to make ourselves the promise apply indeed to us, all the while we also occupy the role of beneficiary. If we were to cancel the promise simply because we wanted to, we would be acting contrary to the reasons that we – we ourselves – have to make the promise. This identity between agent and recipient does not render the promises we make ourselves empty gestures, as when we might think we could give ourselves some money by passing it from our right hand to our left.[4] For self-made promises have an effect on our conduct, corresponding to what has been promised. But it does account for the distinctive character of such promises. Moreover, duties to ourselves, if they exist, must reflect, as I explain toward the end, the intimate relation we cannot fail to have to our own person.

For now, it is enough to observe that Singer's first argument collapses because it fails to recognize the importance of our capacity to divide ourselves into two in order to take on obligations to ourselves. Immanuel Kant too appealed to such a capacity in order to make sense of the concept of duties to oneself, a concept that he admitted, at the beginning of the "Doctrine of Virtue" in his *Metaphysics of Morals*, can seem contradictory for reasons similar to those invoked by Singer.[5] In order to be truly free, Kant argued, and so able to have any moral obligations at all, we must not only be able to act for reasons, for the exercise of this ability may be determined by antecedent causes and therefore result in actions that are only events among other events in the causal order of nature. We also need to have a freedom that consists in dividing ourselves into two – a sensuous being (*Sinnenwesen*) who is part of the natural order and a rational being (*Vernunftwesen*) with the capacity to rise above that order of cause and effect – in order to impose on ourselves principles that indicate what we should consider to be reasons for action and that enable us therefore to begin on our own, without causal antecedents, a series of changes in the world. On Kant's view we thus impose on ourselves not only such principles but also, as a precondition, the general obligation to affirm – to exercise instead of evading – this very capacity of self-determination that enables us to act freely according to reasons, a capacity that constitutes the essence of our humanity. As a

[4] Cf. Wittgenstein, *Philosophische Untersuchungen*, §268.

[5] Kant, *Metaphysics of Morals*, Doctrine of Virtue, Part One, Introduction, §§1–3.

result, Kant went so far as to say that the fundamental duty to ourselves to respect our own freedom and hence the moral law we then freely impose on ourselves underlies all our moral duties to others.

I cite this Kantian theory only as an example, however. It does not describe in a satisfactory way the self-division that lies at the basis of the idea of duties to oneself. First of all, a conception of freedom as external to the causal order of the world, a conception that Kant himself, both in the passage cited and elsewhere, admitted to be "incomprehensible" (*unbegreiflich*) because foreign to everything that forms part of our experience, seems as inessential as it is extravagant. I have already made this point at the beginning (Section 2.1) of Chapter 1. And as I will explain in Chapter 7, a better account of free action is that our actions are free to the extent that they are motivated by reasons, or more exactly by our best understanding of the reasons relevant in the given situation. Secondly, the kind of self-division Kant had in mind rests on his doctrine of the "autonomy" of reason, which holds that reason, being essentially self-legislating, determines by principles it imposes on itself what may count as reasons for belief and for action. Chapter 5 is devoted to showing why this doctrine is incoherent: when we do impose on ourselves principles of thought and action that would not otherwise carry any authority for us, it is only because we see reasons to do so. But more particularly, in the case of the obligations to ourselves that we incur voluntarily, as when we make a promise to ourselves, it is essential – as I have observed – that we believe we have reasons to take on these obligations. Only on this condition can these obligations turn out to be other than fake obligations that we can cancel simply at will.

As for Singer's argument (2), which holds that it makes no sense to say we have rights with regard to ourselves, it is less serious. Such a way of speaking would certainly be bizarre. But if it is not in fact strange to say that we owe certain things to ourselves, it appears possible to conclude that in these cases the existence of a duty does not imply a correlative right, because the language of rights has been developed to protect the individual against offenses by other individuals. In any case, it is in no way odd to say that we are correct to expect that we will respect our obligations to ourselves, such as keeping the promises we have made to ourselves, and to complain about ourselves when we fail to do so.

Obviously, this defense of the idea of duties to oneself remains incomplete in various ways. It has not explained, for instance, why the ways in which we ought to act with respect to ourselves should be understood to be *moral* duties. Why is this not instead a matter of individual prudence?

I return to this question later (Section 2.3), when examining what the moral point of view itself implies about the existence of duties to oneself.

2.2 Further Difficulties

Before that, however, I must continue to survey the standard arguments against this idea, not only to underscore how problematic it is, but also to better understand in the process what would have to be nature of such duties if they in fact exist. We should note, to begin with, that so far we have only considered those supposed duties to oneself that would belong to the class of duties voluntarily assumed – that is, obligations in the strict sense – from which the person to whom the obligation is owed is typically entitled, if he so wishes, to release the individual so obligated. But obviously not all duties are of this kind. Think, for example, of the duties not to torture, not to cause harm to someone for the pure pleasure of doing so, or not to let perish people who are dying from hunger. We are not released from these duties if the other person says, for some perverse reason, that he or she does not mind being treated in these ways. Now, do there not exist duties to oneself of this kind as well? Are they not indeed among the most fundamental duties we have, for instance the duty to respect our own bodily integrity? Do we not have the duty to avoid gratuitously causing pain or harm to ourselves, a duty that – unlike the first class of duties to oneself – applies to us independently of any voluntary act on our part and from which we are not entitled, even in principle, to release ourselves?

Singer mentions in passing the view that there exist duties of this type. But it is only in order to declare – in what can be called his argument (3) – that they are not really duties *to* oneself but rather duties *regarding* oneself, and that if it is asked to whom they are due, the answer must be society or the rest of humanity.[6] In taking this tack, he is adopting a secularized version of the traditional view that duties concerning ourselves are duties we owe to God, our creator. To the extent, however, that we today believe that we ought not to be servile or gratuitously cause ourselves pain or harm, our thought is ordinarily that we owe this, not to God or to society,

[6] Singer, "On Duties to Oneself," 204. Vincent Descombes endorses a similar analysis for many cases in which we say we owe it to ourselves to do or not to do certain things, for instance, not to abandon our sense of honor. These are cases, he claims (*Le complément de sujet*, Paris: Gallimard, 2014, 302, 314), in which it is in reality to some social group that we owe such things. That may be sometimes so, but clearly not always. I may believe I owe it to myself to keep my sense of honor, whether or not there happen to exist any social groups that expect this of me.

but quite simply to ourselves.[7] In what way is this simpler, and to my mind more plausible view unsatisfactory or incoherent? Singer does not say.

More recently, the French philosopher Ruwen Ogien took up the cause from Singer and set out in his book, *L'éthique aujourd'hui*, to show that in this respect as in others, nothing counts in favor of the notion of duties to oneself.[8] This project formed part of the "moral minimalism" by which he sought to reduce the legitimate demands of morality to the sole requirement of not doing harm to others. I find this conception unacceptable for a number of reasons.[9] Among them are precisely those I see as counting in favor of the belief that we have moral duties not only to others but also to ourselves. Nonetheless, the arguments Ogien advanced, like those of Singer, are among the objections one is naturally inclined to raise. If I now proceed to criticize them in turn, it is not, with a few exceptions, in order to deny them any value at all. They simply do not have the decisive force they are thought to possess. The status of the idea of duties to oneself seems to me, as I said at the start, ambiguous and difficult to settle in any definitive way.

What are then the principal objections by which Ogien seeks to show that the notion of duties to oneself is incoherent or poorly conceived? He takes over Singer's first argument concerning supposed obligations to oneself, an argument I have already examined and that has moreover long been something of a commonplace.[10] But he adds many others, beginning with his own version of what I termed Singer's argument (3). That argument, it will be recalled, was directed against the view that there exist duties to ourselves, such as not doing ourselves gratuitous harm, that we do not incur by our own voluntary acts and that we cannot release ourselves from. Unfortunately, his version is no more plausible than Singer's. In order to dismiss the possibility of this sort of duties to oneself, Ogien argues that duties that cannot be cancelled by those who form their object are not really duties to persons (either to others or to oneself), but instead

[7] It seems to have been Christian Wolff who at the beginning of the eighteenth century introduced this latter conception into philosophy, and in this he was followed by Kant. See J. B. Schneewind, *The Invention of Autonomy* (Cambridge: Cambridge University Press, 1998), 440.

[8] R. Ogien, *L'éthique aujourd'hui. Maximalistes et minimalistes* (Paris: Gallimard, 2007), 25–57. He cites Singer as an inspiration at 218.

[9] For a critique of Ogien's programme, see not only my essay "L'éthique à sa place," *Critique* 706 (March 2006), 208–219, but also the insightful book by Nathalie Maillard, *Faut-il être minimaliste en éthique?* (Genève: Labor et Fides, 2014), whose arguments in favor of the concept of duties to oneself I largely endorse.

[10] Ogien, 34–39. See, for example, Thomas Hobbes, *Leviathan*, II.26, §2: "Nor is it possible for any person to be bound to himself, because he that can bind can release, and, therefore, he that is bound to himself only is not bound."

to "impersonal moral principles."[11] It makes no sense to say, however, that one has a duty to a moral principle. One can have the duty to respect the principle, but heeding it consists precisely in recognizing the duty it imposes with regard to certain persons. In short, every moral principle we must respect indicates some duty we owe to individuals. If there exist impersonal moral principles requiring us to treat ourselves in certain ways, then there exist as well moral duties to ourselves.

Take, for instance, the supposed duty we have to ourselves not to be servile, not to abase ourselves before others. According to Kant, seeking to gain the approval of another by making ourselves into a simple instrument of their will, refusing to exercise our own capacity of judgment, amounts to causing an affront to "the humanity in our own person."[12] To this claim, Ogien replies in a further argument against the concept of non-voluntary duties to oneself – let us call it argument (4). It is that "so-called moral duties to oneself are in reality duties to abstract entities such as nature or the human species," or, in the case at hand, to humanity.[13] Farther on (Section 2.4), I myself express reservations about the idea, suggested by Kant's remark that we should respect the humanity in our own person as in that of others, that the basis of our duties to ourselves is strictly identical to the basis of our duties to others. I believe that it embodies instead an extra element deriving from the special relation we bear essentially to ourselves. But for the moment, I want simply to point out against this new argument that insofar as it makes sense to speak of duties to abstract entities – in itself a rather misleading way of speaking – such duties must consist in duties to the individuals exemplifying these abstractions. There can be no love for humanity that does not involve love for at least some of its members (though there have been people to attempt the impossible). The same is true for respecting humanity: it cannot mean anything other than respecting human beings. If I have the duty to respect humanity wherever it may be found, without exception and thus in my own person as elsewhere, it follows that I have a duty to respect myself as a human being.

With a further argument (5), according to which "so-called moral duties to oneself are not duties but rather precepts of prudence," Ogien seems to me to have conceded the essential point.[14] This argument is no doubt, along with argument (1), the one most commonly urged against the notion of moral duties to oneself in general. However, it presupposes – for such is the nature of precepts of prudence – that it makes sense to say of an individual

[11] Ogien, 40. [12] Kant, *Metaphysics of Morals*, Doctrine of Virtue, Part One, Book I, §11.
[13] Ogien, 41. [14] Ibid., 48.

that he *ought* to do something, to take care of his health or to develop his talents, *out of regard for his own good*, and that he ought to do so, whatever may be his desires at the moment. The language of prudence resembles closely the language of morality. What then determines that such duties of prudence should nonetheless be distinguished from duties that are properly moral, instead of constituting one class of moral duties among others? One might think this is merely a question of terminology. But the question becomes more substantial if it turns out, as I have already suggested, that these duties to oneself, termed duties of prudence, derive from the same source as duties generally recognized as moral. This possibility I examine in Section 2.3.

For now, let us proceed to Ogien's next argument (6). It holds that "the moral component of a supposed duty to oneself always concerns other people."[15] In the supposed duties of this sort that may appear most clearly to belong to morality, for example, in those forbidding greed, servility, or lying insofar as it consists in betraying the truthfulness at which the exercise of reason naturally aims – here as elsewhere Ogien is following closely Kant's discussion in the *Metaphysics of Morals*[16] – their moral character derives entirely, he argues, from the way they "relate to other people (*sont relatifs à autrui*)." The actions they forbid are contrary to morality only in virtue of their harmful effect on other individuals.

This thesis seems to me clearly untenable. Although lying, greed, and servility can certainly have negative effects on others that justify condemning them in this respect – lying serves to deceive others, greed deprives them of the resources they may need, servility encourages in them the lust for domination – we condemn these sorts of actions as well, if not in the first instance, because of the wrong to oneself that they involve. This is clear in the case of servility. The principal reason not to be servile is that in seeking the approval of others to the point of making myself a simple instrument of their will, I am forsaking my own dignity, whatever encouragement I may thereby be giving to other people's bad habits.

Lying is a somewhat more complex case, since the principal wrong it involves, intending to deceive, generally consists in the harm it does to others. But it is not incorrect to see in it as well a wrong that one does to oneself. To present as true what one believes to be false means knowingly to misuse the very purpose of speech, an essential capacity of our humanity, which is to communicate what we take to be true. (This purpose

[15] Ibid., 53: "l'élément moral du devoir envers soi-même, c'est ce qui concerne autrui."

[16] Kant, Doctrine of Virtue, Part One, Book I, §§9–12.

underlies the elementary fact that to assert something is to assert it as true). No doubt, as I said, the wrong one does to someone else in seeking to deceive them is ordinarily a greater harm. Sometimes, too, the act of lying may be justified if the lie is relatively insignificant but produces some enormous benefit, or – more defensibly – if it serves to prevent a considerable evil. On these two last points I depart from the rigoristic position that Kant adopts in his discussion of this subject.[17] But Kant is undeniably right to maintain that every lie as such, independently of its possible consequences, seems to us to sully in the individual who commits it "the dignity of humanity in his own person." This is evident in the contempt we continue to have for the inveterate liar who will deceive us no more, as well in the disgust we cannot help but feel when we find ourselves forced to lie for some meritorious reason.

It may be true, therefore, that the acts governed by supposed duties to oneself also have consequences that make them subject to duties to others and that these consequences often constitute the principal reason why we ought or ought not to act in a certain way. This does not change the fact that the relation to ourselves that is involved in these acts is an object of blame or praise and thus appears to form part of the domain of morality. Up to this point, I have been considering "perfect" duties, that is, duties that require strict obedience. But the situation is the same with what one could hold to be "imperfect" duties to oneself, duties that may be fulfilled with a certain latitude of choice, such as the duty to develop one's talents. The person who squanders them or lets them go to waste, do we not blame him for what he does to himself and not merely, supposing this to be true, because he thereby deprives the rest of humanity of the benefits that developing his talents would have provided them?

Let us move on to Ogien's final argument, according to which, (7) "the notion of duties to oneself contradicts the principle of [individual] freedom." It poses, he claims, "a moral and political problem," since it seems to have "as its principal function to deny our freedom to make what we want of our life and to make use of our body as we wish, even when we do not cause any harm to others."[18] Now, in part, this argument presupposes

[17] Kant, §9. For his absolute prohibition of lying, see, of course, his famous – or infamous – essay, "Über ein vermeintliches Recht aus Menschenliebe zu lügen" ("On a Supposed Right to Lie out of Love of Humanity"), in Kant, *Gesammelte Werke*, Akademie-Ausgabe, VIII, 425–430.

[18] Ogien, 57: "La notion de devoir moral envers soi-même contredit le principe de liberté. . . En effet, l'argument de « devoir moral envers soi-même » semble avoir comme fonction principale de nier notre liberté de faire ce que nous voulons de notre vie et de disposer de notre corps comme nous l'entendons, même lorsque nous ne causons aucun tort à autrui."

what is meant to be proven, namely that we ought to be morally speaking free to make of our lives what we want, provided that we do not wrong other individuals. After all, the fact that individual liberty is not a supreme value is shown by the very principle that forbids harm to others. But in addition, it is necessary to distinguish between the realm of morality and the realm of the political. There are countless examples of action we regard as morally doubtful or quite simply wrong, without thinking of making them the object of state intervention or legal enforcement. Indeed, precisely insofar as the idea of moral duties to oneself has proven to be so controversial, we have good reason to require that the principles of our political life remain neutral in this respect. The present question, however, is a question about the bounds of morality, not about the limits of state power.

Ogien's various arguments against the concept of duties to oneself, arguments that he is far from being the only one to advance, do not therefore seem to me any more decisive than Singer's. We often say, to ourselves as well as to others, that we owe certain things to ourselves and even sometimes that we owe them to ourselves morally: we owe it to ourselves to make a greater effort next time, we owe it to ourselves morally not to base our life upon a lie. In my view, it is only with the greatest hesitation that we should reject as a confusion a way of thinking that forms so deep-seated a part of everyday life, and then only after having examined the motivations for its entrenchment. And yet, it is difficult as well to shake off the impression that something is not right in the notion of duties to ourselves. I repeat the argument I presented at the beginning as constituting the most powerful objection: Is it not the function of morality to have us look beyond ourselves, to concern ourselves with the good of others instead of continuing, as we habitually do, to think about things in terms of how they may serve our own good?

In the following, I try to explain why it is to be expected that we come to feel divided between these two positions. We find ourselves drawn in two contrary directions because of our ability to adopt both of two fundamentally different relations to the world. As we move back and forth between these two perspectives, the notion of moral duties to oneself can appear either confused or instead quite coherent.

2.3 The Impersonal and Personal Points of View

Chapter 1 (Section 1.2) described at length these two fundamental attitudes toward the world. On the one hand, we often live our lives from within, pursuing our own projects and looking at the things and people around us from this point of view. We are likely then to take into account other people's view of the world, but only in order to better calculate how we may strategically achieve our ends. Or we may indeed attach importance to the well-being of certain individuals and not solely to our own, but only because we have a special affection for them or because they are bound to us by ties of family, profession, or culture. Their own good enters our thinking in virtue of their occupying a place in the conception of the world we hold on the basis of our own concerns. It is only natural that we adopt this perspective, since it is the direct expression of what makes each of us the individual we are. Each of us has our own life to live. No one else can live it for us, substituting themselves for us in the choices by which we decide how we will think and act. As a result, we are inclined in our deliberations to take into account only those things or persons that may resist or contribute to the realization of our purposes. We inhabit then a perspective in which everything refers back to ourselves. This perspective is not necessarily *egoistic*, since our concern can extend to the good of others who are important to us in some way. But it is a perspective that is fundamentally *egocentric*, centered on those concerns that happen to be ours.

On the other hand, we manage, sometimes at least, to recognize the limits of such a perspective, to escape our spontaneous egocentrism by heeding in ourselves a force for self-transcendence that can be called the voice of conscience. For the moral point of view, as I also explained in Chapter 1 (Section 1.5), demands of us that we look beyond ourselves and see in the good of others reasons for action that are independent of our own concerns and particular attachments. When, for example, we help someone because of how we may profit from this act, securing the favorable reaction of others or enjoying the satisfaction of doing a fine deed, we are not really acting as morality requires. We need instead to take a direct interest in this person's good, as devoid of ulterior considerations as the self-love in which we take an immediate interest in our own good. Just as we do not care about ourselves because we are someone we feel particularly close to or because we hope to receive some benefit in return, but simply because "it is me," so we should care about any other person simply because it is he or she. The moral point of view, as the Bible often declares, demands that we love our neighbor as ourselves.

This point of view is one we can embrace because we are able to adopt a completely different attitude toward the world than the one we ordinarily occupy. Instead of living our life from within, we have the capacity to stand back and to look at ourselves from the outside, in the third person, as one individual among others in a world that goes its way independently of our concerns. I have already had occasion (Section 2.1) to mention this capacity when I pointed out how we are able to treat ourselves as being enough of another person that we can make ourselves a promise. But it plays a much deeper and more pervasive role than that. Not only does it underlie our moral thinking as a whole; it also enables us to develop the understanding that there exists a reality altogether independent of our experience. This capacity we have to take up an impersonal view of things is a remarkable power of ours. It is not marveled at enough. Other animals can think, reason, and in some measure reflect, yet this capacity lies beyond their power. No dog, no ape, however intelligent it may be, is able to conceive of itself as simply one dog or ape among others, but always sees and deals with the world from the point of view that is its own.

I do not want to suggest that it is always better to step back and look at our life from the outside. On the contrary, we cease then to be natural and at one with ourselves in the way that often gives our lives vigor and direction. Here is an example. We can assume toward our particular attachments the same kind of reflective attitude that morality demands we adopt with respect to people in general. We can, that is, take our bearings from properly moral reasons for treating those close to us in appropriate ways, instead of following as before the feelings and interests that gave rise to these attachments. In this spirit, we can then tell ourselves, from a duly impersonal point of view, that this is the way *one ought* to act with regard to a friend or spouse. However, it can seem a greater sign of friendship or love – and ordinarily our friend or spouse will far prefer – if we help them or do them a favor, not because it is our duty, but simply because we like or love them. I already had occasion in Chapter 1 (Section 1.5) to endorse on this score Bernard Williams's quip that aiming at their good, not simply because of the affection we feel for them, but also on the supposition that this is what our attachment to them requires of us morally, involves "one thought too many."[19] The moral point of view is not, contrary to moralistic presumptions, the point of view from which we should always act. My aim here is simply to describe this point of view and the capacity of mind that makes it possible.

Now, because morality depends on this distancing from self by which we cease to live immersed in our individual lives, it appears to consist

[19] Bernard Williams, "Persons, Character, and Morality," reprinted in *Moral Luck* (Cambridge: Cambridge University Press, 1981), 18.

essentially in a set of duties that refer us beyond ourselves and toward others. It seems not to have a place for duties to oneself. Is it not precisely the function of morality to pry us loose from our habitual tendency to concern ourselves with our own person and our particular needs and interests? This, as I have said, is the most significant argument that counts against the idea of duties to oneself.

Yet at precisely this point there can arise a contrary line of thought that seems – such is *the first hypothesis* I propose in favor of the opposite view – to restore the rejected notion. Whence the sense of perplexity that so easily surrounds this subject. For if morality demands that we transcend absorption in our particular projects in order to rise to an impersonal point of view, does it not follow that what we owe morally to others we owe equally to ourselves, since this point of view requires us to regard ourselves as simply one person among others, having no more but also no less importance than the rest of humanity? It is, after all, a basic rule of morality not to make an exception for oneself! The concept of duties to oneself would seem therefore to have its source in the very perspective from which we should understand our duties to others.

This is by no means to say that duties to oneself constitute the source of duties to others. Such a view can be found in Kant, as I have noted (Section 2.1). We cannot, he claimed, be subject to duties in regard to others except insofar as we freely impose on ourselves the duty of respecting the moral law that lies at the basis of those duties. Only because we thus owe it to ourselves to be moral beings can we come to be obligated to others.[20] This tack derives, however, from his general doctrine of the "autonomy" of reason, and I have already (Section 2.1) pointed to the trouble with that conception. Basic principles of thought and action cannot draw their authority from our having imposed them on ourselves, since imposing principles on ourselves is something we must see reasons to do, reasons, likely involving existing principles, that we regard as having an antecedent authority for our conduct. Whenever we do impose on ourselves moral principles that would not be otherwise binding on us – and the circumstance is rare, as when we give ourselves the rule of never making a promise it will be difficult to keep – we must presume that there exist moral reasons or principles for doing so (promises ought to be kept). As I explain in Chapter 5, reason cannot be, contrary to Kant, fundamentally self-legislating. It consists instead in our capacity of being responsive

[20] Kant, *Metaphysics of Morals*, Doctrine of virtue, Part One, Introduction, §2.

to reasons. There is, therefore, no basis for holding with Kant that duties to oneself are the foundation of duties to others.[21]

So no, the hypothesis I am advancing is not that one kind of duty is the source of the other. Instead, it is that the impersonal point of view is the source of both – both duties to others as well as duties to ourselves. This means, among other things, that even if one would like to conceive of the latter sort of duties as duties of individual prudence, they will count no less as moral duties.

2.4 How Duties to Oneself May Make Sense

Nonetheless, this first hypothesis is but a point of departure for the rehabilitation of the idea of duties to oneself. It is not sufficient. For having some moral duty to myself, if this sort of duty can be said to exist, does not consist simply in my being one human being among others, as though the duty I have not to demean myself before others were simply the application to my individual case of the general duty of demeaning no one. What are commonly held to be our duties to ourselves embody for the most part a distinct character reflecting the special relation that we have to ourselves and that differs fundamentally from the relation we can have to other people. Moreover, their dependence on the particular character of our essential relation to ourselves is nothing strange. In general, our duties depend on the relation in which we stand to those to whom they are owed.[22] For instance, even though it is not always desirable to draw back from our particular attachments and the particular affections at their basis in order to determine what we owe to these individuals from an impersonal point of view, the duties we then acknowledge reflect the relations in which we stand to them. What we owe morally to a friend is different from what we owe morally to our children or spouse, just as it is different from what we owe to those to whom we have made a promise or from whom we have borrowed. The duties we owe to every human being as such, independently of any particular relation to them – to respect their bodily integrity or to aid them when in distress – are but one kind of duty among others, and they proceed from our general relation to others that is our common humanity.

[21] V. Descombes appears to hold that if apparent duties to oneself are not in reality duties to someone else (see note 6), then they rest on the Kantian notion of autonomy, which he, like I, regards as incoherent (*Le complément de sujet*, 302–322). However, I disagree with him that the idea of duties to oneself goes hand in hand with the idea of autonomy.

[22] Cf. W. D. Ross, *The Right and the Good* (Oxford: Oxford University Press, 1930), chapter 2.

Now the relation to ourselves that lies at the source of the duties we are thought to have to ourselves has to do with the way we count as responsible for our thoughts and actions. At bottom, this responsibility is of a more intimate nature than a merely causal relation. It does not consist simply in our possessing a control over what we think and do that is much more complete than our power over the conduct of others. This exceptional control is itself but an expression of the capacity to choose among possibilities that no one else can exercise in our place. And this capacity of choice expresses, in turn, the fundamental relation to ourselves that makes each of us the self or subject we are. It is that in all that we think, feel, or do we *guide ourselves by reasons*, or at least by what we take to be reasons.

As I will detail in Chapter 8 (Section 8.3), there are two distinct respects in which this is so. Not only do the various elements of our mental life take shape in response to reasons; they function as they do by indicating reasons for what we should then think and do. We cannot, for instance, come to believe something unless we regard it as true, and that means unless we take there to be reasons to think it is true. But in addition, believing something consists in being disposed to think and act in accord with the presumed truth of what is believed, and hence in accord with the further reasons for thought and action its presumed truth (in conjunction with other parts of our outlook) points us to. So too with desires. We cannot desire something without perceiving, correctly or not, some reason to desire it, and every desire, whether momentary or habitual, disposes us, all else being equal, to think and act in accord with the presumed value of its object – that is, to heed the reasons for thought and action it points us to. It is in virtue of this fundamental relation to ourselves that consists in guiding ourselves by reasons that we are selves at all, living our lives as no one else can do in our place and counting thereby as responsible for what we think and do.

My *second hypothesis* is, then, that this constitutive relation we have to ourselves explains the special character of what appear to be duties to oneself. I have already indicated (Section 2.1) how the promises we make to ourselves differ in this regard from other promises: the person to whom they are addressed (ourselves) is not free to cancel them at will, since the reasons to which we are responding in making them are reasons that hold for us apart from our also being the object or addressee of these promises. But the hypothesis fits as well the duties to oneself that we do not voluntarily incur. Thus, the duty to develop our talents rests on the fact that we alone can choose which of our possibilities we will set out to cultivate. We have no parallel duty to develop the talents of others for the simple reason that we are, strictly speaking, incapable of doing so. In the end, that can only be their own affair. So too for the duty not to abase ourselves before others. Servility does not consist in treating ourselves as though we were merely an animal or in making ourselves an object of ridicule, as we might do to someone else in order to humiliate them. For we might, like certain comedians or in order to amuse our friends, freely choose to act in such ways without being commanded to do so and hence without making ourselves in any way servile. Servility consists instead in renouncing to choose for ourselves, in subordinating ourselves of our own accord to the arbitrary will of another, whatever may be the action we will then be commanded to perform. This form of behavior, which amounts to turning our capacity for choice against itself, can only be directed against our own person.

As for the apparent duty not to base one's life on a lie, we have already seen how lying in general seems to involve a wrong one does to oneself, in addition to the wrong done to others in trying to deceive them: one is knowingly abusing the purpose of that essential capacity of our humanity that is speech. But the duty not to lie to myself is something different than the duty not to lie to someone who happens to be me, and the wrong it prohibits is of a different kind from the two wrongs involved in any act of lying. In this case it is a matter of not undermining my integrity as the agent of my acts.

For in order to succeed in lying to myself, I must – in the very act of lying and not merely as the object of the lie – hide from myself what I am doing, telling myself, for example, some plausible though deliberately false story in order to get myself to believe the lie. If, for example, I am going to convince myself that I am a great runner despite always coming in last, I must invent various excuses for why I did not happen to run so well on those occasions. In lying to myself, I have to rid myself of an awareness that this is what I am doing, since otherwise I cannot be deceived by the lie. It is a general fact, as I have noted, that we cannot believe what we take to be false, at least so long as we take it to be so. At bottom, the wrong I am doing consists, then, in turning my ability to act against itself. When we act, our intention, whether fulfilled or not, is to know what we are doing. But when I lie to myself, I am acting in a way that keeps me designedly ignorant of the action I am really engaged in. This is not something I can do to anyone else's power of action: by arranging the situation in an appropriate way, I can make it so that they are ignorant of what they are doing, but I cannot make them make themselves ignorant of it. There is, to be sure, a significant difference, morally speaking, between telling oneself a little lie in order to acquire the confidence to do something difficult and basing one's whole life on a lie. A minor lie of the former sort may be pardonable in virtue of its benefits, just like certain lies one may tell others, even though it is still wrong in itself. But the important thing to observe is that the case of lying to oneself confirms the general rule: the specific character of duties to ourselves rests on relations we can have only to ourselves.[23]

The reader will have no doubt noticed that in pursuing my two hypotheses, the argument has shifted from the impersonal perspective, which underlies the moral point of view as such, back to the perspective in which we live our lives from within, our attention focused on our own person and on the world as it appears in the light of our individual projects. This should not be surprising. Let me summarize the course of the argument. Since the standpoint of morality requires us to think impersonally and to consider ourselves as simply one individual among others, it would appear to require us to see ourselves too as an object of moral concern – not more so than others, but also not less. To this extent, there must, it seems, exist duties to oneself. Such was the reasoning of my first hypothesis. But if our duties to others depend on the relations in which we stand to them, the duties we have to ourselves must involve, such was the import of my second hypothesis, the relation in which we stand to ourselves. And this brings us back to the perspective in which we live our lives from within and in which the intimate relation each of us has to ourselves therefore takes center stage.

The concept of duties to oneself assumes therefore its full contours when the moral point of view combines with the point of view each of us occupies in living our lives from within as the life we alone can live. This is what I meant in suggesting at various points that the ambiguous status of this notion results from a movement *back and forth* between the two fundamental attitudes toward the world we can assume, the personal and the impersonal perspectives. In adopting the moral point of view, we put aside a concern for our own person, and in this regard the idea of duties to oneself seems nonsensical. The whole point of morality is to break the hold that our personal projects and attachments have on our thinking. Yet in taking up this impersonal point of view, in which we figure as but one individual among others, we must, it seems, focus our moral attention upon ourselves as well. We cannot count for more, but we also cannot

[23] For more on what is involved in self-deception, see my discussion in *The Autonomy of Morality* (Cambridge: Cambridge University Press, 2008), chapter 9, §§3–4.

count for less. Thus we are led back to our concern for ourselves, for it is with an eye to the special relation we have to our own person that we must determine what we owe morally to ourselves. And yet focusing on how to relate properly to ourselves can seem, from the impersonal standpoint of morality, nothing but an impediment to the main business of learning to counter the natural tendency to privilege our own interests over those of others. In this light, the idea of duties to oneself looks ill-conceived. But again, concerning ourselves with people's good impersonally cannot mean refusing to give any consideration at all to our own. And so on.

The preceding reflections have not, then, been intended to settle, once and for all, the question whether there do exist moral duties to oneself. My aim has been to reconstruct, by means of two hypotheses, how such a belief can plausibly arise as well as to indicate why it continues to be problematic. The difficulty stems from the fundamental duality of our nature, divided as we are between the natural tendency to live our lives from within and the capacity to look at ourselves from without.

CHAPTER 3

The Ethics of Reading

This chapter, like the preceding one, explores some unexpected consequences of the account of the moral point of view with which I began. However, what can be meant by this chapter's title is not immediately obvious. The phrase has become popular in contemporary literary theory, largely through the influence of J. Hillis Miller. What it suggests is that reading is an activity that raises questions of an ethical character. Yet why this should be so can seem puzzling, and the writings of literary theorists who invoke the phrase have done little to dispel the obscurity. Miller's own remarks are more helpful than most. Reading, he declares, looks like an act of ethical significance in two ways, since it entails both a responsibility-to and a responsibility-for:

> On the one hand it is a response to something, responsible to it, responsive to it, respectful of it. In any ethical moment there is an imperative, some 'I must' or *Ich kann nicht anders*. I *must* do this. I cannot do otherwise. If the response is not one of necessity, grounded in some 'must,' if it is a freedom to do what one likes, for example to make a literary text mean what one likes, then it is not ethical.

On the other hand, Miller continues,

> I must take responsibility for my response and for the further effects, interpersonal, institutional, social, political, or historical, of my act of reading.[1]

These points are pertinent, though also rather vague. In particular, are we to suppose that reading is *like* an act with an ethical character in that it too is, or should be, responsive to a demand, or that it *is itself* such an act? And how can the latter be true, if that to which the act of reading owes a responsibility is not a person, but rather a text, or the meaning of the text? Miller does not address these questions. Moreover, even if he does better

[1] J. Hillis Miller, *The Ethics of Reading* (New York: Columbia University Press, 1987), 4, 43.

than many contemporary literary theorists in recognizing that there is such a thing as the objective meaning of a text to which we as readers should be responsible, it is by no means clear how exactly he understands this notion. So I shall set out on my own and begin from the beginning.

My aim will be to show that the idea of an ethics of reading is not, in fact, the confusion it may seem at first to be. It turns out, on the contrary, to be an idea of real significance. It places some of the key questions of philosophical hermeneutics – that is, of the theory of interpretation – in a new and illuminating setting. But even more strikingly, the ethics of reading gives powerful expression to the essence of ethical thinking itself.

3.1 The Reading Relation

Consider the term "ethics" itself. In the philosophical tradition, ethics as a discipline has been concerned with two distinct but interrelated questions: how we ought to live in order to live well, and how we are to treat one another and perhaps other living beings as well. In recent times, the term has also been used to refer, more specifically, to the first of these subjects, living well, in contrast to the second, treating others well, which is then commonly classified as "morality," though I will not follow such usage here. Now, in what way does reading constitute an ethical phenomenon in either of these two regards? No doubt we live richer lives if we read some good books, and there are likewise many cases in which reading various materials (ranging from newspapers to the Bible, say), and reading them well, can deepen our understanding of how we ought to act with regard to others. Sometimes too, how we read a book can itself have a significant impact on the lives of other people, if we make public our understanding and interpretation of the book. That is a possibility belonging to what Miller had in mind by the element of responsibility-for. All these cases concern the ethical consequences of reading.

However, the idea of an "ethics of reading" suggests, I believe, something more profound and also less familiar, namely that our very relation as readers to what we read – to books or, more generally, to texts – is a matter of ethical import. This was Miller's thought in referring to the idea of a responsibility-to. In order for reading to enrich our lives, in order for it to play a role in how we go on to treat others, we must first read, and the idea is that the act of reading, in and of itself, involves an essentially ethical task of being responsible to what we read. Yet how can a reader's responsibility to what a text says not merely resemble in certain respects our ethical responsibility to other people, but constitute in itself an ethical relation?

This is the question I will pursue, leaving aside further questions having to do with the consequences of reading, both for our own lives and for the lives of others. As the final section (Section 3.5) will show, the ethical relation to others that the act of reading does in fact involve is one that embodies the very core of the moral point of view. I have already, in Chapter 1, explained the essential features of this perspective. However, moral thinking can turn out to be relevant in important ways we may not at first anticipate.

One of the most basic facts about our relation as readers to texts is that this relation is asymmetrical. We can read the text, but the text cannot read us. Sometimes, it is true, literary theorists talk about "being read by the text," but this is a metaphorical phrase, referring to the experience of being challenged by the text to reflect on some of our central assumptions, an experience we can have only in and through our reading of the text. Reading is an act, initiated and performed by an agent, and texts themselves are not agents or persons: texts speak to us only when they are read, and read by us. Now if the reading relation is inherently asymmetrical, and if it is moreover a relation, not to another person but to something else, namely to a text, how can it be a relation that is, in itself, of an ethical character?

One may feel that I have left out another equally essential feature of our relation as readers to what we read: though the text that we read is not another person, it was written by a person to embody in certain respects their thought and feeling. I think this point is right and, moreover, absolutely crucial. If texts are not conceived as being the expression of their authors' intention, then the practice of reading cannot itself be of intrinsic ethical significance. We may consider the ways that reading enriches the lives of readers or gives them instruction about how to treat others well, and in this sense we can talk about the ethical importance of reading, that is, about its beneficial consequences. But there can be an "ethics of reading" for which the activity of reading is itself a matter of ethical moment and our responsibility as readers to what the text says or means truly an ethical responsibility, only if the relation of reader to text is ultimately a relation of the reader to another person. Now who can this other person be, if not the author of the text? And in what can our responsibility as readers to the text consist, if not in seeking faithfully to grasp what the author meant in writing it as he or she did?

However, I want to postpone a clarification of the key, if problematic, notion of "the author's intention" (I shall return to it shortly), in order to focus on a further salient fact about the reading relation, which is that it connects us to another person only indirectly. In the act of reading, the author is not there, but only the text. This fact – the author's essential absence – is of great moment. Certainly the ethics of reading, if such a thing exists, cannot be utterly *sui generis*, since it too must have as its object, as all areas of ethics do, the way we are to act with regard to persons (others or ourselves). Yet it would have the distinctive feature of dealing with how we are to act with regard to someone who is, not merely perhaps for a time, but necessarily absent.

That reading does involve an ethical dimension and that, in virtue of the absence of the author, it gives rise to a special sort of ethical problem are views that Plato expresses in the discussion of writing at the end of his dialogue, the *Phaedrus*. In this passage, the topic is the dangers of writing rather than the responsibilities of reading. But the two are connected, and one of the remarks that Plato has Socrates make points to what must be the fundamental concern of an "ethics of reading." The trouble with a text, Socrates observes, is that, "roaming about everywhere" (*kulindeitai pantachou*), it comes to be read both by those who are intelligent or well-intentioned readers and by those who are not and yet it is by nature unable to defend itself against the abuses of misunderstanding that may be perpetrated by the latter: "When it is wronged (*plemmeloumenos*) and attacked unfairly (*ouk en dikei*), it always stands in need of its father's support, for on its own it can neither defend itself nor come to its own support" (275e). By "its father" is meant, of course, the author of the text. Thus, Plato is claiming that the text itself, unlike apparently its author, cannot correct the misinterpretations by which readers may treat it unfairly as they fail to listen to what it says or distort its meaning for their own purposes.

Now it is essential to distinguish the two parts of Plato's claim. The first (i) is that the text cannot talk back and object to an interpretation of its meaning that has been foisted upon it. Indeed, as Socrates wryly observes, no matter what one may ask of a text, it always – in contrast to a conversation – keeps saying the same thing (275d). The second (ii) is that the author, if he or she were present, could authoritatively correct the erroneous interpretation. We need not accept (ii) – in fact, we ought not to accept it, since authors do not possess that sort of authority (a point about which I will have more to say later) – in order to recognize the crucial importance of (i), the inability of texts to talk back, for the idea of an "ethics of reading." It is entailed by the essential asymmetry of the reading relation that I underscored before. When people have been wronged, they are in principle (if they have not been killed in the process) able to object to their mistreatment. Texts, by contrast, cannot object to how they are mistreated, that is, to how they are inadvertently, carelessly, or deliberately misread. In this fact lies, as I have begun to suggest, the distinctive ethical feature of the reading relation.

The passage from Plato's *Phaedrus* also points to a further assumption on which the idea of an "ethics of reading" must depend. Reading has to be understood as a process in which we interpret what we read – interpret it, that is, in the broad sense of taking or construing the text to say this or that, if only at the grammatical level, though generally our scope is more ambitious. (I will go on later to distinguish some more specific aims of interpretation). For whether a text is treated fairly or wrongly has to do with how we read it and in particular with how faithful our interpretation of what it says is, or at least aims to be, to the text itself. That all reading involves interpretation in the broad sense mentioned ought to be uncontroversial.[2] So too the idea that the ethics of reading, if such a thing exists, concerns our being responsible as readers to the meaning of what we read as we in this sense interpret it. In what follows, I shall take these points for granted. More contentious questions await us.

3.2 Some Basics of Textual Interpretation

One of these questions springs from the fact that for the practice of reading to be itself something of ethical moment, our relation as readers to a text must, as I have mentioned, be ultimately, if not directly, a relation to another person. The text has to be regarded as the expression of its author's intention. Moreover, if misreading the text consists in failing to grasp what the text itself says – and what else could misreading signify, if it is to mean anything at all? – then what the text says, and in this sense its meaning, must be determined by the author's intention. Since I have rejected the idea that the author is the authoritative interpreter of a text's meaning, I need to explain how I think the notion of author's intention should be conceived.

That this notion is indispensable, on at least some construal, should be indisputable, though unfortunately among literary and hermeneutic

[2] The word "interpretation" is sometimes used in the narrower sense of substituting for some problematic expression one that is more understandable. See, for instance, L. Wittgenstein, *Philosophical Investigations* (Chichester: Wiley, 2009), §201. He correctly points out that interpretation (*Deutung*) in this sense must rest on a prior, non-interpretive kind of understanding. However, my broad use of "interpretation" includes this sort of understanding as well, which is indeed the form that reading ordinarily takes.

thinkers it is not. From William Wimsatt and Monroe Beardsley's critique of "the intentional fallacy" to Hans-Georg Gadamer's rejection of the *mens auctoris* or author's intention (*die Meinung des Verfassers*) in favor of what he called "the fusion of horizons" (of text and reader) to structuralist and post-structuralist ideas about "the death of the author," there have been many to deny, often jubilantly with a sense of liberation, that the meaning of a text turns fundamentally on what the author intended to say.[3] Yet texts do not write themselves. They are written by authors and written to some purpose or variety of purposes. If what a text says or means did not depend on the author's intention, we would have no basis for believing, as we do, that to understand the meaning of some problematic passage we should turn first of all, if not exclusively, to other passages of the same text or to other writings of the same author. We consider these things to be obviously pertinent because they have been produced by the very same cause as the passage in question, namely the mind of the given author. And if we then find it necessary to look farther afield, we examine primarily texts by authors of the same time and culture, who may have shared key assumptions with our author, or at past texts that may have influenced the author. The relevance of these materials turns on their causal connection to what the author was thinking in writing the text: they have the same causes as the author's intention, or they had a causal influence on it.

The same is true when we prefer one interpretation of a text to another because it shows better how the different parts and features of the text fit and work together. The coherence we are aiming to discern is that of means adapted to ends, and how can the text show this sort of purposiveness, if not in virtue of its being the expression of the intention with which the author wrote it? Sometimes, as with Henry James's novella, *The Turn of the Screw*, we may believe that a text is so constructed as to frustrate a univocal understanding of the things and events it portrays. That is, we may think it aims to be ambiguous. We may even surmise, if it is a literary text, that it is thus challenging the idea of interpretation as uncovering a hidden key that makes complete sense of a text. Yet we can attribute these

[3] See William Wimsatt and Monroe Beardsley, "The Intentional Fallacy" (1946), chapter I in their book, *The Verbal Icon* (Lexington: University of Kentucky Press, 1954); Hans-Georg Gadamer, *Wahrheit und Methode* (Tübingen: Mohr, 1972 [1960]), XIX, 280–290, 373; and, for a succinct evocation of the themes that have come to dominate structuralist and post-structuralist thinking, the classic essay by Roland Barthes, "La mort de l'auteur" (1968), republished in Barthes, *Le bruissement de la langue* (Paris: Seuil, 1984), 61–67. I have examined Gadamer's hermeneutical theory at length in "Interpretation und Gespräch," chapter VIII of my book, *Das Selbst in seinem Verhältnis zu sich und zu anderen* (Frankfurt: Klostermann, 2017).

aims to the text only if we assume they were the author's in writing it as he did, and grasping how he has accomplished such purposes is then the task of interpretation.

At other times, we may conclude that a text is not ultimately coherent, that it is indeterminate or even contradictory in what it says, not because the author intended it to be so, but instead contrary to any design we may reasonably ascribe to her. Yet we come to this conclusion only because various parts of the text make sense in themselves – that is how we are able to perceive the inconsistencies or gaps in the text as a whole – and what can explain this uneven coherence of the text, if not that the author's intention in writing it as she did was in certain respects confused or unclear?

When we moreover prize such a text for the conflicting elements it contains, believing that the unintended incongruities it displays reflect the genuine complexity of its subject, we can thus credit the text with an insight into reality we deny to the author only if we are relying on the familiar fact that one may be moved to think one thing and also to think another without realizing that one thinks them both, even when their combination reveals something important. For there to be a conflict, each of the conflicting elements, taken singly, must hang together in itself and say one thing, and how can it have this purposive unity if not by being the expression of what the author intended to say in composing it? Such is also the basis on which we may conclude that a text imparts something insightful, though unintended by its author, because of the way its different elements instead support one another: the parts were intended severally, even if the whole they actually constitute was not. In general, we cannot explain how a text may sometimes say more than its author intended it to say except in terms of the author's intentions. In this regard, the old hermeneutical maxim of understanding an author better than he understood himself only makes sense on the assumption that the author's intention plays a fundamental role in determining what a text means.[4]

Indeed, how can we believe we have before us a text at all and not just a random collection of sentences, unless we suppose that its parts are meant to form a whole, that one passage or line is meant to succeed another, and who could have meant these things if not the author? We cannot even regard a string of sounds or marks as forming a sentence with a grammatical meaning, unless we suppose it was produced by someone (not a monkey,

[4] When therefore I say, here and elsewhere, that the author's intention "determines" what the text means, my point is not that the text's meaning is under the author's full control, but simply that its meaning is a function, however complex, of what the author intended in writing it.

not a pencil being blown across a piece of paper) intending to conform to established usage, and we cannot grasp more particularly the point or role of the sentence, without understanding how the speaker or writer intended it in the context. Sometimes, in fact, the same sentence – e.g., "I remember the man holding the cigarette" – may have several different grammatical meanings (depending in this case on whether the participial phrase, "holding the cigarette," refers to part of what is remembered or does not), and establishing which one it actually has in a particular context presupposes some idea of the speaker's intent in uttering it.

As all these rudiments of textual interpretation attest, it is difficult to conceive of what understanding a text would be like if it did not turn on ascertaining the intention of the text's author. In other words, the point is not so much that one *ought* to regard the author's intention as determining what the text means. It is that, however much various theorists may scorn the concept, one *cannot ultimately avoid* doing so.[5] "Anti-intentionalism," to give a name to the position against which I am arguing, overlooks the obvious. Even when we are dealing with a text such as the *Iliad* or the United States Constitution that is not the work of a single author but of many (perhaps now nameless) individuals working over generations, understanding the meaning of the text requires, for the same reasons as in simpler cases, understanding what they severally or together, if not in perfect harmony, intended it to mean. Or consider a case where the person who has signed a legal document is chagrined to learn that what it means and therefore obligates him to is not what he intended. Despite the document speaking in his voice ("I, Joe Smith, do hereby contract to..."), what it means is what its actual author, the lawyer drawing it up, intended it to say in accord with legal practice.

3.3 The Author's Intention

Nonetheless, the proliferation of anti-intentionalist theories has not been entirely baseless. Often they have arisen through a misidentification of what is in fact a legitimate target. Thus, one important factor in their rise has been the ambiguity of the very term, "the author's intention." In some of its senses – what the author set out to say, what she said to herself as she composed the text, what she may have said afterwards about her aims – "the author's intention" need not coincide with the text's

[5] On this point, see P. D. Juhl, *Interpretation* (Princeton: Princeton University Press, 1980), chapter II.

meaning. Contrary to Plato, the author is not the authoritative interpreter of the text she has written. This is another regard in which the hermeneutical maxim of understanding an author better than she understood herself makes good sense. True, the author is usually a commentator of interest, since her remarks about the text stem from the same source, namely her own thought and feeling, as the text itself, much as other works the author wrote or other works of the same cultural milieu can also prove useful (in accord with the same sort of reasoning from common causes) in determining the meaning of the text. Yet usefulness is not the same as conclusiveness. For what the text means consists in what it itself says or contains, and not in what the author may say about it. Though having a conversation differs from reading a text in that the person we are talking to is there to tell us what she meant by some statement, we can still, contrary to what Plato appears to suppose, have reason to question what she tells us. No one is an authoritative, unchallengeable self-interpreter, neither an author nor a speaker.[6] No doubt, skepticism about the idea of authorial intention has been partly fueled by a warranted distrust of the all too frequent attempts to establish the meaning of a text by relying on the author's various comments about it, before or after its composition or even in the body of the work itself. About this last point, however, I shall have shortly a bit more to say.

It will also not do to conceive of the author's intention as E. D. Hirsch has done, even though he was a pioneer in seeking to rehabilitate the concept. According to Hirsch, the author's intention, by which he seeks to define the meaning of a text, consists in what the author "willed to convey."[7] However, not only is "willing" in general, without some further explanation, a notoriously obscure notion, but there can turn out to be a great difference between what we may will – that is, want – to say and what we end up saying in fact, and the question has to do with the meaning of the actual words in a text.

Yet "the author's intention" in still a further sense, namely what the author intended insofar as he realized this intention (or set of intentions) in

[6] As a rule, we do not hesitate to rely on the person himself to tell us the intention with which he is presently acting. But this is not because he has some special, first-person knowledge of his own mental states, but because in acting he may well be expressing or avowing to himself the intention with which he is acting and can thus tell us what he is saying to himself. For more detail, see Chapter 8, Sections 8.4–8.5.

[7] E. D. Hirsch, *Validity in Interpretation* (New Haven: Yale University Press, 1965), 31: "Verbal meaning is whatever someone has willed to convey by a particular sequence of linguistic signs." See also 46–49.

the writing of the text, with whatever degree of awareness or control, must count as determining what the text says or means. For this is the notion presupposed by the elementary features of textual interpretation that I surveyed before. The assumption that other parts of the same work have an immediate bearing on the question of what a problematic passage means, the expectation that the text possesses a coherence of means and ends (or that it is at last partially coherent in this way), the conviction that our object is a text at all and not a random assortment of sentences – all these depend on the idea that the text embodies a defining purpose (or plurality of such purposes), and what can a purpose of this sort be if not, since texts do not write themselves, the author's intention, though his intention, importantly, just insofar as it comes to expression in the text? It is true that authorial intention in this sense of the term – I shall call it the author's *effective* or *realized intention* – cannot be determined without looking at the text itself. But that does not imply that the concept is idle and could be just as well dispensed with. Unless we suppose that the meaning of a text consists in what the author effectively intended in the writing of the text, we cannot, as I have explained, make sense of the most basic things we do in dealing with a text.

This concept of effective intention corresponds, in fact, to the concept of intention that we apply to actions. A person who does something intentionally need not have planned the action in advance, need not, while acting, rehearse or attend explicitly to the aim of the action, and need not be able afterwards to report reliably all that in fact she was attempting to achieve. An action's intention forms part of the action itself, making it the goal-oriented activity it is, instead of a mere physical movement. "Action," moreover, is to be understood here in a broad sense to include acts of saying this or that. What a person meant or intended in speaking as she did is the intention embodied in her very utterances.

This parallel can help to dispel a number of possible confusions. First, just as the intention with which we act or speak need not be the same as the intention we formed prior to acting or speaking, so the author's intention that is actually expressed in the text and thus determines what it means need not reflect any with which he approached the writing of the text. It is, after all, a common experience not to know what to think about some matter until we actually start to talk or write about it.[8] Second, there is the fact that a person's intention in acting, which makes it the action it

[8] This is the theme of the brilliant essay by Heinrich von Kleist, *Über die allmähliche Verfertigung der Gedanken beim Reden* ("On the Gradual Formation of Thoughts While Speaking").

is, may be shaped by social and historical factors that, in their influence on him, are not under his control or that are altogether unknown to him. Things are no different in the case of texts. Though the text's meaning depends on its author's intention as realized in the text, the author may not be, all by himself, the author of his intention. It would be a misunderstanding of the conception of authorial intention I am defending to suppose it entails that the author is the complete master of his words.

The parallel between texts and actions is worth pursuing even further. For instance, just as in a rather complex action (such as weaving a sweater or having a conversation) we may monitor how the whole process is going and adjust each step in the light of how previous steps have turned out, thereby perhaps modifying the very goal we are intending to achieve overall, so the author's intention as realized in a text generally takes shape in and through reflecting about her progress in the writing of that text. Rereading and interpreting what one has already written often form part of the very process of writing. As a result, certain passages may allude to other passages or even claim to explain them. Yet this phenomenon does not undermine the distinction I have drawn between the author's realized or effective intention, which determines the meaning of the text, and the remarks she may have made about its meaning before, during, or after its composition – remarks that may be illuminating but that are not authoritative. For the sort of self-interpretation in question, unlike a remark made by the author from the outside, is one that figures in the text itself. It thus forms an ingredient in what the author effectively intended the text to mean or say, just as an agent's self-monitoring is a feature of the total activity in which she is engaged. It follows, however, that the author's ideas about the meaning of some particular element or passage, insofar as they have come to expression in other parts of the text, are what those other parts say that element or passage means and do not necessarily establish what it really means. Perhaps some aspects of Milton's portrait of Satan, despite the conclusions other parts of *Paradise Lost* clearly intend us to draw, are sympathetic enough to warrant Blake's assertion that Milton was "of the Devil's party without knowing it." Milton may not have been of one mind in the writing of his poem.

In general, I believe, theories of textual interpretation do well to model themselves on the way we interpret in everyday life people's actions and utterances.[9] Any such theory that would have false or absurd consequences

[9] For someone so well versed in hermeneutical theory, Paul Ricœur oddly argued that the hermeneutics of texts applies to actions but not to utterances. See his essay, "Le modèle du texte:

if applied to these phenomena is probably wrong. This principle could be said to be but a corollary of the universality of hermeneutics that Friedrich Schleiermacher proclaimed at the beginning of the nineteenth century, arguing that he found himself using in everyday conversations the same methods of interpretation he held to govern our reading of texts.[10]

Still, however instructive (and too seldom exploited), the parallel between texts and actions or everyday conversations needs to be developed with care. It would be wrong to suppose that an author's intention, insofar as it determines the meaning of a text, must resemble in every respect the intentions with which people act and talk in ordinary life. Indeed, a second source of the present disdain for the idea of authorial intention has been an often justified hostility to the kind of biographical criticism that is content to explain what an author meant by reference to his past experience, his personal and historical circumstances, his various remarks about the work in question, and about any number of other things – that is, in much the same way that we ordinarily make sense of someone's action or words by relying on what we know about his person and situation. For to regard the work as simply a reflection of the author's life and times misses the fact that texts of a literary, philosophical, or scientific character involve a suspension of everyday concerns and a devotion to the special demands

l'action sensée considérée comme un texte" in *Du texte à l'action. Essais d'herméneutique II* (Paris: Seuil, 1986), 183–211. His argument is based on several false dichotomies between spoken and written language – that written language is fixed but spoken language is fleeting (what about speech that is recorded?), that spoken language is addressed to someone present whereas written language is addressed to whoever can read (what about a letter written to a friend?) – as well as on agreement with Plato's assumption that a speaker, unlike an author, is always there to provide an authoritative interpretation of what he meant. From this assumption he then went on to draw the conclusion that what a text means is largely autonomous with regard to the author's intention, thus confusing meaning and significance (a distinction I explain in Section 3.4).

10 Friedrich Schleiermacher, "Über den Begriff der Hermeneutik" (1829), reprinted in Schleiermacher, *Hermeneutik und Kritik*, ed. M. Frank (Frankfurt: Suhrkamp, 1977), 315: "... ich ergreife mich sehr oft mitten im vertraulichen Gespräch auf hermeneutischen Operationen, wenn ich mich mit einem gewöhnlichen Grade des Verstehens nicht begnüge, sondern zu erforschen suche, wie sich wohl in dem Freunde der Übergang von einem Gedanken zum anderen gemacht habe, oder wenn ich nachspüre, mit welchen Ansichten, Urteilen und Bestrebungen es wohl zusammenhängt, dass er sich über einen besprochenen Gegenstand grade so und nicht anders ausdrückt ... Ja, ich gestehe, dass ich diese Ausübung der Hermeneutik im Gebiet der Muttersprache und im unmittelbaren Verkehr mit Menschen für einen sehr wesentlichen Teil des gebildeten Lebens halte, abgesehn von allen philologischen oder theologischen Studien" ("I find myself very often in the middle of a personal conversation involved in hermeneutical operations, if I am not satisfied with the usual level of understanding but want to find out why my friend moved from one thought to another, or if I am wondering what are the views, judgments, and purposes that have led him to speak one way rather than another about the matter under discussion ... Indeed, I confess that I regard the practice of hermeneutics in our mother tongue and in our everyday dealings with men to be an essential part of cultured life, apart from philological or theological studies.")

of the creative imagination and literary form, philosophical depth and argument, or scientific precision and evidence.

And yet, what such a text means remains a matter of what its author, now in the effort to heed those demands, intended it to mean – again insofar as this intention is realized in the text. Although a lyric poet may write his poem from the standpoint of a persona instead of as an expression of his own thought and feeling, this persona is nonetheless a device constructed by the real poet, and grasping the meaning of the poem involves ascertaining his purpose in deploying it. Proust rightly inveighed against Sainte-Beuve's biographical method, complaining that it "consists in not separating the man and the work, in immersing oneself in all sorts of information about the writer, in collecting his correspondence, in questioning those who knew him," and so forth. But he rejected it at bottom because, as he continued, "this method fails to perceive what a bit of familiarity with ourselves easily teaches us: that a book is the product of another *self*" – Proust himself italicized the word – "than that which we manifest in our habits, in society, in our vices."[11] Thus, we should in reading works of literature certainly attend, not just to what they *say*, either directly or through the use of characters and personae, but also to what they *do*, by way of exploring, modifying, problematizing, or extending existing conventions and modes of expression. Yet when we attribute these, as sometimes said, "literary" features to a text, our assumption must be that they too are part of what its author intended it to embody, insofar as that intention was realized in the work. The meaning of a literary text generally involves a concern with form, in more or less intimate conjunction with the content of what it says – but only because, after all, the author meant it to be just such a text.[12]

[11] Marcel Proust, *Contre Sainte-Beuve* (Paris: Gallimard, 1987), 127: "Cette méthode, qui consiste à ne pas séparer l'homme et l'œuvre, à s'entourer de tous les renseignements possibles sur un écrivain, à collationner ses correspondances, à interroger les hommes qui l'ont connu, . . . cette méthode méconnaît ce qu'une fréquentation un peu profonde avec nous-mêmes nous apprend: qu'un livre est le produit d'un autre *moi* que celui que nous manifestons dans nos habitudes, dans la société, dans nos vices."

[12] I mention *en passant* a difficult question that I cannot go into here. How much belongs to the (realized) intention of an author or indeed to an intention in general – all the logical consequences of one's intention or only those of which one is aware at the time? The second answer cannot be right. For when I assert for instance, "The cat is on the mat," I mean to deny, not just that the cat is on the sofa where it was yesterday, but all the possibilities incompatible with what I am asserting, whatever they may be, even if I cannot enumerate them all now. Someone who did not mean that would not understand what it is to assert something. Probably the best answer is that I am denying in my assertion all the contrary possibilities, whatever they may be, that could have occurred to me. In any case, this problem about the content of an intention does not undermine the thesis that the

3.4 Meaning and Significance

We do not, however, read books or poems solely for their textual meaning. We do not aim only, or even principally, to determine what their author meant to say, but seek to discover what they mean for us. We may, for instance, be interested in seeing how a work forms part of a larger cultural movement or in charting its influence on other works. More commonly, we may want to find out how it speaks to our own interests and preoccupations. If it is a legal text (a statute, judicial opinion, or constitutional provision), we may want to ascertain its import for a particular case or social problem. However, all these endeavors require that we first form an idea of what the text itself says or means. For how else can we gauge its relevance in these various ways? And what it means, as I have argued, consists in the author's intention as realized in the text itself. The distinction between a text's *meaning* in this sense and its *significance*, its relevance to the reader's concerns, is therefore indispensable. Others too have recognized its crucial importance, most notably E. D. Hirsch,[13] even if he errs, as I have noted, in the notion of authorial intention he uses to define a text's meaning.

Because in reading we seek to understand not just what the text means but what it means for us, interpretation as commonly practiced involves grasping both its meaning and its significance. We need not always keep the two apart in our reading. Indeed, it may not be easy to do so. Determining meaning and determining significance each call upon a mix of reasoning, imagination, and emotional sensibility, and when we respond to the text in this complex way, we often lose sight of the difference between the two.[14] Ultimately, the only sure method of distinguishing what the text means from what it means for us is to reflect: we have to ask ourselves which parts of our understanding of the text hinge essentially on interests of our own and would have to change if our interests were different. Even then we can encounter the complication that our own concerns may have made us more attentive than we would otherwise be to

meaning of a text lies in the author's realized intention. I am grateful to Rüdiger Bittner for a discussion of this point.

[13] Hirsch, *Validity in Interpretation*, 8f, 140f, 255.

[14] This phenomenon has led various reader-response theories, such as the *Wirkungsästhetik* of Wolfgang Iser (see his book, *The Act of Reading*, Baltimore: Johns Hopkins University Press, 1978 [1976]), to reduce the reader's views about what a text says or means to simply one more aspect of the overall way the reader responds to the text (of what the text "does"), and as a result to run together meaning with significance.

certain aspects of the text itself, so that we must determine whether there is reason, independently of those concerns, to attribute the features in question to the text. Yet all these difficulties are not insuperable. The distinction between meaning and significance is real, as is sufficiently shown by the fact that a text cannot in general prove relevant except in virtue of what it happens to say or mean.

Now it is true: normally, the author's intention is that his work be significant or relevant in certain ways. Probably no author wants his text to be read as merely the expression of his thought and feeling, but instead to be applied by his readers to their own situation. For only then can the work be enjoyed and learned from. As a result, the author may include in the work itself indications about what readers are to make of the text before them.

Yet intended and actual significance are two quite different things. Insofar as intended significance forms part of the author's effective intention, it figures in what the text itself says or means, as perhaps paradigmatically illustrated by the final line of Rilke's sonnet, *Archaïscher Torso Apollos*: "Du mußt dein Leben ändern" – "You have to change the way you live." The significance the text actually acquires depends, by contrast, not just on the text but also on the interests and conceptions of its readers. Think of a political constitution, the intended meaning of some of whose provisions is that certain organs of government are authorized to "interpret" it, that is, to adapt it to changing conditions, even though the way these governmental organs (for instance, constitutional courts) subsequently develop what the document says may differ quite a lot from what its authors could have foreseen. Or think of my command, "Do what you think best!" When you go on to do what you think best, you show that you understand the meaning of my words, even though the particular action you do may not at all be what I was hoping you would do. William Blake may have ultimately intended his "dark Satanic mills" to mean not so much factories or Establishment churches (the two usual interpretations of that famous phrase in his poem, *Jerusalem*) as whatever his readers might understand to be the agencies by which the human soul is destroyed. But if so, then that was his (effective) intention and what the phrase means, and it is to be distinguished from the more specific construals his various readers have subsequently given to the phrase.[15]

[15] I cannot go here into the complex question of what it means to interpret correctly the significance of a text (though see Section 4.3 of the following chapter). In general, it can be said that correctness in this regard depends on two factors: not only must the meaning of the text be correctly understood, but the criteria belonging to the relevant interests of the reader must also be satisfied.

The distinction between meaning and significance allows us to defuse a third reason to distrust the idea of authorial intention. The idea that the meaning of a text is determined by the author's intention does not contradict the fact, as many have supposed, that literary and philosophical works, and certainly the greatest among them, have the ability to speak to readers in continually new ways. Ascertaining all that a text says or means can in itself be sometimes exceedingly difficult and appear to be an unending task. But the inexhaustibility of a text consists fundamentally in its capacity to prove relevant or applicable to the many different sorts of concerns that readers in different contexts and historical circumstances bring to bear. What is inexhaustible is the text's potential for significance, not its meaning, though great works could not have this power to show themselves significant in ever new ways except in virtue of the profundity of what they say or mean.

3.5 Reading and Respect

Having clarified at some length the idea of author's intention, I return now to the ethics of reading. My argument so far has been that if there is such a thing as the ethics of reading, if the reader's relation to a text can count as ethical in character, then this relation must ultimately consist in a relation to another person and that, furthermore, reading does involve such a relation inasmuch as what the text says or means – what we must seek in the first instance to grasp as readers – is what the author effectively intended it to say or mean. I have, however, also observed that the ethical nature of the reading relation would have to be special in kind since it relates us directly, not to the author, who is absent, but to the text, which, unlike a person, is unable to object to how it may be mistreated – that is, to how it may be misread. Moreover, even if the author were there as we read and objected that we were misinterpreting the meaning of what he had written, his interpretation of the text's meaning (of what the text itself says, as opposed to its significance) would not be necessarily correct, nor ours necessarily wrong. What the text means is a matter of what he intended in the very writing of it. No one can speak with absolute authority for the text, and the text cannot defend itself.

Precisely because of this difference between the text and its author – the text is not a person, nor what it says or means the property of the author (though the text as a set of words may well be her legal property, protected by copyright) – one might doubt whether the reading relation can really be an ethical relation. But I disagree. There is indeed such a thing as the ethics of reading. Misreading a text, interpreting falsely what it says or means, does amount to wronging the author when the misreading is not simply inadvertent but the result of carelessness or deliberate distortion, and particularly (though not only) when such misreading is not kept to oneself but given public expression. For consider again the similarity between texts and actions. Actions, like texts, are what they are in virtue of the intentions they express. Now, one way people can be poorly treated is in regard to the intentions with which they have acted. Suppose that someone regards the actions of a certain person as of so little consequence that he fails to see the other's gesture for the generous offer it is, or he finds it useful for his own interests to portray that offer as something altogether different, say, as an attempt at ingratiation. Surely we would think that he has wronged the other person, even though the immediate object of the wrong was the other's action (which has been thoughtlessly or perfidiously construed) and even though that action is neither itself a person (and so cannot defend itself) nor the property of the agent, whose statements after the fact about her intentions are not authoritative. The person has been wronged because what she was doing in acting as she did has been slighted or falsified.

Similarly with authors and texts. I am not suggesting that we wrong the author when we treat her text in ways she may not wish us to. When, for instance, we skim it, read only part of it, or read the end first, or when we find in it a significance for our purposes that she would regard as objectionable, we are not doing her a wrong any more than we wrong a person by reacting to his actions in a way he may not like. But it is a different matter when we misrepresent the meaning itself of the text and we do so not because we have simply made a mistake, but because we cannot bother to get it right or because we find it expedient to distort what it says. Then we are failing to treat the author as she deserves. To appreciate this fact, we need only consider how we would react if the situation were reversed and we were the object of such treatment. Would we not feel angry, and angry because we believed we had been wronged, if someone negligently or willfully misconstrued what we have written? That is how we feel when what we have said is thus falsified, and why should our having written it instead change our reaction?[16]

[16] Even when the meaning of a text is willfully or carelessly distorted in a way that makes it appear better (for instance, more interesting or deeper) than it actually is, the author is still being, if not perhaps wronged, then treated wrongly, just as someone is treated unjustly if his action is similarly misrepresented as being in some way better than it really is.

As I noted, the injustice is of particular moment when the misrepresentation of the author's meaning is not kept to oneself but made public in some way. This point, too, the parallel with actions helps to explain. There is a great difference between forming a careless or deliberately falsifying view of the intention with which someone acted and giving open expression to such a view in what one says or does. The first is not good, but the second is far worse. For it is then no longer a matter of merely a thought, but instead of a deed whose wrongness consists (quite apart from the bad consequences it may have) in demonstrating for others to see the disregard or contempt in which one holds the other person. So too in the case of carelessly or willfully distorting the meaning of an author's text. Doing so openly is an act of disrespect.

Texts do tend to differ from actions in an important regard I have mentioned before. Agents are generally in the vicinity of their actions, such that when their actions are described falsely, or when they believe that they are, they can complain. Texts, by contrast, "roam about everywhere," as Plato notes, and do not have their authors nearby, or necessarily anyone, to stand up for them when they are misread. It might be thought that this difference in fact points to a good reason to doubt that carelessly or purposely misreading a text is to wrong the author. For suppose, one might object, that the author is dead and has been dead for many years or even centuries: How can such misreading really be said to do him a wrong? Such an objection forgets, however, the many ways we believe the dead can be wronged, as when a dying person's last wishes are not respected, the memory of genocide victims is dishonored, or someone's reputation after death is slandered. Here then is another way. Dead authors too, not solely living ones, are wronged by thoughtless or willful misinterpretation, and precisely because they are no longer around at all to protest, such misreading is particularly rife in their case.

To write a text, to express something of oneself in writing, is thus to make oneself especially vulnerable to others. Therein lies, in fact, the ultimate importance of the ethics of reading I am arguing for: it epitomizes the very essence of ethical thinking. Formulated abstractly, the moral point of view consists in seeing in another's good a reason for action on our part, apart from all consideration of our own good.[17] As a result, our moral character shows itself most clearly in the way we treat the vulnerable, those with little power, few resources, or no social standing, since they cannot make it in our interest to treat them well. When our right actions happen

[17] For more detail, see Chapter 1, Sections 1.2 and 1.5.

also to be to our advantage, questions naturally arise (perhaps in our own mind as well) about our real motives and about our underlying attitude toward other people. These worries are allayed when it is seen how we act in situations in which the moral and the expedient no longer coincide, in which others lack the means to induce us to treat them fairly. Now among such situations are those in which we are reading and interpreting what someone has written. How faithful we strive to be to the text and to what its author meant reveals a lot about our moral character in general. Though I will not go so far as to assert that a bad reader cannot be a good person, I doubt that a habitually careless or deliberately manipulative reader is likely to be one. Someone who does not mind distorting what a text says, since the author is not there to complain (whether or not the author correctly grasps the meaning of what he wrote), reveals a disregard for how another asks to be understood, a willingness to twist another's words for his own purposes, that he might just as easily display toward the weak and defenseless when dealing with them directly, in other areas of life.

My claim then is not that careless or willful misreading constitutes a particularly grave offense. There are far worse things one can do to a person than to misread her in this way. The point has to do with what failing thus to respect what people have written shows about the character of those who engage in it, and thus about how they are likely to act in other contexts as well.

I conclude with a somewhat similar observation that Karl Kraus, the great Viennese satirist and moralist in the first part of the twentieth century, made about respect for language itself, whether in speaking or writing (his explicit focus) or in reading as well. It is, he said, a "mental discipline that enjoins the highest measure of responsibility toward the sole thing that can be wronged with impunity, namely language, and that serves like no other to teach respect for every other kind of human good."[18] Kraus's idea in this passage (as in much of his work) was that we should show a regard for our language's rules, traditions, and powers of expression, not solely for the sake of effective communication with others, but because a concern for how we speak and write is ultimately a concern

[18] Karl Kraus, "Die Sprache," in *Magie der Sprache* (Frankfurt: Suhrkamp, 1982), 344: "... einer geistigen Disziplin, die gegenüber dem einzigen, was ungestraft verletzt werden kann, der Sprache, das höchste Maß einer Verantwortung festsetzt und wie keine andere geeignet ist, den Respekt vor jeglichem andern Lebensgut zu lehren." This essay, one of the very last that Kraus published in his review *Die Fackel* (late December 1932), appeared shortly before Hindenburg appointed Hitler chancellor on January 30, 1933.

for the integrity of our own thinking. Language is not a mere tool, but the very medium of our being.

I do not think that respect for language is strictly speaking an ethical attitude since it does not consist in a relation to a person, unless, that is, it embodies a respect for ourselves. But it does, as Kraus indicates, help us to grasp what it really means to respect another. If in our face-to-face interactions with other people we fail to show someone respect, we usually pay some price – the person may retaliate, the law may punish us, other people may form a low opinion of our character – so that we may act in a respectful manner out of fear of the consequences of doing otherwise. In this case, of course, our attitude itself is not really one of respect, as it is when we show others respect without giving any thought to such sanctions. Respect for language, on the other hand, is a respect that can be violated without, as a rule, any ill consequences. The careless use of words, confused or obscurantist modes of expression, rarely get anyone into trouble. (They often put one ahead). That is why, in Kraus's words, a sense of responsibility to the language we speak and write is a form of self-discipline that "serves like no other to teach respect for every other kind of human good." It instills in us the habit of deferring without ulterior motive to what is itself of intrinsic worth.

Now, respect for the actual meaning of a text, as the expression of the author's effective intention in writing it as he did, is indeed, as I have argued, truly ethical in nature. It possesses, however, the same propaedeutic virtue as respect for language. It too can generally be violated with impunity. Thus, seeking as readers to grasp faithfully what a text is saying teaches us to appreciate what is the fundamental principle of all moral thinking: we are to treat everyone well whether or not they (or others) may be able to make it in our interest to do so, just as though they were too weak to retaliate if we do not, just as though they were, like the author of a text, not even there to notice how we are treating them. In this regard, the ethics of reading does not have to do merely with one ethical relation among others. Far from doubtfully forming a province of ethics at all, it points to the very heart of the moral point of view.

CHAPTER 4

The Holes in Holism

4.1 First- and Second-Order Questions

In this chapter, devoted to an examination of one of Ronald Dworkin's last great works, I will go a lot farther in laying out the non-naturalist metaphysics that the nature of moral thinking seems to me to require.

Justice for Hedgehogs was, in fact, Dworkin's philosophically most ambitious book, far more ambitious than its title might suggest.[1] One might suppose that it deals essentially with justice, inferring from the allusion to Isaiah Berlin's famous essay, "The Hedgehog and the Fox," that its principal aim is to offer a grand theory of this subject. Berlin, it will be remembered, used Archilochus' line, "the fox knows many things, but the hedgehog knows one big thing," to contrast two different intellectual attitudes toward the world: the fox, like Berlin himself, recognizes that life gives rise to many diverse and sometimes conflicting ends, which have to be balanced or held together in an uneasy truce, whereas the hedgehog believes that all our proper ends find their place in a single, overarching system.[2] Dworkin was certainly a hedgehog in this sense. However, the unitary vision he develops in this book embraces much more than the nature of justice. His ambition was to tie together into one comprehensive theory all the different domains of value – both ethics, or how we ourselves are to live well, and personal morality, or how we as individuals are to treat others, no less than political morality, which concerns how we are to treat others, justly for instance, as members of a political community. Even the nature of interpretation, as practiced in history, law, and literary criticism, is included, because of its dependence on values. "Value," Dworkin

[1] Dworkin, *Justice for Hedgehogs* (Cambridge, MA: Harvard University Press, 2011). All references to this work will be given in the text as parenthetical citations. About a year before his death in 2013, Ronald Dworkin gave me a set of very valuable comments on a draft of the original version of this chapter. I remain very grateful to him.

[2] Berlin, *The Hedgehog and the Fox* (London: Weidenfeld and Nicolson, 1953).

announces at the beginning of the book, "is one big thing" (1). *Justice for Hedgehogs* is not primarily a book about justice, even if justice is its ultimate target.

So capacious is the theory Dworkin presents that the entire first half of the book is devoted to presenting, as an integral part of the more substantive discussions to follow, an account of the nature of value judgments in general and of what it means for them to be true or false. Generally, philosophers distinguish such "meta-ethical" or second-order questions *about* ethics and morals from the first-order questions *of* ethics and morals that concern what things are in fact good and bad, right and wrong, and they often suppose that these two sorts of questions can be addressed independently of one another – that meta-ethical propositions do not embody any first-order moral commitments. Dworkin wants none of this. He rejects the distinction itself as incoherent (67), maintaining that every supposed meta-ethical claim is really a straightforward moral judgment in disguise.[3] Yet no sooner does he declare that "there are no nonevaluative, second-order, meta-ethical truths about value" than he goes on to deliver, in the next sentence, his own meta-ethical and not discernibly evaluative view about the nature of value judgments: "Value judgments are true, when they are true, not in virtue of any matching [a realm of moral facts, CL], but in virtue of the substantive case that can be made for them" (11). The difference between judgments and judgments about what is involved in those judgments is, then, hardly illusory.

What Dworkin is right to reject is not the distinction between the ethical and the meta-ethical, but rather a particular way of conceiving it. This is the philosophical position he calls "Archimedean" or external skepticism, a position whose most sophisticated version appears in the writings of such contemporary "expressivist quasi-realists" as Allan Gibbard and Simon Blackburn. According to them, we can see reason to believe that some things are good and others bad while at the same time holding, from an outside standpoint, that these judgments do not actually purport to describe the value properties of things, of which in fact there are none, but only serve to express certain sorts of attitudes on our part. I already indicated in Chapter 1 (Section 1.4) some ways in which the expressivist analysis fails to capture key features of our first-order moral judgments, and I will broaden this criticism in Chapter 6. However, Dworkin's reasons for rejecting this two-tier kind of analysis are different

[3] This view was first developed in Dworkin's essay, "Objectivity and Truth: You'd Better Believe It," *Philosophy & Public Affairs* 25 (2), Spring 1996, 87–139.

from mine. As we have just seen, he denies the existence of any distinction in the realm of value between a judgment being true and its being rationally justified by a "substantive case" having been made for it. I disagree.

This equation between being true and being justified has in his eyes other virtues as well. It plays an essential role in his rejection of the value pluralism that Berlin defended. If the truth of our value judgments is fixed by argument and not by some independent order of values, then the nature of any of our values turns on the justification it can receive from our other commitments. Conflict between our values as well as what can look like their ultimate plurality are therefore only apparent. In ethics and personal morality as in political morality, "integration is a necessary condition of truth," Dworkin claims. "We do not secure fully persuasive conceptions of our several political values unless our conceptions . . . mesh" (5–6). With this claim I also disagree, as I explain toward the end.

Dworkin's book is thus the work of a consummate hedgehog. The meta-ethical and the ethical, reflections on method and arguments of substance, ethics, morality, and politics, even hermeneutics, are brought together into one, all-encompassing theory. *Justice for Hedgehogs* is a magnificent work, always engaging, if not, I believe, always persuasive. I shall focus on the general conception of value propounded in the first half – Parts One ("Independence") and Two ("Interpretation") – and on the way it lays the groundwork for the discussions of ethics, personal morality, and political morality in Parts Three through Five. For my theme here, as in this book as a whole, is with how reflection on the nature of our moral thinking leads inevitably to questions – I would say "metaphysical" questions – about the nature of the world itself. About the details of his ethical, moral, and political views, many of them familiar from Dworkin's earlier writings such as *Life's Dominion* (1993) and *Sovereign Virtue* (2000), I shall have less to say. There will be occasion to conclude, however, with an examination of his argument against value pluralism.

4.2 Truth and Morals

In ordinary life, we think of our ethical and moral judgments as being true or false, and by their truth and falsity we mean nothing very different from the truth and falsity of our empirical judgments. If we declare that lying when convenient is wrong, we intend to be saying what is the case independently of ourselves or anyone believing that it is so. In particular, we do not understand ourselves as simply expressing our negative attitude toward such a practice, but instead as stating a fact about what is really the case, independent of the disapproval we may feel, since we regard the wrongness of that sort of action as justifying our disapproval. Or so we may well think, if untouched by philosophical worries. Yet as Dworkin observes (29), grounds for doubt are lying in wait. If we ask what makes an ethical or moral judgment true and how we come to know any such truths, our confidence can begin to waver. In the case of perception, what makes our judgments true is the perceived objects having the qualities we see them to have, and we come to have perceptual knowledge in virtue of the way these objects act causally on our senses, a way that can be studied by empirical science itself. How can there be any parallel account of ethical and moral judgments? Throughout the book, Dworkin has a great deal of sport with "realist" attempts to portray ethical and moral facts as states of the world that we somehow grasp and that somehow render our judgments true or false. Are we to suppose, he jokes, that these facts consist in configurations of moral particles or "morons" that act on us as physical particles do when we acquire our beliefs about the physical world (9, 29, etc.)?

Nonetheless, the conclusion is not, Dworkin insists, that our ordinary understanding of ethical and moral judgments as true or false is a mistake. Nor should we infer that it only makes sense within our practices of evaluation, given their purposes, since the world itself lacks all distinctions of value, and that these judgments ultimately serve therefore only to express attitudes of approval or disapproval on our part, even if rather complex ones about how we and others ought to act whatever may be our attitudes at the time. The latter view is the sophisticated form of Archimedean or external skepticism developed by Gibbard and Blackburn. The trouble with their expressivist quasi-realism, Dworkin argues, is that one cannot hold consistently the two propositions they want to combine, namely (i) that within the practice of ethical and moral evaluation, certain judgments are well justified by reasons and thus count as true and (ii) that these same judgments, when viewed philosophically from outside that practice, cannot really count as true. What sense can be given to the notion (ii) that they cannot really count as true, if not that, contrary to (i), there fail after all to be good reasons to think they are true (43, 62f)?

I think Dworkin is right here. To put his point generally, truth cannot be relativized to a framework. This is plain from the difficulties of such philosophers as Kant and Carnap in their attempts to distinguish "empirical" from "transcendental" or "internal" from "external" standpoints. One cannot assert within a given framework of thought that objects are indeed subject to causal laws, that numbers indeed do exist, or that lying is indeed wrong, and then claim, without self-contradiction, that outside that framework – transcendentally, externally, or meta-ethically – such statements are not really true. If looking at the situation in the broadest possible way, considering how that framework of thought fits in with everything else we know, we conclude that its judgments cannot really be true, then they are in fact false, even within that framework. In Chapter 6 (Sections 6.6–6.7), I pursue a similar argument against framework-relativity in considerably more detail.

As mentioned earlier, Dworkin believes that his refutation of Archimedean skepticism entails the incoherence of the very idea of meta-ethics. We must discard, he infers, the supposed distinction between first-order questions about what is right and wrong and second-order questions about what is meant in calling various things right or wrong: "meta-ethics rests upon a mistake" (67). However, this conclusion misidentifies the error in Archimedean skepticism, which is not the distinction itself, but rather the idea that we can coherently assert as true at one level what we deny to be true at the other. We can reject this latter idea yet still seek an answer to the indisputably second-order question of *what* the truth of moral judgments consists in.

Moreover, Dworkin himself, as I pointed out earlier, presents an answer to this meta-ethical question: "Moral judgments are made true, when they are true, by an adequate moral argument for their truth" (37; also 11). The truth of value judgments does not consist in their matching some independent reality of values, though it is perfectly proper to say, as we ordinarily do, that such judgments aim to get it right, to be stating a fact, about what is really valuable or not, independently of our attitudes toward the subject. For what we then mean, according to Dworkin, is that those judgments rest upon arguments that justify their acceptance, whatever approval or disapproval we may feel. It has to be said that the term "adequate" seems ill-chosen. The phrase "an adequate argument for the truth of moral judgments" can suggest that the argument is a *means* to ascertaining their truth, as though their truth were some separate state of affairs, whereas Dworkin's position is that the truth of a moral judgment is nothing other than the valid argument that justifies it. As he says, "the moral realm is the realm of argument, not brute, raw fact" (11). Moreover, an argument might be deemed "adequate," in one sense of the term, if it established the truth of some proposition without offering the deepest or most illuminating grounds for that proposition; such an argument would not seem to be what *makes* that proposition true. A better formulation occurs later on: "the truth about morality just is what the best case shows" (122).

Such is, in outline, Dworkin's conception of the nature of ethical and moral truth. It is intended to cut a middle way between what he regards as the outlandish metaphysics of realist theories of value and the irredeemable subjectivism of expressivist approaches. It vindicates, he believes, in a down-to-earth yet wholehearted way our ordinary understanding of value judgments as true or false independently of any attitudes of approval or disapproval. This conception faces a host of problems, however. They all stem, I believe, from the futility of trying to have objectivity without objects, a status Dworkin has not been alone in aiming to secure for values.[4]

An immediate difficulty is that it looks odd, if not circular, to say that what makes a judgment true is an argument for its truth. One would have thought that what makes a judgment *true* (as opposed to justified) has to do with what it purports to be *about*, and what a judgment is about is not any argument offered on its behalf.

Another difficulty should be apparent from my remarks about how an argument may be "adequate" without being deep. In general, justification is a response to doubt, and thus an argument does not count as justifying some proposition simply because it may be sound, its conclusion following from premises that are true. It must also be suitable for resolving the doubts that its addressee, whether others or ourselves, has about the conclusion, where "suitability" means that its premises must be truths that the addressee already accepts or could come to accept without first having to agree to the conclusion. Whether an argument justifies its conclusion, whether it is in that sense a good argument, depends therefore on what happens to be the standpoint of its intended recipient. An argument may be a good one if addressed to certain persons, and a bad one, for all its soundness, if addressed to others. However, the truth of a judgment – even of an ethical or moral judgment, if "truth" in this case is to mean anything like what it means elsewhere – cannot depend on and vary with the standpoint of its addressee. How then can it be maintained that "moral judgments are made true, when they are true, by an adequate moral argument for their truth" (37)?

There is a further difficulty, one that Dworkin himself brings up, though fails to dispel. As he observes (69), our empirical beliefs are justified

[4] See for instance Hilary Putnam, *Ethics without Ontology* (Cambridge, MA: Harvard University Press, 2004), chapter 3, whose very title is "Objectivity without Objects."

insofar as their being true explains why we hold them. This is because evidence for a belief has to be causally dependent on what the belief purports to describe: pig tracks show that a pig walked through the yard only if a pig (not a neighbor using a pig's foot) made the tracks. How then can our ethical and moral beliefs count as justified unless in their case too the facts they describe – some things being good or bad, right or wrong – form part of the causal explanation of why we hold them? And how can that be so unless realism about values is correct, despite all the mocking remarks about "morons"? Dworkin tries to meet this challenge by denying that our ethical or moral beliefs can be causally explained by what makes them true: "there is no causal interaction between moral truth and moral opinion" (70; also 12, 76). That is why, he argues, we do not talk about having "evidence" for our ethical or moral beliefs (82). What makes them true are not ethical or moral facts in the world, of whose existence we might gather evidence, but rather arguments that justify them. In their case, justification has nothing to do with explanation.

This response will not do for several reasons. First, if Dworkin were right that moral beliefs are not made true by moral facts in the world but rather by good arguments, then their being true, understood in this sense, would in fact explain why we hold them, when we hold them because they are justified. After all, cannot sound arguments play a causal role in the formation of belief or in the strengthening of beliefs already held? Though certainly assuming that moral arguments can produce conviction (why else would he have written the books he did?), Dworkin denies, however, that the soundness itself of those arguments – which means, according to him, the truth of the conclusions they justify – can be causally responsible for the moral beliefs we acquire on their basis. That is what he means by the striking sentence, "People's personal histories, rather than any encounters with moral truth, cause their convictions" (47; also 79f, 419). Yet to deny that moral belief can be produced by sound argument, and precisely in virtue of the argument being sound, is to deny that moral thinking is a rational activity. If there really were, as Dworkin claims, a "radical independence of the truth of conviction from the manner of its production" (445), deliberation in the moral realm would not really be deliberation. For when we set out to deliberate rationally, whatever the domain, we intend that our thinking be shaped, not simply by arguments that happen to be sound, but by the very soundness of those arguments. Otherwise, it will be a matter of luck that we accept the right arguments. Given his own account of moral truth, Dworkin ought not to deny, therefore, that moral opinions may be explained causally by their truth. And if instead we do not equate moral truth with moral argument, as I believe we should not, the same point holds: wanting our deliberation to be shaped by the soundness of the arguments we embrace entails wanting it to be constrained by truth, namely by the truth of the premises and the conclusion. In general, whenever we think about what we should believe or do, we intend that our thinking be guided by the truth.

There is a second, related defect in Dworkin's effort to dissociate justification and explanation in the realm of value. It emerges when we look more closely at the way in which justified beliefs are causally dependent on their justifying arguments. In general, an argument is supposed to point to reasons for endorsing its conclusion. Accepting an argument therefore means being moved, that is, being caused, by those reasons to believe what they justify. In the case of empirical arguments, the reasons consist in the evidence for the conclusion. But it is important to note that the evidence is not simply the various physical or psychological facts adduced, but these facts insofar as they count in favor of the conclusion. (One might agree to the facts and yet deny that they support the conclusion). In general, as I argued in Chapter 1 (Section 1.3), this relation of "counting in favor of," in which empirical facts can stand with regard to our possibilities of thought and action, is what reasons consist in, and the relation is normative in character just as reasons are: what one has a reason to think or do is what one *ought* to think or do, all else being equal. Consequently, when we are moved by empirical arguments to accept their conclusions, the beliefs we thereby form are beliefs caused by something normative in character, namely the reasons or evidence justifying their acceptance. The same must also be true when we are moved by arguments indicating how we should act.

Now if all this is so, it ceases to be absurd, as Dworkin supposes, to think that moral beliefs can be caused by moral facts, just because the latter are not physical in nature. While moral beliefs cannot be understood as being about the arguments that justify them, they can be plausibly understood as being about the reasons for action, reasons of a decisive kind having to do principally[5] with the treatment of others, that such arguments are intended to point out: the belief that lying is morally wrong is the belief that there are impersonal reasons, based in the good of others, not to lie. What moral beliefs are about would thus be moral facts (facts involving moral reasons) that make them true, when they are true, and that causally explain them, when those beliefs are held in virtue of justifying arguments.

[5] If not exclusively. See Chapter 2 on the idea of duties to oneself.

Justification and explanation would be as tightly linked in their case as in the case of empirical beliefs. If we do not normally talk of having "evidence" for our moral beliefs, that is because the reasons for action that are their object do not generally produce intermediate phenomena that are our means of access to them – though we do sometimes take what a person of judgment says about a particular case as good evidence for what is the right action in the circumstances.

A lot more needs to be said, of course, about this kind of realist conception. It certainly faces important difficulties of its own. Yet they largely turn, I believe, on the general problem of how to make sense of something we ordinarily believe, namely that reasons can be causes. I turn to this problem in Chapters 6 (Section 6.8) and 7, as I fill in this realism further. Here, the main point is to show that Dworkin has too little to say in his otherwise wide-ranging book about so basic a question as the nature of reasons.[6] He fails to see that reasons are much like the "morons" he takes so much pleasure in ridiculing. They too, though nonphysical in character, must be understood as causally responsible for the beliefs we acquire by reasoned argument, and when these beliefs are themselves about reasons, as I think moral beliefs are, then what makes them true explains causally our having them. Moral reasons are the objects that make possible the objectivity of moral beliefs.

4.3 Interpretation

Dworkin draws a number of consequences from his account of "truth in morals." The broadest is the thesis that ethical and moral reasoning form one instance among others of "interpretive reasoning" (38, 102). In an essential respect, he asserts, making ethical or moral judgments and reflecting on our values is like interpreting actions, utterances, and texts: we are engaged in determining what certain of our convictions mean in practice or mean for one another, just as we "speak of the meaning or significance of a passage in a poem or a play, of the point of a clause in a particular statute, of the motives that produced a particular dream, of the ambitions or understandings that shape an event or an age." In general, interpretation speaks the "language of intention or purpose" (125). In this regard, it differs fundamentally from the other main kind of intellectual inquiry, scientific understanding, which deals with phenomena that lack

[6] His discussion of the subject is limited to pp. 49–51 and 439–446.

intention or purpose or approaches them in abstraction from the extent to which they do so.

According to Dworkin, this difference in subject matter entails profound differences in the methods and goals of the two forms of inquiry, including their very notions of truth. He champions what he calls an "all-embracing dualism" between interpretation and science (124, 152–155). It is something of a return to the efforts of German philosophers at the turn of the nineteenth and twentieth centuries to contrast the *Geistes-* and *Naturwissenschaften*. Dworkin's professed aim is to reverse what he sees as the baleful tendency ever since the early modern Scientific Revolution to distort the nature of interpretation by forcing it into the mold of scientific reasoning (417). The preceding discussion suggests that in using his account of moral thinking as a model for a theory of interpretation, he may have been led to overdraw the dissimilarities between interpretative and scientific inquiry. That suspicion will be confirmed.

As we have seen, Dworkin holds that what makes an ethical or moral judgment true is an adequate argument for its truth. He says the same about interpretation in general (151ff, 176f). There, too, truth matters, and interpretation, as he rightly insists against skeptics, relativists, and post-modernists, would not be anything like it is if difference in opinion were not taken to be a sign of disagreement (128). But what the truth of an interpretation consists in, on his view, is the successful case that is made for it. Of course, what counts as a successful case depends on the sort of interpretation one is pursuing; seeking to comprehend an historical event is not like working out the import of a legal statute. Dworkin distinguishes three main genres (135–136). In "collaborative" interpretation, as in the interpretation of laws or literary texts, people try to understand something someone has created in order to carry on the project its creator or author has initiated. "Explanatory" interpretation, most at home in historical inquiry, does not collaborate with the phenomena it investigates, but aims instead to establish their significance for the audience it addresses. Finally, "conceptual" interpretation undertakes to determine the meaning of certain problematic concepts; unlike the other two genres, it does not seek to interpret what others have produced in the past (some text or some set of events), since its object is a concept that belongs to the community and it hopes by its efforts to change that object for the better, to clarify and refine it.

Whenever we interpret, we must therefore understand as well the specific interpretive practice in which we are engaged, and because the purposes of these practices can themselves be differently understood, interpretation is always at work on both levels at once: we are endeavoring to discover the best way of making sense of some phenomenon so as to satisfy what we take to be the proper purposes of the interpretive activity in which we are involved. This is what Dworkin calls his "value theory" of interpretation (130–134, 149–152), since it emphasizes the essential role that value judgments – about the best way of making sense of something in accord with the best account of our purposes in doing so – play in all interpretive activity. Ethical and moral reasoning may be one type of interpretive enterprise among others, forming a species of "conceptual" interpretation (157). But values set the terms of all interpretation, and that is why, according to Dworkin, truth in interpretation is a matter of successful argument. In general, an interpretation of some object is true "when it best realizes, for that object, the purposes properly assigned to the interpretive practice properly identified as pertinent" (131).

This account of interpretation, especially in regard to how it describes literary and legal interpretation and historical interpretation, seems off the mark, however, and for the same reason that his account of the truth of moral and ethical judgments fails. When we seek to understand a text or an historical event, our target is that object itself. What makes our interpretation true, if it is true, is thus not our argument for attributing to that object a certain meaning or purpose, which is but a means for arriving at the truth, but rather that object actually having the meaning or purpose we attribute to it. What is it, moreover, for a text or event to have a specific meaning or purpose? Dworkin largely rejects the "psychological state" theory of interpretation according to which "interpretive claims are made true . . . by actual or counterfactual facts about the mental states of one or more people" (128). This conception may sometimes hold for conversational interpretation, he admits, but does not apply more generally (129). Yet historical interpretation clearly attempts to discover the actual assumptions and purposes of the individuals it studies. It must do so in order then to work out the significance of past actions for the audience it now addresses. When, for example, historians analyze the events that led to the French Revolution, they are certainly organizing them within a present-day perspective unavailable to the agents involved, who had no idea of preparing the way for "the French Revolution." Nonetheless, they cannot show how those actions resulted in what has come to be known as the Revolution, unless they first describe what those actions themselves were like and thus what the agents' intentions were at the time. Even though historical interpretation generally focuses on the significance of past events, it must still as a prerequisite reconstruct the "mental states," the actual intentions or purposes, of the individuals involved. And again, the judgments it makes about the significance of those events are not, any more than its judgments about past intentions, rendered true by the arguments used to justify them. What makes them true is instead the past events really having the causal importance for later developments that those judgments describe them as having.

The situation is similar in literary interpretation. I have already discussed this subject at length in Chapter 3 (Sections 3.3–3.4). But let me repeat here the substance of my argument.

We may be interested in pursuing a text's significance for our present-day interests. But that endeavor requires that we first determine what the text means – how else can we gauge its relevance? – and what it means must consist in the author's intention. The latter is, of course, an ambiguous concept. In some senses of the term – what the author set out to say, what he said to himself as he composed the text, what he may have said afterwards about his intentions – "the author's intention" need not coincide with the text's meaning. But what the author intended insofar as he realized this intention in the composition of the text must surely count as what the text itself means. Texts do not write themselves. They are written by authors and written to some purpose or mixture of purposes. If we did not suppose that the text was the expression of the author's intention, we would have no basis for thinking, as we do, that to understand the meaning of some problematic passage we do best to turn first to other passages of the same text or to other things that author wrote. The same is true of legal interpretation, even though Dworkin denies it (129–130, 149–150), and even though the case is more complex, since the author of a legal statute is a collective agent (a legislature) whose identity and therefore whose authorial intention is defined by institutional rules.

Dworkin does not consider these aspects of textual interpretation. Otherwise, he could not so easily dismiss the concept of author's intention (130, 150) as well as the distinction (135, 141), on which I have been leaning, between the *meaning* of a work, defined by the author's realized intention, and its *significance*, which is its relevance to the concerns of others (including ourselves). Even though normally part of the author's intention is that the work be in some way significant for its readers, intended and actual significance are two quite different things. And even though literary interpretation does not as a rule aim simply at discovering authors' intentions, any more than historical inquiry generally aims at simply determining what, apart from its importance, people in the past were intending to achieve, but seeks as well, if not most of all (as is obviously so in legal interpretation), to understand how the text may speak to our present interests, understanding a text's significance presupposes a grasp of its author's intention.

Moreover, what makes the interpretation of significance true is, as with the interpretation of meaning, things being as it argues them to be – in this case the work having the relevance ascribed – and not the argument itself. That is why literary and historical modes of interpretation can indeed adduce *evidence* for their claims about meaning or significance. In arguing for an interpretation of either, we often cite features of a work or of past actions or features of their relation to our present concerns as being indicative of, because causally dependent on, the meaning or significance we attribute to the work or actions. We may contend that a particular passage reveals what the poem as a whole intends to convey; we may point out how events, before a certain person intervened, were not heading in the direction we know they ultimately took, in order to argue that this person's actions were the decisive catalyst. In sum, the difference in subject matter between scientific and interpretive inquiry does not entail a difference in their respective notions of truth.

4.4 Pluralism

As we saw at the beginning, Dworkin is skeptical about the distinction between second-order views about the nature of value and first-order value judgments themselves. This skepticism, I showed (Section 4.1), is unfounded. He himself, moreover, relies upon just such a distinction. Nonetheless, he also holds that his (effectively second-order) account of what makes value or interpretative judgments true, namely the decisive arguments offered in their favor, serves to justify his (first-order) conviction that value pluralism is wrong. Here is his reasoning. Empirical and scientific judgments, Dworkin claims, can be "barely true": the fact that makes any such judgment true could have not been the case even though the world was not otherwise any different (114). If there were value facts – sets of "morons," as he scoffs – then value judgments could also be barely true. But since there are not, since "an interpretive justification that draws on a complex of values" (154) is what makes any such judgment true, values themselves are defined by their interpretive interconnections (153–155, 263, 343, 352). There cannot then be an ultimate plurality of distinct values. Interpretation, whatever its domain, is, in Dworkin's view, "pervasively holistic" (154). In order to understand any meaning-embodying phenomenon, we must figure out how it fits with related phenomena, and so we must discover how they all make sense together. We interpret responsibly, he holds, insofar as we take to heart this imperative.

An immediate objection is that scientific judgments cannot in reality be barely true in Dworkin's sense, at least given what we know about the natural world. For any empirical fact exists only because of its causal connections with other such facts, so that if it did not obtain, those other facts would have to be different as well. In the natural world, everything hangs together too, in the distinctive way that natural phenomena do so. Yet this interconnectedness does not prevent an empirical judgment from being true in virtue of the fact it purports to describe. Why then cannot the same be so in the domain of value judgments? Once again, there does not appear to be the dichotomy between scientific and interpretive inquiry that Dworkin imagines.

However, let us look more closely at what he says about the holistic character of interpretation, to see whether it really supports his rejection of value pluralism. I begin with how he formulates in holistic terms a frequent way of contrasting "morality" and "ethics." We become morally responsible agents, Dworkin holds, by trying to combine all our different obligations and concerns for others into a coherent whole (101), just as we become ethically responsible when we seek to shape our various interests and projects into an overall way of life that makes most sense personally to us (203–205). Since this ethical sort of responsibility is interpretive in character, it should also impel us, he continues, to see whether there is reason, not simply to incorporate morality into our conception of living well as a set of side-constraints, but instead to regard a moral concern for others as part and parcel of our very concern to live well ourselves (202, 255). We should want to integrate ethics with morality as two mutually supportive dimensions of concern, for "integrity" in this sense is what the holism of interpretation requires.[7] In general, the "correct understanding" of any two principles that apply to the same domain is, according to Dworkin, "an understanding of each that finds support in our understanding of the other" (263).

The linchpin of his effort to integrate ethics and morality is what he calls "Kant's principle": the reason to think it important how our own life goes must be a reason to think it important how anyone's life goes (19, 260).

[7] The theme of "integrity," as well as some other elements of Dworkin's theory of interpretation, goes back to his book *Law's Empire* (Cambridge, MA: Harvard University Press, 1986), especially chapter 6.

This principle seems to me true. We cannot value our own humanity (to use Kant's term), we cannot value our own pursuit of a good life, simply because it is ours. For why should we feel any interest in that pursuit of ours, unless we suppose that it is something of value in itself? As a general matter, I cannot coherently consider anything I possess (an object, an ability, a goal) to be good just because it is mine; I must think that it is itself good, whoever may similarly have it, if I am to prize the fact that it happens to be mine. In this sense, if not in others, William Godwin was right to complain, "What magic is there in the pronoun 'my', that should justify us in overturning the decisions of everlasting truth?"[8]

Thus, the so-called Kantian principle shows that we cannot value living well ourselves without also having to recognize the importance of others living well. But that falls short of the sort of integration Dworkin believes necessary. After all, recognizing that others living well must matter if my living well is to matter does not entail believing that others living well matters *as much* as mine does to me. As everyone would surely acknowledge, self-concern and concern for others often appear to conflict. How are the conflicts to be addressed? Integrity, he argues, demands that we seek something more fundamental than a "balance" between the two perspectives, ranking their contrary demands in various ways depending on the kind of case at hand (261ff). Ranking presupposes the existence of conflict, even if it may consist in a rational way of adjudicating it. Instead, he claims, we must find a way of interpreting these two kinds of concern that not only looks correct about each but also makes them mutually supportive. In other words, we must show how the conflicts are in fact only apparent.

Dworkin devotes Part Four of his book to examining how the proper scope of different elements of morality – aiding, not harming, and promise-keeping – can be defined on the basis of the Kantian principle that the reason we have to value our own pursuit of living well is a reason to value that of others. The result is meant to be an understanding of both our responsibility for ourselves and our responsibility to others that dissolves the conflicts between them by specifying more carefully what they each involve. Dworkin's strategy in these passages is to imagine a situation where the two kinds of concern appear to conflict, to determine (in accord with the Kantian principle) which of the possible courses of action we have most reason to choose, and then to regard this solution of the conflict as

[8] William Godwin, *Enquiry Concerning Political Justice* (1798), Book 2, chapter 2 (London: Penguin, 1985, 170).

refining our understanding of what self-concern and concern for others really mean. The conflict should thus turn out to be illusory.

This is how he aims to deal with value conflict in general, as an earlier discussion of that subject makes explicit (118–120). We may sometimes think – his example there – that honesty and kindness conflict, as when we wonder whether we should tell a friend just how bad we find an essay of his about which he has asked us our opinion. But if we decide, says Dworkin, that the right thing is to tell him the truth, we are thereby concluding that this action is not really cruel, and if we decide that we ought instead to tell him what he would like to hear, we are thereby concluding that to do so is not really to be dishonest. "What is the right thing to do?" and "Is the apparent conflict real?" are not, he declares, independent questions. "There are no genuine conflicts in values," no need to balance or rank our values. Value conflict is "illusory and temporary."

A first thing to observe about this strategy of argument is that it does not show that value pluralism is false. That is because pluralism, at least for Isaiah Berlin, was fundamentally a theory, not about the ubiquity of value conflict, but about the ultimate *sources* of value. It is, as he once defined it, "the conception that there are many different ends that men may seek and still be fully rational."[9] In other words, our different values cannot be traced back to some single master value (pleasure, freedom, or reason), which they variously express or promote. Value conflict Berlin saw as a corollary of this ultimate heterogeneity. He may have exaggerated the extent to which our values really conflict, but that does not entail that his pluralism was a mistake. The ethical and the moral, as Dworkin conceives them, seem themselves to constitute two distinct sources of value.

Secondly, Dworkin's strategy does not in many cases succeed in showing that value conflicts are merely apparent. Telling our friend what he would like to hear, instead of our real opinion, because we think it the best thing to do is still being dishonest, even if pardonably so. More fundamentally, the Kantian principle, as indicated before, does not by itself dissolve many of the well-known conflicts between self-concern and concern for others. Though I cannot see value in my own pursuit of a good life without recognizing that others living well is similarly valuable, nothing in

[9] Isaiah Berlin, "The Pursuit of the Ideal," in *The Crooked Timber of Humanity* (New York: Knopf, 1991), 11. Cf. the definition later in the same volume: "To look upon life as affording a plurality of values, equally genuine, equally ultimate, above all equally objective; incapable, therefore, of being ordered in a timeless hierarchy, or judged in terms of some one absolute standard" (79).

that principle prevents me, as already noted, from valuing my pursuit *more* precisely because it is mine. The pronoun "my" is not without all force. Whence those difficult conflicts we all face between doing well ourselves and doing well by others.

What has gone wrong? Like many self-described "holists," Dworkin has failed to recognize that a proper understanding of the nature of any one of our values depends, not on all our moral and ethical convictions that may prove relevant when that value is in play, but only on those that serve to explain why that value itself embodies something of importance, why it ought to command our attention and commitment. Explaining the importance of a value and explaining why, in certain situations, pursuing this value ought to yield to the pursuit of some other value are not the same thing. In the latter case, our understanding of why the first value matters remains unchanged. So the conflict between that value and the other, and thus their ultimate plurality, are real, not merely apparent, even if we may believe we have reason to subordinate, in such situations, the one to the other.

What allows us to explain why a given value is of importance, without bringing in all our other values, is that, contrary to Dworkin, evaluative judgments are as a whole true or false, not in virtue of arguments justifying the belief they are true or false, but rather in virtue of specific facts that make them so. This holds even for our judgments about the nature of particular values themselves. A value is a good, and what is good is, as a general matter, what there is reason to pursue. Thus, the facts that make our understanding of the nature of a value correct are the reasons explaining why it represents a way of being and acting we should pursue. Honesty and kindness are separate values because the reasons for their importance are distinct. Conflicts between them can thus be real, not merely apparent. There is indeed an intimate connection between second-order reflection about the nature of value and first-order value judgments. But it is altogether contrary to the one Dworkin alleges. A realism about value of the kind I have proposed points to why value pluralism is likely to be true and why we must therefore reckon with having to make judgments about one value being more important than another in particular circumstances. However metaphysically ambitious this realism may be, it puts me then in the company of the fox, not the hedgehog.

In subsequent chapters of this book, I say more about this realism about values, primarily in developing in far greater detail the realist account of reasons that undergirds it.

PART II

Self and World

CHAPTER 5

Kant and the Meanings of Autonomy

"Autonomy" is a philosophical notion that people continually invoke without hesitation, as though everyone agreed that what it signifies is a good thing. That, in my view, is a sign that they do not know exactly what they mean by the term, or that different people mean different things by it. Indeed, the term has a number of distinct, established meanings. With Kant, "autonomy" became a key concept of philosophy. But it would be a mistake to assume that everything we understand today by "autonomy" stands in a necessary relation to Kant's own concept of it. According to Kant's idea of autonomy, the ground of validity for not only moral but for all principles of thought and action consists in the self-legislation of reason, which is therefore to be considered the source of their validity. As Kant said of the moral law,

> The will is not merely subject to the law but subject to it in such a way that it must be viewed *as also giving the law to itself* [*als selbstgesetzgebend*] and just because of this as first subject to the law (of which it can regard itself as the author [*Urheber*]).[1]

In this chapter, my aim is to contrast the Kantian conception of autonomy as self-legislation with other meanings of the word and consider to what extent that conception itself is coherent.

[1] Kant, *Grundlegung zur Metaphysik der Sitten*, Akademie-Ausgabe (Berlin: Königlich Preußische Akademie der Wissenschaften, 1902–), IV, 431: "Der Wille wird also nicht lediglich dem Gesetz unterworfen, sondern so unterworfen, dass er auch *als selbstgesetzgebend* und eben um deswillen allererst dem Gesetze (davon er selbst sich als Urheber betrachten kann) unterworfen angesehen werden muss." In subsequent references to Kant's writings, I will abbreviate the Akademie-Ausgabe as AA. Here and elsewhere I have used Mary Gregor's translation, *Groundwork of the Metaphysics of Morals* (Cambridge: Cambridge University Press, 1998), though I have sometimes modified it.

5.1 Political and Legal Prehistory

As is well known, the word "autonomy" had a long history before Kant took it over in his *Grundlegung zur Metaphysik der Sitten* of 1785.[2] Two things about this prehistory are interesting. First, the term "autonomy" was used almost exclusively in political or legal contexts without being extended to the domain of moral philosophy and without being applied to the general philosophical question of how rational beings are related to the principles of their thought and action. Second, neither the political nor the legal meaning of the word provided a precise or even suggestive model for the way in which Kant would develop the concept of autonomy in these other and broader contexts.

The Greeks did not use "*autonomia*" with reference to individuals, but only with reference to political communities, using it in particular to describe those that do not stand under the rule of foreign powers or a tyrant. Such communities are autonomous insofar as they live according to their own laws, that is, by the laws that they have chosen to regulate their common life. That does not mean that they base the authority of these laws solely on their own will or their own legislation. Even if the laws become legally binding by having been decided upon by the appropriate procedures, it could be and often is the case – not only in antiquity – that the community has imposed those laws on itself because it (or, more precisely, its representatives) is convinced of their antecedent moral validity. This shows that a system of positive law does not offer a model of what Kant understands by "autonomy," and not only because his concept of autonomy refers to individual rational beings and not to communities. Even more significant is the fact that law can be understood as ultimately resting, as I indicated, on an already existing and presumably valid system of norms, namely on morality. Kant's concept of autonomy, by contrast, is supposed to explain the nature of morality itself and thus not only the binding force (*Verbindlichkeit*) or obligatory character of moral rules but also their very validity (*Gültigkeit*) or correctness.[3]

[2] On the history of the concept, see Rosemarie Pohlmann, "Autonomie," in: *Historisches Wörterbuch der Philosophie*, ed. J. Ritter, vol. 1, (Basel: Schwabe, 1971), 701–719.

[3] Kant stresses this last distinction because the morally correct thing to do also becomes obligatory or binding for rational beings like us who (unlike God, who necessarily acts morally) may be inclined to act otherwise and who are therefore required to subordinate our inclinations to what is morally correct. In this chapter devoted to Kant's theory of autonomy, I will generally use the two terms, validity and bindingness, together, since the aim of that theory is to explain them both. In the rest of the book, I use one or the other term, as it is appropriate.

In the early modern period, "autonomy" continued to be used in this political sense. At the same time, however, a new, legal meaning emerged. The term "autonomy" came to designate the authority for self-legislation or for legal self-determination that a municipality, an organization, or even an individual (for example, a member of the nobility or a property owner) enjoys within the framework of a given, overarching legal order. Such a public or private legal authority is exercised when, for instance, a city council passes a law or a citizen sells his house. In these cases, the validity of the ordinance or the sale of the real estate depends upon the decisions of the responsible city officials or of the owner. But this kind of autonomy is obviously a local phenomenon, which is defined and limited by an already existing legal order. It too could therefore hardly serve as a model for the Kantian conception, according to which autonomy not only applies to the realm of morality *as a whole* and even more generally to the nature of reason itself but is supposed to *explain* the validity of all the laws and principles they involve.

Such then was the situation up until Kant. "Autonomous" in the political sense were communities that live by their own laws, that is, by laws that they themselves have approved. "Autonomous" in the legal sense were municipalities or individuals that are authorized by an overarching legal system to pass laws or to engage in legal transactions. Nothing in this context would have prepared us for the radical and quite general claim with which Kant expressly introduces the word "autonomy" to designate the fundamental nature of every rational being as such: "Autonomy of the will is the quality of the will wherein the will is a law to itself (independently of any quality of the objects of the will)."[4] One can understand why Kant chose the term "autonomy" for his doctrine of the self-legislation of reason. But his reasons stemmed more from etymological considerations than from established linguistic usage. Christian Wolff, whose writings had shaped not only substantively but also terminologically the German philosophical landscape of the time, used the expression only in its political meaning.

Moreover, Kant did not begin talking about "autonomy" at all until quite late, for the first time in fact in the *Groundwork* of 1785, and there he used the concept exclusively in the new meaning he was introducing. In the lectures on moral philosophy that he regularly held in the mid-1770s,

[4] Kant, *Grundlegung*, AA IV, 440: "Autonomie des Willens ist die Beschaffenheit des Willens, dadurch derselbe ihm selbst (unabhängig von aller Beschaffenheit der Gegenstände des Willens) ein Gesetz ist."

not only is the word missing but the concept as well, if we are able to trust the transcripts. In them, Kant was already presenting the laws of morality as universal, categorically necessary rules of action that, in the case of human beings, who can be inclined otherwise, become categorically binding obligations. However, he asserted as well that we can grasp not only their validity, but also their obligatory character or (as I shall also say) their bindingness through our understanding (*Verstand*) alone, without reference to the will of God and – there is no mention of this at all – without reference to any self-legislating activity on our part.[5]

Since Kant's concept of autonomy seems untenable to me, I am tempted to say: too bad he did not remain with this conception. For the only significant weakness of the lectures on moral philosophy of the 1770s is Kant's assumption that the understanding by itself cannot provide a sufficient motive for action:

> If I judge by the understanding that the action is morally good, then I am still very far from doing this action of which I have so judged ... To be sure, the understanding can judge, but to give this judgment of the understanding a force so that it becomes a motive to impel the will to carry out the action, that is the philosophers' stone.[6]

If the understanding were indeed motivationally inert, then it would be equally unable to move us to revise our existing beliefs or to draw conclusions. Since that seems obviously false, it cannot be excluded from the outset, as Kant supposes, that the understanding is also capable of moving us to perform those actions whose correctness it indicates. According to the Kant of these lectures, however, carrying out, if not recognizing, a moral law can only take place (legal coercion and social pressure aside) through "moral feeling" as it has been formed by habituation or through an anticipation of God's rewards and punishments.[7] Or, to be more exact, that is his general position. For in another passage Kant concedes that the understanding does possess "a moving force" (*bewegende Kraft*) insofar as it resists "immoral actions ... because they

[5] Kant, *Vorlesung zur Moralphilosophie*, ed. W. Stark (Berlin: De Gruyter, 2004), 55–73, 79. This recent edition is based on the "Kaehler" transcript of 1773–1775. For an English translation based on similar transcripts, see Kant, *Lectures on Ethics* (Cambridge: Cambridge University Press, 1997), 65–73, 76. When Kant writes in these lectures, "All obligation is either external or internal" (49 and 62, respectively), he is not referring to the bindingness of a moral law, but rather to the "motivating grounds" (*Bewegungsgründe*) (50 and 62, respectively) – one's own will (*Willkür*) or someone else's – by which a person is moved to comply with the law.

[6] Kant, *Lectures on Ethics*, 71. The corresponding passage in the *Vorlesung zur Moralphilosophie* is at pp. 68–69.

[7] Kant, *Lectures on Ethics*, 71, 68–69; *Vorlesung zur Moralphilosophie*, 67–69, 61–62.

run counter to the use of its rule." But then he adds that this motivational force of the understanding is not in fact sufficient to prevail over the opposing impulses (*elateres*) of sensuality.[8] Kant's concession is on the right track. But the added qualification is not. If the understanding can resist, why can it not sometimes prevail? In addition, moral feeling and reverence for God can only gain the upper hand by pointing to reasons for not giving in to those impulses, and thus they themselves involve an exercise of the understanding. Naturally, one can be driven by temptations to act against one's better judgment, and good habits, which involve proper feelings, are the best protection against such temptations. But phenomena of this sort cannot be well understood by means of a crude dichotomy between understanding and feeling.

Later, in the *Groundwork*, Kant came to the conclusion that moral feeling and the fear of God are inappropriate motives for moral action. But this change did not lead him to question the assumption of the motivational inertness of the understanding. (In Section 5.4, I return to the continuing role of this assumption in Kant.) Instead, the "critical philosophy" that comes to expression in the *Groundwork* leaves behind the conceptual framework of the earlier lectures on ethics. The understanding is no longer credited with the capacity of comprehending the bindingness of moral rules since their bindingness, like the bindingness and indeed the validity of all the principles of our thought and action, has now ceased to be regarded as strictly speaking an object of knowledge, but instead as a product of self-legislating reason. That, of course, is Kant's doctrine of autonomy. All in all, I prefer, with the reservations mentioned, the standpoint of the earlier lectures on ethics.

As I will explain later, Kant's concept of autonomy implicitly underlies his conception of theoretical reason as well, although the term itself does not appear in either edition of the *Critique of Pure Reason* (1781, 1787). However, it is interesting to note for which attitudes of mind Kant never used the term, even though they too consist in the exercise of reason, even though he also treated them extensively, and even though we ourselves tend to speak of them as paradigm forms of autonomy (so that careless commentators sometimes refer to his treatment of them as "Kant's doctrine of autonomy"). We commonly call people "autonomous" who think for themselves or who do what is right regardless of reward or threat. Kant's usage is completely different. He did indeed ascribe an important role in his moral philosophy to these capacities of thinking for oneself and

[8] *Lectures on Ethics*, 72; *Vorlesung zur Moralphilosophie*, 70–71.

of governing oneself, but he never designated them as "autonomy." There is a good reason for this. Such cases have to do with the relation that we in our thinking and acting have to other people (or to God), whereas Kant reserved the term "autonomy" or "self-legislation" for the relation in which we can stand to the principles or laws themselves of thought and action. Yet that does not mean, as we will see, that he did not think of trying to explain these capacities by means of his concept of autonomy. On the contrary, he claimed that only on its basis are they explicable.

I turn now to a closer examination of both phenomena – thinking for oneself and self-governance – in order to show to what extent Kant correctly analyzed them without appealing to his concept of autonomy and how he then went astray when he attempted to found them on this concept.

5.2 Thinking for Oneself

The text in which Kant directly takes up the phenomenon of thinking for oneself is his famous essay of 1784, "An Answer to the Question: What Is Enlightenment?" In it he summons his readers: "*Sapere aude*! Have the courage to make use of your own understanding!"[9] He explains the nature of this independence of mind primarily through a discussion of its opposite, the immaturity that consists in letting others tell us what and how we should think. Clearly, Kant does not mean to assert that someone who thinks independently never relies on the knowledge of experts or on the reports of eyewitnesses. The essential thing is that one trusts the statements of others only when one perceives oneself good reasons for believing in their reliability, if not, of course, in their infallibility.

For Kant, then, the essence of enlightenment is the determination to think for oneself without another's supervision. Unfortunately, he offers only an individualist kind of explanation for why this commitment has been relatively rare until his own time: it is a "self-imposed immaturity," to which most people have surrendered out of "laziness and cowardice." According to this diagnosis, political and religious powers have succeeded in preventing the development of independent thinking simply by virtue of exploiting the inhibition in using their own reason for which these people have themselves been responsible. Kant has missed the important role of various social, intellectual, and even religious movements (for

[9] Kant, "Beantwortung der Frage: Was ist Aufklärung?," AA VIII, 35. English translation: "What Is Enlightenment?," in Kant, *Political Writings* (Cambridge: Cambridge University Press, 1991), 17.

instance, the Reformation) in actively producing and encouraging, to cite his own words, "the spirit of a rational valuing of one's own worth and of each individual's calling to think for himself."[10] Thinking for oneself is a way of living that has to be learned.

However, what I would like to underscore is that Kant does not use the word "autonomy" a single time in this essay, either to designate thinking for oneself or to explain the conditions of its possibility – and this, it will be recalled, only one year before the publication of the *Groundwork of the Metaphysics of Morals*. The concept does not occur implicitly, either. In a passage concerned with the question whether one age may take it upon itself to limit through certain agreements the right to think for oneself in a subsequent age, Kant does remark that "the touchstone of whatever can be decided upon as law for a people lies in the question: whether a people could impose such a law upon itself?"[11] But this statement invokes the political concept of autonomy, which, as I mentioned, leaves open the ultimate basis of the self-imposed law: a people can subject itself to a law and thereby make it legally binding because it is convinced that this law is in itself already morally valid.

It should not really be surprising that Kant's essay on enlightenment does not use the term "autonomy" or rely on his own (eventual) concept of it. Thinking for oneself – a disposition that we ourselves habitually refer to as "autonomy" – and autonomy in the Kantian sense are two entirely different things. The former concerns our relation to other people, the latter our relation to the principles of our thought and action. Kant proceeds in this essay as if he could adequately analyze the capacity of thinking for oneself without going into the nature of the validity and bindingness of the principles in accord with which we exercise this capacity. This assumption is correct, and indeed so much so that everything he says there about independence of thought remains untouched even if – as I believe necessary – we completely reject his account of the latter subject, namely his doctrine of autonomy.

What by contrast we ought to find striking, if not quite surprising, is the way in which Kant, two years later, takes up again the theme of thinking for oneself. Toward the end of his essay "What Is Orientation in Thinking?" (1786), he seeks to distinguish three meanings of the expression "freedom of thought" (*die Freiheit zu denken*), which is but another name for "thinking for oneself." This freedom, he claims, consists not only in not being prevented by the "civil coercion" of the state or by social

[10] Ibid., 36. English translation, 18. [11] Ibid., 39. English translation, 20.

pressure (through "coercion of conscience") from following one's own thinking wherever it leads. It must also, thirdly, be understood as the "subjection of reason to no other laws than those which it gives to itself." This is a clear allusion to the autonomy of reason as defined in the *Groundwork* one year before. I quoted his definition at the beginning:

> Hence the will is not merely subject to the law but subject to it in such a way that it must be viewed *as also giving the law to itself* [*als selbstgesetzgebend*] and just because of this as first subject to the law (of which it can regard itself as the author [*Urheber*]).[12]

In this subsequent essay, Kant is thus, without using the term itself, extending his concept of "autonomy" from morality to the domain of theoretical reason. In a footnote, he goes so far as to characterize the third sense of "freedom of thought" by means of a formulation that directly recalls the first formula of the moral law from the *Groundwork*, including its reference to self-legislation:

> To make use of one's own reason means nothing more than to ask oneself, concerning everything one is supposed to accept, whether one finds it possible to make the reasons why one accepts something or the rule that follows from what one accepts a universal principle for the use of one's reason.[13]

Self-legislation on the basis of universalizable rules or maxims holds, says Kant, as much for theoretical as for practical reason – since, as he asserts near the beginning of the *Groundwork*, "there can, in the end, be only one and the same reason, which must be distinguished merely in its application"[14] – and thus constitutes the essence of thinking for oneself as the correct exercise of one's own reason.

Why is there such a departure from the more modest approach of "What Is Enlightenment?" Why does Kant now consider it necessary to bring in his conception of autonomy, if not the term itself, and to claim that thinking for oneself is possible only when reason gives itself its own laws or principles? The answer lies no doubt in the fact that this concept was introduced formally for the first time in the *Groundwork*, that is, one year after the essay on enlightenment, but only one year before the essay on orientation in thinking. The year 1785 was indeed a crucial one in

[12] Kant, *Grundlegung*, AA IV, 431; *Groundwork of the Metaphysics of Morals*, 39.

[13] Kant, "Was heißt: sich im Denken orientieren?," AA VIII, 146–147; *Political Writings*, 249. The first formula of the moral law is: "Act only in accordance with that maxim through which you can at the same time will that it become a universal law" (*Grundlegung*, AA IV, 421; *Groundwork*, 31).

[14] Kant, *Grundlegung*, AA IV, 391; *Groundwork*, 5.

Kant's development, a year in which he achieved through the formulation of the concept of autonomy a much deeper understanding of the foundations of his philosophical project as a whole.

In "What Is Orientation in Thinking," Kant explains the necessity of appealing to this concept by claiming that freedom of thought in the two other senses mentioned – which correspond to the understanding of thinking for oneself in the essay on enlightenment – can only be guaranteed through the self-legislation of reason. "If reason," Kant writes, "does not will (*will*) to be subject to the law it gives to itself, it must bow under the yoke of laws which another gives it."[15]

That is, however, an astonishingly bad argument. It is first of all clumsy in relying on a confusing contrast between "reason," which is a faculty, but which Kant treats here (as elsewhere) as though it were an agent in itself, and "another" (*ein Anderer*), which manifestly can only be a human being (or God). This sort of confusion shows clearly that Kant is running together the two distinct problematics of reason's relation to its principles, on the one hand, and a rational being's relation to other such beings, on the other.

But second, and more profoundly, the argument presupposes that we cannot be subject to any law governing our thinking without it having been imposed on us – if not by ourselves (through our own reason), then by someone else. Why such an implausible presupposition? Kant is clearly appealing to the notion "no law without a legislator," a notion that is as questionable as it is familiar. For who imposed on us, for instance, the logical law of non-contradiction, the principle according to which we ought to avoid contradictions in our thinking? It makes no sense to speak of the imposition of a law of this kind, since, among other things, any reason one might see for such an imposition or for the acceptance of such an imposition would have to presuppose the validity of the law in question. Why can this example not serve as a model for other, more complicated cases? The fundamental laws of thought would then be principles that exist in their own right and whose validity we therefore simply have to acknowledge, a conception I will defend in what follows (Sections 5.4–5.5). The notion of "no law without a lawgiver" is an inheritance of the Judeo-Christian tradition, in which God is held to be the creator of absolutely everything. Its continuing influence has led many to suppose without question that if the laws or principles of thought and action have

[15] Kant, AA VIII, 145; *Political Writings*, 248.

not been legislated by God, then they must have been imposed by us. This is one religious inheritance (among others) it would be good to get beyond.

The essay "What Is Enlightenment?" offers, then, a far better account of the nature of thinking for oneself. Precisely because Kant does not even pose there the question about the relation in which we stand to the principles of our thinking, this essay heeds the point I have made repeatedly: thinking for oneself is a disposition that has to do with our relation as rational beings to other such beings, and not with our relation as rational beings to the principles guiding our thought and action or to reasons in general and to the basis of their validity and bindingness. We are ourselves used to describing the ability to think for oneself without the tutelage of political, religious, or other authorities as "the autonomy of the individual." There is nothing wrong with doing so, so long as we do not confuse this ability with what Kant himself terms "autonomy." And so long as we (unlike Kant) recognize that these two relations – that of the individual to other individuals and that of reason to its principles – should be treated in relative independence from one other. There have certainly been attempts to explain the validity of some principles on which we rely by the fact that we belong to a particular cultural or social tradition and thus to base the latter relation on the former, precisely with the aim of calling into question the claims of individual autonomy. Such an aim is understandable: thinking for oneself is not a value immune to criticism. It is, however, a mistake to pursue that goal in this manner. It would be better to regard tradition as the necessary vehicle of principles whose validity itself exists independently of their having been passed down through tradition.[16] For surely it would be odd for us to believe that a principle, quite apart from its content, is binding on us solely because earlier generations happened to have observed it.

In any case, it is clear that autonomy, as Kant understands it, does not – contrary to his essay on orientation – represent an essential presupposition of the capacity to think for oneself. Escaping the tutelage of others in order to think and act by our own lights is quite compatible with the belief that the principles by which we then proceed have an antecedent validity that our reason does not establish, but instead must acknowledge. There is, as I will explain in Section 5.4, the additional fact that Kant's opposing view, his very idea of autonomy, is fundamentally incoherent.

[16] For more on this point, see my book, *The Autonomy of Morality* (Cambridge: Cambridge University Press, 2008), chapter 1.

5.3 Self-Governance

I turn now to the second attitude of mind that we often call "autonomy," but that Kant never does, although he discusses it extensively and even attempts, as in the case of thinking for oneself, to explain its possibility by means of the concept of autonomy he introduced. It is the readiness to do what is right without consideration of any threats or rewards by a higher power, divine or human. Following J. B. Schneewind, I will refer to this disposition as "self-governance." It is not to be confused with "self-legislation" or "autonomy" in the Kantian sense.[17]

St. Paul, in his *Letter to the Romans*, had such a disposition in mind when he wrote:

> When the Gentiles, who do not have the law, do by nature things required by the law, they are a law for themselves, even though they do not have the law. They show that the work of the law is written in their hearts, their conscience bearing witness to it and their deliberations among themselves sometimes accusing and sometimes excusing them. (2:14–15)

By the expression "the law" those commandments are meant through which God has instructed us how we should treat one another morally. Although the Gentiles did not receive such a law from God, they nevertheless are, Paul is saying, capable of behaving as God's commandments demand when they follow their conscience (*syneidesis*). Thus they are "a law for themselves" (*heautois eisin nomos*), by which Paul certainly does not mean that the Gentiles view their own reason as the author of the distinction between right and wrong, but rather that in their conduct they follow their conscience, which bears witness (*symmaturein*) to what are in effect the requirements of the law. Self-governance is thus the ability to follow one's sense of right and wrong without the need of any higher outside authority. It presupposes not only that one can distinguish oneself between right and wrong but also, and especially, that one can find in oneself the motives for doing what is right.

In our day, a capacity of this kind is often described as "autonomy." There is nothing wrong about doing so. It can make sense to say that autonomy consists in what Paul terms "being a law for oneself" (*heautōi einai nomos*). Self-governance, together with thinking for oneself, is indeed one of the unproblematic things that can be called "autonomy" in the individual realm. One should simply realize that it is not what Kant

[17] Schneewind, J. B., *The Invention of Autonomy* (Cambridge: Cambridge University Press, 1998).

understood by "autonomy," and that it does not presuppose such a conception. Someone who acts on the basis of his sense of right and wrong without the incentive of external commands does not need to assume that the standards he invokes receive their validity or bindingness from his reason instead of assuming that his reason is what enables him to grasp these standards as the objective truths they are. Self-governance is a capacity of mind that has to do solely with the motivation, not with the principles, of moral action.

Kant, however, was of a different opinion: not in the lectures on moral philosophy of the 1770s, in which he essentially neglected the phenomenon of self-governance, mentioning only moral feeling and reverence for God as internal motives for moral action,[18] but in the *Groundwork* of 1785. There he places the ability to do what is right for its own sake explicitly at the center of his account of moral action and goes on to insist that this ability is possible solely through the self-legislation of reason he calls "autonomy." Let us look more closely at these two aspects of his position in the *Groundwork*.

As is well known, Kant in this work draws a fundamental distinction between acting "in conformity with duty" (*pflichtmäßig*) and acting "out of duty" (*aus Pflicht*). One can act in conformity with one's duty for any number of motives: out of self-interest, out of sympathy for others, out of fear of legal sanctions, out of hope for God's reward. But one only acts morally, Kant claims, when one acts out of duty, that is, out of the intention to do what is right simply and solely because it is right, independently even of one's changing feelings of sympathy. He calls this attitude "respect for the law," defining respect as "the consciousness of the subordination of my will to a law without the intervention of other influences on my mind," a subordination that is a self-subordination under the moral law, since respect is described as a "self-effected feeling" (*selbstgewirktes Gefühl*).[19] This is a conception of what I have called "self-governance," and indeed a rather strict one, inasmuch as it excludes all feelings of sympathy and compassion. Moreover, Kant does not at this point in the book connect the "self-effected feeling" of respect for the law with the idea of self-legislation, which he only later on in the *Groundwork* introduces under the name of "autonomy."

[18] Oddly, he cites there in passing (*Vorlesung zur Moralphilosophie*, 62; *Lectures on Ethics*, 68) the passage from St. Paul without apparently perceiving its implications.

[19] Kant, *Grundlegung*, AA IV, 401n; *Groundwork*, 14n.

It is true that in that same passage in which he brings up the concept of respect he offers the following clarification: "The *object* of respect is therefore simply the *law*, and indeed the law that we impose (*auferlegen*) upon *ourselves* and yet as necessary in itself." Yet the self-imposition of the law that he is talking about here – at least if we limit ourselves to what the statement literally says – is not the self-legislation of autonomy, which according to a later passage in the *Groundwork* (I have quoted it before) consists in the will being "not merely subject to the law but subject to it in such a way that it must be viewed as also giving the law to itself and just because of this as first subject to the law (of which it can regard itself as the author [*Urheber*])" (GMS, p. 431/GMM, p. 39). For what Kant means in that earlier passage is the self-subordination or subordination of one's own conduct under a law that, as he remarks, is viewed as "necessary in itself" (*an sich notwendig*), that is, as in itself unconditionally valid and binding. Nothing is said about the origin of its validity and bindingness. Nothing is said, for instance, to suggest that one is only subject to the law because, as the later passage says, one is its author. Up to this point, Kant is speaking solely of a motivational structure that can be characterized quite appropriately as "self-governance." We "impose" such a law on ourselves in that we apply it as a constraint, understood to be inherently valid, on whatever we may choose to do. One could even speak in this case of "self-legislation" as well, albeit in a very different sense from the one that Kant himself preferred and that implies authorship of the law in question.

But Kant did not, of course, let matters rest there. When he turns to explaining how this attitude of respect is possible, Kant reaches for his concept of autonomy. In order to be able to act solely out of respect for the moral law, without ulterior motives (or "interest," as he says) and not on the basis of our essentially variable feelings of sympathy, we have to regard ourselves, he says, as the authors of this law, that is, of its very validity and bindingness. We have to regard ourselves as – to repeat again the passage in which he introduces the concept of autonomy – "not merely subject to the law but subject to it in such a way that it [our will] must be viewed as also giving the law to itself and just because of this as first subject to the law (of which it can regard itself as the author)." Yet, the claim that respect can be explained only through autonomy is not one that Kant demonstrates convincingly.

His main argument, which I must cite at length, goes as follows:

> If we look back upon all previous efforts that have ever been made to discover the principle of morality, we need not wonder now why all of them

> had to fail. It was seen that the human being is bound to laws by his duty, but it never occurred to them that he is subject only to laws of *his own though universal legislation* [*seiner eigenen und dennoch allgemeinen Gesetzgebung*] ... For, if one thought of him only as subject to a law (whatever it may be), this law had to carry with it some interest by way of attraction or constraint, since it did not as a law arise from *his* will; in order to conform with the law, his will had instead to be constrained by *something else* to act in a certain way. By this quite necessary consequence, however, all the labor to find a supreme ground of duty was irretrievably lost. For, one never arrived at duty but instead at the necessity of an action from a certain interest. This might be one's own or another's interest. But then the imperative had to turn out always conditional and could not be fit for a moral command. I will therefore call this basic principle the principle of the *autonomy* of the will in contrast with every other, which I accordingly count as *heteronomy*.[20]

To put the argument more succinctly: for Kant, it is supposedly a "necessary consequence" (*notwendige Folgerung*) that, if one thinks of oneself as subject to a moral law without simultaneously considering oneself as (through one's reason) its author, an action out of respect for this law becomes impossible, since one then can act in accord with this law only on the condition that one intends to satisfy or advance some interest. One cannot, in other words, do what is morally required simply because it is the right thing to do. Kant is even of the opinion that one can more generally, in whatever realm, only guide oneself by reason if reason itself institutes or lays down the principles by which it operates. Later in the *Groundwork* he says precisely that, in a generalization of his doctrine of autonomy that is apparently meant to hold no less for theoretical than for practical reason:

> Now, one cannot possibly think of reason as consciously receiving direction from any other quarter (*anderwärts her*) with respect to its judgments, since the subject would then attribute the determination of his judgment not to his reason but to an impulse (*Antrieb*). Reason must regard itself as the author (*Urheberin*) of its principles, independently of alien influences. Consequently, as practical reason or as the will of a rational being it must be regarded of itself as free.[21]

These two passages do not offer a very good argument, however. I will sketch here why this is so. A more detailed account follows in Section 5.4.

[20] Kant, *Grundlegung*, AA IV, 432–433; *Groundwork*, 40–41.
[21] Kant, *Grundlegung*, AA IV, 448; *Groundwork*, 54.

It is not true that in general we can regard a reason for thinking or doing something as valid only if we either consider ourselves the author of its validity or instead appeal to some given interest that would be satisfied or furthered if we were to think or act in that way.[22] For in any case where we indeed bestowed on some consideration the status, which it otherwise would not have, of being an unconditionally valid reason for thought or action, we would have to see reasons to give it that authority, and since these reasons could not themselves rest on any of our given interests, they would have to be regarded as valid in their own right, independently of our authorship as well as of our interests. If there would then have to be reasons of this sort, why could not moral reasons figure among them? The "necessary consequence" of which Kant speaks does not exist. Acting out of respect for moral principles, which constitutes Kant's conception of self-governance and which we ourselves may call "autonomy," is entirely possible without autonomy in the Kantian sense.

Let me summarize what has been said thus far. "Autonomy" can mean many different things. Before Kant, the word had a political meaning – the ability of a community to live by its own laws – as well as a legal meaning – the authority to proceed self-legislatively within an overarching legal order – both of which could not have been especially influential for Kant's definition of the concept. These days we often designate as autonomy in the individual realm the ability to think without the guidance of another or to do what is right without regard to reward or punishment. However, thinking for oneself and self-governance are not what Kant himself understood by "autonomy," namely a self-legislation that establishes the very validity (and thus bindingness) of the principles of thought and action. He did believe as well that thinking for oneself and respect for the demands of morality are only possible on the basis of an autonomy of this sort. But in that, as I have indicated, he was mistaken.

5.4 Kant's Concept of Autonomy

Yet what about Kant's concept of autonomy itself? Up to this point, I have tried to show that thinking for oneself and self-governance do not depend

[22] Note that if this argument is supposed to be compatible with the argument of the "Orientation" essay – namely, that thinking for oneself presupposes autonomy, since a law or principle of action to which one is subject but which one has not given oneself must be a law that someone else has imposed – then Kant is presuming that a law that one views as valid solely on the basis of some interest is either a law one imposes on oneself in order to satisfy that interest or else is a law imposed by someone else whom one considers it is in one's interest to obey.

on autonomy in the Kantian sense. Both are dispositions of mind that, however exactly we may wish to analyze them, are essentially coherent, if not to say invaluable. In both these senses, there is indeed what we may call "autonomy." But autonomy as Kant understood it is another matter. I have already on several occasions indicated in passing that the autonomy of reason, in which reason is understood as the author of the validity of the principles of thought and action, is in my view a questionable and even contradictory concept. This point I now want to argue more closely.

Since the question concerns the very coherence of Kant's idea of autonomy, it is good to remind ourselves first of this idea's actual scope and of its deepest motivations. Although the term "autonomy" appears for the first time in the *Groundwork*, the concept itself underlies not only his moral philosophy but also his "critical philosophy" as a whole. Near the end of Section 5.3, I quoted the passage from the *Groundwork* in which theoretical reason, no less than practical reason, is called the "author (*Urheberin*) of its principles." Even in writings, such as the *Critique of Pure Reason*, where the word does not occur, the concept is clearly at work. One need only think of the famous passage in the preface to the second edition of the *Critique*, which declares that "reason has insight only into that which it produces after a plan of its own."[23] For Kant, reason gives itself its own laws or principles in every sphere of its employment, and it does so in a way that makes it the author of their authority.

The fundamental concern that led him to this position is not difficult to grasp. Ever since the scientific revolution of the seventeenth century, a naturalistic picture of the world as a realm of value-neutral facts has become increasingly dominant. As a result, all principles of thought and action, all distinctions between good and bad, right and wrong, justified and unjustified, have seemed to be ultimately intelligible (leaving God aside) only as norms of our own creation. One version of this view found in the eighteenth century its paradigmatic expression in the philosophy of David Hume: all such distinctions arise from given feelings and desires, so that reason can only be the "slave of the passions." Kant was too much of a rationalist to be attracted to this approach for very long, although for a while he partially embraced it in the realm of moral philosophy.[24] Traces of this temporary temptation still appear in his lectures on moral philosophy of the 1770s, particularly in the thesis, previously discussed, that the understanding, though capable of grasping moral principles, is unable to

[23] Kant, *Kritik der reinen Vernunft*, B XIII.
[24] See Dieter Henrich, "Über Kants früheste Ethik," *Kant-Studien* 54(4) (1963), 404–431.

move us to act accordingly except on the basis of some affective state, for instance, a "moral feeling." Kant could not remain satisfied with this jumble of rationalistic and sensualistic elements, not only because of his doubts about the supposedly necessary role of feelings in the motivation of moral action but also because the idea that the understanding can grasp or perceive basic principles was a remnant of an older rationalism that no longer appeared compatible with the new naturalistic world-picture. How could principles, given their character of being valid and binding, occupy any place in the world of Newtonian physics from which everything normative has disappeared?

Kant therefore saw himself obliged to place rationalism on a new foundation. In his "critical philosophy," principles are no longer perceived by the understanding as an object of knowledge, but rather are produced by self-legislating reason, in some cases with regard to given interests, in others independently of them and categorically. Kant's concept of autonomy was thus supposed to provide the solution to a problem that had become pressing with the development of modern science: What can it mean to live according to reason when the world itself no longer contains any directives that we could grasp in order to know how to think or act? The answer was to see in reason the source and author of its own principles. That this conception of reason fits so well into the naturalistic view of the world, which has come to be ever more widely accepted (whether rightly is a question to which I shall return), explains why, despite some rather obvious objections, it has exercised so great an influence for more than two centuries. It had in Kant's eyes the further advantage that reason – now conceived as a self-legislating faculty in contrast to the understanding, which was still deemed a motivationally inert, because merely perceptual or cognizing, faculty – could count in virtue of its self-activity as able to motivate action without the aid of any given feelings and, thereby, to become, as he said, "practical."

The difficulty is that, on closer examination, talk of the self-legislation of reason does not appear to make sense. The claim that the authority of principles is our own work is contradictory, even when one insists that we do not establish them arbitrarily but rather through the exercise of our reason. Insofar as we can speak meaningfully at all about imposing a principle on ourselves that would otherwise not be valid and binding, such self-legislation can take place only on the condition that we *see reasons* to adopt this principle. These reasons themselves have to possess, then, an authority that cannot be explained by the supposed autonomy of reason. Their validity has to be *acknowledged*, and that means by a faculty of reason that must be understood as in this respect essentially receptive, not self-legislating.

In order to appreciate the contradictory nature of the Kantian conception, let us examine a few cases in which it is indisputable that rules acquire their validity through self-legislation. Consider, for instance, the rules that govern the release of new drugs or that regulate traffic on the road. Not only are there reasons for adopting such rules, reasons that show that it is appropriate or corresponds to our interests to set them up. Equally obvious is the fact that the authority of these reasons – their ability to justify the establishment of such rules – is not something created by the exercise of our reason. These reasons are valid independently of our doing, and we employ our reason in order to recognize their validity, not in order to institute it. That means, in turn, that even the authority of a self-imposed rule cannot depend completely on the exercise of our reason, since it rests on the recognized authority of the reasons justifying the institution of that rule. Thus, I can, for example, in view of my tendency to promise too much, give myself the rule not to make in the future any important promise without drawing up a list of everything I have already promised, and a necessary condition for my being bound by this rule is that I have imposed it upon myself. But that is not, of course, a sufficient condition for its bindingness, which also derives from the underlying principle that I am aiming to honor – namely, that promises are to be kept or maybe that a good reputation is to be maintained.

In the end, there must always be reasons, whether principles or not, whose independent validity we simply acknowledge. (Principles themselves are rules designating standing reasons of thought or action that generally outweigh competing considerations). Acknowledgment is the basis on which we must, if rational, embrace those principles of thought and action that are not the special rules I have been mentioning. When it does appear necessary to adduce reasons for these principles, they are generally reasons to believe that the principles are valid, not reasons to decide that they are to be established as valid.

5.5 Reason and World

Thus it becomes evident what the nature of reason really is. Reason cannot be essentially self-legislating, since it must always draw its bearings from reasons that prescribe to it how it is to proceed. In general, as Aristotle observed, a mental faculty (*dynamis*) is defined in terms of what constitutes its characteristic exercise (*energeia*), and this activity must in turn be defined in terms of the sort of objects (*antikeimena*) toward which it is directed.[25] Reason, we accordingly may say, is thus to be understood as a faculty whose exercise basically consists in reasoning, and reasoning in turn consists in *responding to reasons*.

According to Kant, by contrast, "[reason] has to view itself as the author of its principles, independently of alien influences (*unabhängig von fremden Einflüssen*)."[26] It should now be clear how false this assertion is. In relying on reasons whose authority it must presuppose, reason is very far from being "dependent on alien influences," as the second half of Kant's statement would entail. The implicit opposition between "instituting one's own principles" and "being subject to alien influences" is a false dichotomy. For reasons are hardly foreign bodies with respect to reason. They are precisely that to which we must respond if we are to be able to exercise our reason at all. Responding to, guiding oneself by, reasons means, furthermore, grasping them in such a way that one is moved to think or act accordingly. Reason is thus at one and the same time cognitive and motivating, a combination that Kant ridiculed already in his lectures on moral philosophy of the 1770s as a "philosophers' stone" (*Stein des Weisen*) and that he continued to dismiss, though wrongly, as impossible to the end.[27]

The objection I have raised against Kant's concept of autonomy is not unknown, and adherents of the Kantian tradition have devised various strategies to escape it. I cannot discuss all of them here,[28] but a few words should be said about the influential response developed by Christine Korsgaard. The particular interest of her reformulation of the Kantian idea

[25] Aristotle, *De anima*, II.4. In my view, much of modern philosophy, from Descartes to Kant and beyond, has wrongly rejected this position and held instead that the essential faculties of the mind can be understood independently of how the mind fits into the world. I discuss this point in some detail in "Das philosophische Interesse an Selbsterkenntnis," in Oliver Koch (ed.), *Subjekt und Person. Beiträge zu einem Schlüsselthema der klassischen deutschen Philosophie* (Hamburg: Meiner-Verlag, 2019), 23–39.

[26] Kant, *Grundlegung*, AA IV, 448; *Groundwork*, 54. In this passage (see note 21), Kant claims that if reason "would consciously receive direction from any other quarter with respect to its judgments," it would not then be reason but rather some "impulse" (*Antrieb*) that ultimately determines one's judgment. That Kant does not even mention the possibility of reason receiving direction from *reasons* stems from his (naturalistic) assumption that the world, with which reason deals, cannot contain anything normative.

[27] Kant, *Vorlesung zur Moralphilosophie*, 69; *Lectures on Ethics*, 71. Reason as the "critical" Kant conceived it is motivating only because it is not cognitive but rather self-legislating. See Section 5.4.

[28] I have discussed Robert Brandom's version of the concept of autonomy in *Vernunft und Subjektivität* (Berlin: Suhrkamp, 2012), 37–38, and in *Das Selbst in seinem Verhältnis zu sich und zu anderen* (Frankfurt: Klostermann, 2017), 42n. See also note 30 later in this chapter.

of autonomy lies in the fact that she dispenses with the terms "giving" and "imposing" in order to avoid the implication that a law that one gives oneself has to be a law that one could also *not* give oneself and that one thus requires a reason for imposing. According to Korsgaard, the fundamental principles of thought and action are to be understood as "constitutive" of them.[29] They guide, she says, these activities by virtue of making up their very essence, similarly to the way the rules of chess determine what is and is not a valid move in chess. In this sense, we would ourselves, insofar as we think or act, be the authors of these principles, yet without having the choice of imposing them on ourselves or not. For not to adhere to them would mean no longer to think or do anything intelligible, just as moving a rook diagonally is not to make a foolish move but to make no move at all in the game of chess.

Now, Korsgaard is right that some of the fundamental principles she mentions – for instance, the principle of non-contradiction or the principle that to will an end is to will the corresponding means (though not, I think, any moral principles) – are "constitutive" in the sense indicated: they concern the conditions of possibility of coherent thought and action. But that does not yield a justification of the idea of autonomy. For what is it that actually makes a particular principle constitutive? To recognize that in assenting to a contradiction we are failing to think anything meaningful is to see that the rule of avoiding all contradiction has a validity we must respect in order to think coherently at all. It is therefore the universal validity of this principle that explains its being constitutive and not the other way around. Only in virtue of possessing an unconditional authority for all possible thought does it count as a constitutive principle of coherent thinking. For only so can we explain to ourselves *why* we cannot conceive of any meaningful thought at odds with this principle and why we are thus not really thinking anything at all, if we violate it. Someone who says to herself, "I aim to abide by the principle of contradiction because otherwise I would not be thinking anything intelligible," would, if she were to think the matter through to the end, understand by that: "I aim to abide by the principle of contradiction because its unconditional authority for any kind of thinking I might possibly do makes it a principle of all intelligible thought." The concept of autonomy can thus not be saved by the fact that some principles are so close to us that we are not free to accept them or not. On the contrary, this phenomenon makes clear to

[29] Korsgaard, *Self-Constitution* (Oxford: Oxford University Press, 2009), 32, 67, 81. See also Korsgaard, *The Sources of Normativity* (Cambridge: Cambridge University Press, 1996), 235–236.

what extent our innermost being is constituted by its relation to a normative order of reasons of whose authority we are not the author.[30]

I observed before (Section 5.4) how Kant's concept of autonomy and the naturalistic worldview appear made for one other. If reason, however, is no longer to be understood as self-legislating, but instead as responding to reasons that already exist, then we must develop another view of the world that fits this conception of reason. That is no small task, and here, in closing, I will make only a few brief remarks to indicate what is in my view the correct route to take.

First, we should remember that naturalism is a metaphysics and not a theorem of the modern natural sciences. If we want to work out another view of the world that makes comprehensible how something like reasons can exist to which reason must respond, it is not to challenge the truth of modern science, but instead to understand better what it means that its claim to truth is well-founded. The task is thus to develop another metaphysics according to which reasons form part of the structure of reality, that is, of the world itself, if we understand the world – to adopt Wittgenstein's phrase – as everything that is the case, independently of whatever opinions we might have about it.

In Chapter 1 (Sections 1.3–1.4), I already sketched what this alternative metaphysics, this different conception of the ultimate structure of reality, would look like. The next two chapters, especially Chapter 7, will go into far more detail than what I say here. The following should suffice for present purposes. Reasons, as I insisted there, do not consist in anything of a physical or psychological nature since they are essentially normative in character. To have a reason to do X means that one *ought* to do X if nothing else counts against it. For when the reason to do something – for instance, to go swimming because one has some free time – is sufficient without being so decisive that it would be right to say one "ought" to go swimming, this is because in such a case there are several options, all equally justified: one ought to make good use of one's free time, but in which of the available ways is relatively indifferent.[31]

[30] Nothing I have said in criticism of either the "self-imposition" or "constitution" version of the idea of autonomy turns essentially on the supposed subject of autonomy being an individual and not a collectivity. So I do not see how a Hegelian effort to conceive in terms of social practices how reason can give itself its laws provides any sort of way out. For an attempt, see Robert Pippin, *Hegel's Practical Philosophy. Rational Agency as Ethical Life* (Cambridge: Cambridge University Press, 2008), chapters 3–4.

[31] I return to this point in the next chapter, note 25.

Furthermore, reasons to think or do something exist independently of our beliefs about what reasons we have. For these beliefs may be true or false, corresponding or not to the reasons at hand. There is no such thing as bad reasons, only bad conceptions of what reasons there are. Because reasons are both irreducibly normative yet also real, I characterized this picture of the world in Chapter 1 (Section 1.4) as a kind of "platonism." Reasons are like Plato's forms in that they constitute a third, essentially normative dimension of reality, distinct from both nature and mind.

Yet, as I also cautioned, this sort of platonism is nothing outlandish. Reasons are not being said to occupy some ethereal realm, detached from the world of things and minds. Reasons necessarily depend on the physical and psychological facts that are relevant for our thought and action. To have a reason to do X means that something in the circumstances in which we find ourselves counts in favor of doing X. Reasons consist in a certain kind of relation, the relation of counting-in-favor-of, in which phenomena of the natural world, physical or psychological facts, stand to our possibilities of thought and action. Reasons have therefore not only a normative but also a *relational* character and exist only insofar as there exist beings like us, who have possibilities that they can take up.[32] At the same time, reasons are not thereby any less objective, since relations too can form part of reality, independent of our conceptions of them. This kind of platonism hews closely, therefore, to our everyday ways of thinking. When we reflect about what we should believe or do, we presume, first of all, that there exists something we do not yet know but want to discover, namely the reasons to believe or do one thing rather than another. We also presume that these reasons consist in the relevance of the given circumstances to our possibilities of thought and action. The chief theses of the platonism I am defending, the reality and relationality or reasons, mirror these two elementary truths.

"In itself," abstracting from the existence of rational beings, the world obviously contains no reasons. But once such beings exist, the world is no longer normatively mute but takes on a new dimension, consisting in the relevance of various physical and psychological facts to the possibilities of these beings. Normative distinctions do not arise through our own

[32] This means, as I explain in Chapter 7, that there is an intimate connection between reason, as the capacity to respond to reasons, and freedom, which consists not simply in having possibilities but in being able to choose among them. It also means that not just we but the higher animals as well have the capacity of reason, if to a lesser degree.

doing, as though we were the authors of their authority, but rather as a result of our very existence. No doubt, this kind of platonism as well as the allied conception of reason as responsiveness to reasons will strike Kant-impressed thinkers as a fallback into a "pre-critical" style of rationalism. But as I declared in the Introduction, that is a badge I wear with honor.

CHAPTER 6

Moral Philosophy and Metaphysical Evasion

There are many ways in which moral philosophy and metaphysics might be thought to intersect. In part, this is due to what have been in the history of philosophy different ideas about the nature of metaphysics itself. As I explained in the Introduction, I follow the basic definition that emerged in Aristotle's school, where the term "*ta meta ta physika*" was first introduced. By "metaphysics" I mean the enterprise of working out a conception of what the world, in the sense of all that exists, is ultimately like, determining how the various dimensions of our experience fit together in the overall scheme of things. In twentieth-century philosophy, from logical positivism to phenomenology, "metaphysics" often functioned as a term of opprobrium, used to designate irresponsible, unfounded, or outdated modes of philosophical thinking. In many quarters, this usage still persists. Yet I am convinced that even "anti-metaphysical" or "post-metaphysical" thinkers rely, if only implicitly, on metaphysical assumptions in the sense I have indicated.

In this chapter, I take up the question of what we must understand the world to be like if we regard moral judgments, or more generally normative judgments about how we ought to think or act, as more than basically the expression of attitudes of approval and disapproval. Suppose that we regard them instead as fundamentally aiming to get it right, to embody knowledge of how we should indeed comport ourselves. Then how are reasons for belief and action, which are thus the central object of their knowledge-claims, to be understood? What does it mean to say – what is entailed by saying – that they exist? I pursue this question by examining the recent writings of Derek Parfit and T. M. Scanlon.[1] Their thought, in its strengths and weaknesses, is instructive. Both of them hold that normative judgments are true or false and are thus able to embody, not merely

[1] Both Parfit and Scanlon gave me generous and helpful comments on the original versions of the parts of this chapter devoted to their work. I am very grateful to them.

approval or commitment, but also knowledge of the reasons there are. Yet both recoil from following through on the ontological implications of their views. Both fail to acknowledge the metaphysics that the objective existence of reasons really entails, but that I, by contrast, am determined to embrace.

6.1 Anti-Naturalism

Derek Parfit's *On What Matters* is a monumental work.[2] The first two volumes, published in 2011, total 1,400 pages and tackle at length the deepest problems having to do not only with the foundations of morality but also with the nature of practical reason in general. Draft versions of the book circulated widely in the philosophical world for more than a decade, and the names of those who commented on the manuscript fill three pages of acknowledgments. The central chapters devoted to moral theory draw on material that Parfit originally presented in a series of Tanner Lectures at Berkeley in 2002. In published form, they are surrounded by a long introductory section on the objectivity of reasons and an even more extensive concluding section (a 350-page monograph in its own right) on the topic of normativity – plus essays by the commentators at the Berkeley lectures (Susan Wolf, Allen Wood, and T. M. Scanlon, to whom Barbara Herman has been added) along with the author's responses. Then, in 2017, a third volume of 450 pages appeared. Pursuing further reflections on his two main themes of ethical principles and the nature of reasons, it also contains extensive replies to the critical essays that were published in a separate volume and that deal with his views about the second of these topics.[3] *On What Matters* has already established itself as a philosophical classic.

Remarkably, this book, for all its extraordinary length, is a pleasure to read. Every chapter and section, every word, has a point. The prose is always clear, and there are sometimes sentences of a crisp eloquence. The primary reason for the book's size is Parfit's determination to settle in a definitive way some of the deepest disagreements that have riven the field of moral philosophy. The persistence of these disagreements manifestly fills him with alarm. "If we cannot resolve our disagreements," he exclaims

[2] Parfit, Derek, *On What Matters*, volumes I and II (Oxford: Oxford University Press, 2011), volume III (Oxford: Oxford University Press, 2017). In Sections 6.1–6.4, references to this book, by volume and page number, will be given in the text as parenthetical citations.

[3] Peter Singer (ed.), *Does Anything Really Matter? Essays on Parfit on Objectivity* (Oxford: Oxford University Press, 2017).

at one point, "that would give us reasons to doubt that there are *any* true principles. There might be nothing that morality *turns out to be*, since morality might be an illusion" (II, 155). Volume II contains a short autobiographical section (II, 426–430) indicating why the drive to overcome disagreement led him, even though his original object was the fundamental principles of morality, to focus nearly half of his book on the nature of reasons and normative judgments and on related "metaethical" questions. This passage, tellingly entitled "Disagreements," offers a good starting point for discussing the main themes of *On What Matters*.

"I became a philosopher," Parfit there reflects, "so that I would have more time to think about what matters," in other words, to figure out what we have reason to care about. This project led to his first book, *Reasons and Persons*, and to one of its central and most famous conclusions: since no sense can be made of the idea that each of us is an enduring self over time, "personal identity is not what matters" in the way our own lives go, but rather the connectedness of experiences.[4] As he went on, however, to pursue the question posed at the end of that book – on what "Non-Religious Ethics" can we agree, now that we are finally learning to free our moral thinking from belief in God? – worries arose about the sorts of differences he encountered between his views and those of other philosophers. "We seemed to disagree not only about what matters, but also about what it would *be* for things to matter, and about whether anything *could* matter."

What Parfit means is that he found himself at odds with the prevailing conception of what a reason is. In his view, nothing can matter unless there are objective reasons to prefer one course of action to another – reasons, that is, that depend on facts about the world, whatever may happen to be our desires or aims, and not on facts about what would satisfy our present desires or the desires we would have if fully informed about the relevant facts (I, 45). Indeed, all reasons must be essentially objective reasons, he claims, for when we believe our desires or aims give us reason to act in some way, we are supposing that there are underlying reasons, based on the objects of those desires or aims, to satisfy or pursue them at all. Since reasons are normative in character – to have a reason to do something is for that action to be one that, all else being equal, we *ought* to do (I, 33) – nothing can therefore matter unless among the facts that exist are also normative facts, involving objective reasons, about how we ought to live (II, 425).

[4] Parfit, Derek, *Reasons and Persons* (Oxford: Oxford University Press, 1984), 217.

However, the dominant view of reasons is instead that they are subjective, dependent on people's desires and attitudes. Partly this view flourishes, according to Parfit, because the relation between desires and reasons is not thought through carefully enough (I, 65–67). But a principal source, he also holds (I, 109; II, 363), is the widespread acceptance of the naturalistic conception that physical and psychological things of the sort studied by the natural sciences are the only things that exist (II, 265, 305). This metaphysics of naturalism admits, to be sure, psychological facts about what we regard as mattering. But it has no room for facts about what really does matter (II, 425, 601). For these would be normative facts about the objective reasons, grounded in the way the world is, to care about one thing rather than another, facts about what ought to matter to us. It should be plain from earlier chapters how sympathetic I am to this theme of *On What Matters.*

Ethics, as Parfit conceives it, aims to arrive at a body of fundamental truths concerning what is indeed right and good. Thus, the prevalence of subjectivist views about reasons led him to realize that many must in effect regard the very enterprise in which he was engaged as essentially pointless. If naturalism were true and there were no normative facts, Parfit bleakly observes, then he and others who share his view would have wasted much of their lives. "Our consolation would be only that it wouldn't matter that we had wasted much of our lives, since we would have learnt that nothing matters" (II, 367). Whence his need to examine at length these metaethical and even metaphysical questions and vindicate his idea of moral philosophy.

The opposition comes in for unsparing criticism. Subjectivists, he argues, incoherently help themselves to assumptions that only make sense on objectivist grounds, as when (his example is Harry Frankfurt) they suppose that our desires give us reasons for action only when we are fully informed about the objects of our desires – a view that entails in reality that facts about those objects themselves are what give us the reasons to desire them (I, 91–101). Or (like Bernard Williams) they apparently lack altogether the normative concept of a reason, which designates the way certain physical or psychological facts *count in favor* of some action, since they mean by "reasons" only such considerations as might happen to *motivate* us (II, 435).[5]

[5] I think Parfit misunderstands Williams's position. Williams did have the concept of a normative reason; he simply believed that the only normative reasons that exist are "internal" reasons. See his definition of an internal reason in *Making Sense of Humanity* (Cambridge: Cambridge University

Naturalists, however sophisticated, are in no better a position. If (like the so-called Cornell realists) they acknowledge the existence of normative facts, but then identify them with natural (that is, physical or psychological) facts in the way that facts about heat can be said to amount to facts about molecular kinetic energy, they commit the mistake of confusing the natural property that may make some action right with the irreducibly normative property of its being right (II, 295–377). Or if, on the contrary (here the target is expressivists such as Allan Gibbard), they hold that normative claims do not purport to describe anything at all, but only express certain attitudes of approval or disapproval, then they must deny that anything – beliefs as well as actions – can *be* rational, as opposed to being judged rational, with the awkward result that "it could not be rational to believe anything, including Gibbard's view" (II, 410). Naturalism undermines itself: "If Metaphysical Naturalism were true, we could not have reasons to have any particular beliefs . . . So it could not be true that we *ought* to accept Naturalism . . . For us to be able to argue rationally about whether Naturalism is true, Naturalism must be false" (I, 110). This is a very important point. In large part, naturalism – particularly in its emotivist and expressivist versions – arose as a denial of the existence of moral facts, supposedly incompatible with a scientific worldview. But whatever it has claimed about moral reasons or reasons for action would apply equally to reasons for belief, so that there also could not exist reasons to accept the scientific theories it esteems or this philosophical position itself.[6]

It should be noted, however, that in this passage Parfit is criticizing Gibbard's expressivism as principally expounded in *Wise Choices, Apt Feelings*. At the time of writing the first two volumes of *On What Matters*, he appears not to have realized how far Gibbard's expressivism, when reformulated as a form of "quasi-realism" in *Thinking How to Live*, can mimic the sorts of things someone says who believes that normative judgments are true or false and can thus embody knowledge.[7] Given a minimalist conception of truth according to which asserting a proposition

Press, 1995), 35: "A has a reason to φ only if he could reach the conclusion to φ by a *sound* deliberative route from the motivations he already has" (emphasis added). "Sound" is clearly a normative term.

[6] The point is developed in considerable detail by Terence Cuneo, *The Normative Web* (Oxford: Oxford University Press, 2007). See too my book *The Autonomy of Morality* (Cambridge: Cambridge University Press, 2008), chapter 5, §7.

[7] In this regard, Gibbard's *Thinking How to Live* (Cambridge, MA: Harvard University Press, 2003) supersedes *Wise Choices, Apt Feelings* (Cambridge, MA: Harvard University Press, 1990).

as true comes to no more than just asserting that proposition, judgments about reasons too, even though they serve fundamentally to express attitudes of endorsement, can count as true or false. As I noted in Chapter 1 (Section 1.3), Gibbard thus continues to deny that they serve to describe the way things really are, that reasons for belief or action obtain independently of our attitudes toward them. The idea that "R is a reason to do X," he still holds, is to be explained "in terms of the psychological notion of a person's weighing R in favor of doing X."[8] His naturalism is uncompromised. In volume III of *On What Matters*, Parfit examines more closely the claims of this quasi-realism, and we will see later (Section 6.4) what, if anything, he is in a position to say against it.

"Non-naturalist cognitivism" is one name (there are others) that Parfit gives to the position he himself defends: normative judgments are to be understood as being true or false of irreducibly normative facts that involve objective, that is, object-given reasons for belief and action. Such judgments can go wrong, not only because they may be mistaken about the non-normative facts on which reasons depend or because of errors of logic, but also because they fail to describe correctly the reasons themselves to which they purport to refer. Chapter 1 in this book will have made plain that this is a position I share. The parts of his account I have summarized so far – the objectivity of reasons and the anti-naturalism that goes with it – are on the mark. Parfit has failed, however, to acknowledge fully what these views entail. I will come to this point shortly (Section 6.4). But first let us turn to what he says about morality itself. Parfit's two principal concerns – clarifying the nature of reasons and developing a substantive ethical theory – intersect in fact at various points.

6.2 The Triple Theory

On What Matters challenges many widespread views about the foundations of morality as well. Yet Parfit's attitude toward disagreement in the area of substantive moral theory is very different from the way he deals with opposing views about the nature of reasons. To subjectivism and naturalism he gives no quarter. These conceptions are simply wrong. With regard, however, to the debate between Kantianism, contractualism, and consequentialism (utilitarianism is one species), which has dominated moral philosophy over the past several centuries, his approach is more irenic.

[8] Gibbard, *Thinking How to Live*, 190. For his unwavering allegiance to naturalism in this later book, see xi and 194.

The aim is to show that the three most plausible versions of these theories, namely the contractualist core of Kant's theory,[9] T. M. Scanlon's somewhat similar contractualism, and rule-consequentialism, do not really conflict, but instead converge. When these theories are properly formulated, they each yield as rationally justified the same set of moral principles. In order to put them in their proper form, Parfit relies on a series of hypothetical examples, many with picturesque names such as "Fatal Belief," "Tunnel," "Surgery," "Earthquake," and "Desperate Plight." (The use of such scenarios is a hallmark of his philosophical style.) When we reflect on these cases, he claims, we will see reason to endorse particular judgments that oblige us to revise in various ways one or the other of these moral theories. Then it can be shown by general argument that the three theories, thus modified, agree in their conclusions. Thus he argues that if, as the Kantian contractualist would hold, everyone ought to follow the principles whose universal acceptance everyone could rationally will, and if the reasons to choose these principles are to be determined from an impartial point of view and without appealing to any antecedent beliefs about what is morally wrong, then the principles chosen would be those whose universal acceptance would make things go best, as the rule-consequentialist would favor (I, 378–411).

The result is what Parfit calls "the Triple Theory." It states that

> an act is wrong if and only if, or just when, such acts are disallowed by some principle that is
>
> (1) one of the principles whose being universal laws would make things go best [Rule-consequentialism],
> (2) one of the only principles whose being universal laws everyone could rationally will or choose [Kantian contractualism], and
> (3) a principle that no one could reasonably reject [Scanlonian contractualism] (I, 412–413).

The Kantian, contractualist, and consequentialist traditions have been climbing the same mountain, he likes to say ("Climbing the Mountain" was an earlier draft title of the book), and at the peak, where each is at its best, their paths merge.

The idea that these three forms of moral theory, and particularly the Kantian and consequentialist forms, so often viewed as inherently antagonistic, in reality ultimately converge is held to draw support from the

[9] In Parfit's usage, any theory counts as "contractualist" that "appeals to the principles that everyone could rationally choose to be universally accepted" (I, 20).

objectivity of reasons. In order to dispel common worries about the frequency of moral disagreement (II, 546), Parfit argues that if reasons for action depend, not on our desires, but instead on facts about things in the world, then the more carefully we consider these facts, the more we should tend to agree in our normative and indeed in our moral judgments. To the extent therefore that proponents of different moral theories revise them to fit their improved judgments about what we ought to do in particular cases, these theories should themselves come to coincide in what they say is morally right and wrong. The chances of convergence would be slight, if reasons for action turned on what happen to be people's desires and attitudes.

Now, in fact, the three components of the Triple Theory are not on the same footing. The Kantian component shapes the other two, and that is why the three theories tend to coincide. As is well known, rule-consequentialism reduces to act-consequentialism if its rationale is consequentialist – if, that is, making things go best overall, in the aggregate, is what ultimately matters – since adhering to some rule of action can then only be justified insofar as it entails doing the act whose consequences represent the greatest net amount of good (otherwise, one has given in to rule-worship). And yet, act-consequentialism notoriously conflicts with many of our deepest moral beliefs. Parfit avoids this difficulty by holding that rule-consequentialism has to abandon the idea that how well things go is what ultimately matters. It must instead regard as of ultimate importance the following of those rules or principles of action whose universal acceptance everyone could rationally will or choose. In other words, it has to be founded on Kantian contractualism. The Triple Theory, as Parfit puts it, is "only *one-third* consequentialist." The principles of action it recommends are optimific at the level just of principle, but "it is not consequentialist either in its claims about *why* we ought to follow these principles, or in its claims about which *acts* are wrong" (I, 417–418).

The situation is not so different with respect to the third component. Against Scanlon's own understanding of his contractualist formula – "an act is wrong just when such acts are disallowed by some principle no one could reasonably reject" – Parfit argues that the reasons one may consider for rejecting some principle should include not just what one has reason to prefer for oneself but also in some circumstances how benefits and burdens are distributed (II, 191–212), as well as how things would go best, impersonally speaking (II, 214–243). In that case, he continues, the principles justified by Scanlon's formula will be those that everyone could rationally will to be universal laws (I, 411–412; II, 244–259). Again, the

Kantian element proves to be more basic. Parfit's Triple Theory is much like the Trinity: in the three-in-one, one of the three enjoys a priority over the other two. Let us look, therefore, in some more detail at what he makes of Kant the Father.

6.3 Parfit and Kant

Parfit is by no means a true-blue Kantian. He rejects as inadequate or incoherent a great many of Kant's most famous ideas and formulas. Kant may have declared that "consistency is a philosopher's greatest duty." But if the *Groundwork of the Metaphysics of Morals* "gives us more new and fruitful ideas than all the philosophers of several centuries," Parfit also believes that "of the qualities that enable Kant to achieve so much, one is inconsistency" (I, xlii, 183). The *Groundwork*, he jokes, deserves the old Oxford grade of alpha gamma: it contains nothing mediocre, but only passages of sheer brilliance and originality, alongside passages that are confused and deeply wrong-headed (I, xliv). The aim is not therefore fidelity to Kant. "My two masters," says Parfit in the preface, "are Sidgwick and Kant," and though he adds that "Kant is the greatest moral philosopher since the ancient Greeks," he also values the clarity, precision, and detailed argument for which Sidgwick's *Methods of Ethics* provides the model. He seeks therefore to separate Kant's insights from all the errors, to formulate them as carefully as possible, and to develop them into what may be called "a Kantian moral theory."

What then are the parts of Kant's moral theory that Parfit rejects? One is the well-known "formula of humanity" according to which we should always treat others never merely as means but always also as ends. Treating people as ends, Parfit claims, cannot mean treating them in ways to which they can or would consent, since coercion and deception, in which consent is not possible, are at times justified. It has to mean treating them in ways to which they could rationally consent. Yet in some cases, someone's not actually having agreed to some action of ours (such as taking their car without asking), even if the person could rationally have consented to it, makes that action wrong; in other cases, the reasons for which someone cannot rationally consent to some action appeal to the very fact of its being wrong (I, 200–211). Rational consent, he concludes, cannot therefore provide a "supreme" (that is, ultimate) principle of morality. Nor can the deficiency be made good by the first half of the humanity formula. Among other reasons, the idea that harming people without their consent is treating them merely as means – which Parfit understands as both using them in some way and regarding them as mere tools – is incorrect on three counts: (i) when we harm them as a means to some end (for instance, breaking the leg of an assailant), we may not be treating *them* as means; (ii) even if we are then treating them as means, we may not treating them *merely* as means; and (iii) even if we *are* treating them merely as means, we may not be acting wrongly, since the wrongness of the act generally consists in what we do and not in our attitude in doing it (I, 221). Furthermore, as he observes with reference to the Holocaust, there are worse things one can do than treat people merely as means (I, 228).

Another prominent element of Kant's moral theory that Parfit discards is the notion of a "maxim," as used in the "formula of universal law": "act only on those maxims that you can will to be universal laws." By maxims or "subjective principles of action" Kant meant policies by which we act such as "never cheat" or "always look at things from the other's point of view," and the trouble, Parfit argues, is that a policy may (like "never lie") not tell us everything morally relevant about the act done on its basis (was the lie told to just anyone or to a would-be murderer?); it may even (like "always do what is best for myself") refer not so much to the act as to its motive. In order to determine which acts are morally right and wrong, the universalization criterion needs to be applied to acts themselves, under their morally relevant description (I, 289–298).

However, Parfit's most fundamental departure from Kant is one he does not bring up himself. It is pointed out to him by Scanlon (II, 118–121), and even then, in his reply to Scanlon's commentary, he appears far more interested in other matters, although its implications are profound. The idea of a reason, as we have seen, is basic for Parfit's thought. Thus, when he refers, as in the Triple Theory, to rationally willing some principle of action, he understands it as dependent on our having reasons to endorse that principle. Kant, by contrast, understood what we can rationally will as what we can will compatibly with being a rational agent. In his eyes, Scanlon remarks, rationality is the fundamental concept, and the idea of reasons can have only a derivative status. Indeed, according to Scanlon, Parfit expressed surprise in an earlier version of his book that Kant did not employ the idea of a reason in the normative sense that he makes central. Throughout *On What Matters* (e.g., I, 47ff.), Parfit describes rationality as a matter of *responding* to reasons (or to what would be reasons if our relevant beliefs were true), since reasons are objective. Kant never talked this way, and not by accident, since for him our reason is not so much responsive as "autonomous" or "self-legislating." "Reason," says the *Groundwork*, "must look upon itself as the author (*Urheberin*) of its principles independently of alien influences."[10] Principles that we will or legislate for ourselves insofar as we are rational beings tell us what facts can count as reasons to think or do this or that.

Parfit rejects this Kantian doctrine, once it is called to his attention. Claims about what we could will consistently with regarding ourselves as rational agents would be "too restricted and too weak" (II, 191). I would go further. As I argued in Chapter 5, Kant's conviction that rationality is a more basic notion than that of reasons makes no sense. Reason is a faculty whose exercise consists in reasoning, and reasoning entails figuring out on the basis of our existing beliefs and desires what else we have reason to think, want, or do. As rational beings, we regulate our conduct by reasons and principles we presume to be valid; their authority for our thought and action is something we understand ourselves as grasping, not as instituting ourselves. In those limited cases where we do refuse to act in a certain way because it would be inconsistent with being a rational agent or we give ourselves some principle of action (such as never to borrow) that would not otherwise be authoritative for us, we must see reasons to deem that action inconsistent with being rational or reasons (such as the obligation to repay one's debts along with our own propensity to borrow more than we can repay) to impose on ourselves that principle. Ultimately, exercising reason always involves responding to reasons. This is Parfit's view as well. So he appears not to recognize fully how much he in fact differs from Kant on this fundamental matter.

Why, one might ask, was Kant convinced that how we ought to act depends, not on reasons we must grasp, but instead on principles of action that we impose on ourselves consistently with being rational agents and that determine what facts can count as reasons? Scanlon (not to mention Parfit) does not go into this question. Kant's motivations are not difficult to discern, however. I discussed them in Chapter 5 (Section 5.4). If reason is essentially responsive to reasons,[11] then reasons must somehow form part of the fabric of the world. Yet how can anything essentially normative figure in the disenchanted, naturalistic picture of the world, devoid of value and directives – "*le silence éternel de ces espaces infinis*," as Pascal put it – that modern science has (supposedly) taught us to accept? If morality, Kant believed, is to have a rational foundation, then reason itself, not anything to which reason responds, must provide it. Contemporary

[10] Kant, *Grundlegung zur Metaphysik der Sitten*, in *Gesammelte Schriften*, Akademie-Ausgabe (Berlin: de Gruyter, 1902), vol. IV, 448.

[11] I develop this conception of reason further in Section 7.1, Chapter 7.

neo-Kantians such as Christine Korsgaard sometimes make this assumption explicit: "The ethics of autonomy is the only one consistent with the metaphysics of the modern world." Reasons, she argues, are not the object of reflection, but rather its outcome, "a kind of reflective success." When we say that we have a reason to do something, we are not reporting a discovery; we are expressing our confidence that acting this way exemplifies the "practical identity," the conception of what makes life worth living, to which we hold allegiance.[12]

Parfit does discuss Korsgaard's Kantian anti-realism about reasons, though not in regard to its metaphysical basis. He focuses instead on her claim that normative realists, wrongly supposing that practical reasoning aims at acquiring true beliefs about reasons, cannot explain how reasons "get a grip" on the agent, how they can move the person to think or act as they direct. This claim, he objects, confuses normativity, which is a matter of what reasons are, with questions of motivation (II, 418–424). Here he misses Korsgaard's point. She is exploiting one of Hume's principal arguments against moral rationalism in order to show what reasons actually are.[13] Since thinking we have a reason to do something does, all else being equal, move us to act accordingly, but since beliefs on their own cannot motivate, judgments about the reasons we have cannot be understood as expressions of belief, true or false of some domain of normative facts, but instead as expressions of desire. Korsgaard herself conceives of the essentially conative attitude such judgments express as commitment and endorsement rather than desire: reasons are "a kind of reflective success." But no matter. The argument itself is poor. What Parfit ought to have objected to is the second premise in the argument, namely the assumption that beliefs alone cannot motivate.[14] He should have begun by countering that they can certainly do so when they are beliefs about reasons.[15] More generally, however, it is a mistake to suppose that belief as such is

[12] Christine Korsgaard, *The Sources of Normativity* (Cambridge: Cambridge University Press, 1996), 5, 93–96, 100–107, 119–121.

[13] See, for instance, Hume, *A Treatise of Human Nature* (Oxford: Oxford University Press, 1975), 462: "'Tis impossible that the distinction betwixt moral good and evil can be made by reason; since that distinction has an influence on our actions, of which reason alone is incapable." Hume, of course, was equally wedded to a purely naturalistic conception of the world.

[14] See my critique of the Humean argument, with reference to Korsgaard, in *The Autonomy of Morality*, 133–135. Parfit appears, in fact, to accept the second premise when he elsewhere considers the Humean argument: II, 381–382.

[15] In *Moral Realism: A Defence* (Oxford: Oxford University Press, 2003), 122, Russ Shafer-Landau also replies to the Humean argument in this way. But he fails to see the broader point that no belief, whatever its object, is motivationally inert, probably because he does not inquire into the nature of belief in general.

motivationally inert. To believe that *p* is not to have an especially vivid idea of *p* (as Hume himself imagined), nor is it simply to hold that *p* is true. Rather, it is to be disposed to think and act in accord with the presumed truth of *p*. (For more detail, see Chapter 7, Section 7.7, and Chapter 8, Section 8.3). Someone who says he believes it is raining but whose thought and action are not in any relevant way shaped by the assumed truth of that proposition would not be said to believe what he says he does. Thus, in particular, to believe that we have a reason to do something is, in the absence of countervailing reasons, to be moved to act in accord with that reason.

In his preface, Parfit acknowledges indirectly that the Kantian conception of reason is a doctrine to which he stands opposed, not simply because it is inadequate, but as a matter of principle. Korsgaard's critique of "dogmatic rationalism" (her term of abuse for normative realism) "rouse[d] me from my undogmatic slumbers," he says waggishly (I, xlv). Indeed, her underlying "metaphysics of the modern world," according to which the realm of facts about which beliefs can be true or false cannot contain anything normative, is one that Parfit is committed to overthrowing. For it is nothing other than the naturalism he rejects in the name of the objectivity of reasons. Parfit does not appear willing, however, to accept fully the metaphysical implications of his own conception of reason. Nor does he notice a difficulty that this conception poses for his moral philosophy, namely the Triple Theory. To these problems I now turn.

6.4 Ontological Ambivalences

Naturalism is a false metaphysics because there are, not only physical and psychological facts, but also normative facts involving reasons that indicate what we ought to believe, or want, or do. Reasons, Parfit maintains, figure among the things that exist. Of course, reasons are not strictly speaking "things," sitting next to other things such as hungry people and the food in our hands. Reasons consist in the import that physical and psychological facts involving such things have for our conduct. Like many today (myself included), Parfit characterizes the nature of reasons in terms of the idea of "counting in favor of": "facts give us reasons ... when they count in favor of our having some attitude, or our acting in some way" (I, 31). In effect, though Parfit does not quite say so, reasons are therefore *relational* in nature. They consist in the relation of counting-in-favor-of in which facts in the world (including psychological facts about our own mental states) stand to our possibilities of thought and action. Relations depend on their relata. Thus, reasons are, as Parfit says, fact- or object-given. They also depend on our having the possibilities they favor – though these possibilities, it should be noted, are not simply ones we have, but ones we can choose to realize (rocks and trees have possibilities, but they have no reasons).[16] Yet relations, though they depend on their relata, need not be fully explicable in terms of the properties of those relata alone. So in this case: neither the facts that give us reasons nor the possibilities we thereby have reason to take up are (as a rule) normative in character, unlike the reasons themselves. Up to this point, Parfit and I are in full agreement.

Reasons exist, Parfit declares, since we cannot coherently deny the existence of normative facts in virtue of which our judgments about what we ought to think or do are true or false. Yet at the same time he balks at making any "positive ontological claims" about reasons, refusing consequently to call his position one of "realism" (II, 823) and preferring instead not only the term "non-naturalist cognitivism" but also "non-realist cognitivism" (III, 56). Normative judgments are not made true by describing or corresponding to some part of reality (III, 4, 59, 227). Reasons, he cautions, should be said to exist only in a "wide" and not in "some ontological" sense (II, 469, 479, 481, 618). What can Parfit have in mind with so perplexing a distinction? Surely something is amiss when he writes that reasons, like numbers, possibilities, and other supposedly less than full-fledged existents he puts on a List B, "exist in a non-ontological sense" (II, 481). (In philosophy, there may be, as J. L. Austin quipped, "the bit where you say it and the bit where you take it back," but the two do not usually come in such rapid succession). Let us look then at the philosophical concerns that drive him to such paradoxical formulations and that means at his efforts to explain the different senses of "exist."

Chief among these concerns is that reasons cannot be said to exist in space and time, unlike the more tangible things he puts on his List A – rocks, stars, and human beings – that do, he says, exist in an ontological sense (II, 464–487). Yet why should figuring in space and time serve as a criterion of full-fledged, "ontological" existence? Naturalism is a metaphysics, as Parfit acknowledges (I, 109–110) – that is, a supposedly comprehensive account of what there is, and only a metaphysics can replace a metaphysics. He should not therefore want his "non-naturalist cognitivism" to be a "non-metaphysical cognitivism" as well (II, 475). Actually, there would seem to be no difficulty in thinking that reasons

[16] As I explain in the next chapter, the intimate connection between reason and freedom lies precisely in our capacity of responding to reasons.

exist in time, as we can say that a reason obtains at a certain time or that it holds at all times. Space, however, is another matter. Reasons do not exist in space, nor do they have spatial dimensions. Since being in space would indeed appear to be a defining feature of anything "natural," anything physical or psychological in character, rejecting naturalism ought to mean denying to space a decisive role in determining the nature of existence. It is as though Parfit continues to let naturalism set the bounds of his thinking.

Parfit asserts that truths about reasons "have no ontological implications" (II, 486). But even in his favored, narrow sense of "ontological," this is not so. Since reasons depend on natural facts – on facts giving us these reasons and on facts having to do with our possibilities of thought and action – the existence of a reason in the "wide" sense would have to imply the existence of other things in the strict "ontological" sense. He groups reasons with possibilities and numbers, counting on the reluctance of his readers to grant that the latter two kinds of things exist in the same sense as rocks and stars (II, 475–487, 719–749). Reasons, he declares, do not exist in an "ontologically weighty sense," just as not only ghosts but also possibilities and numbers fail to do so (III, 60–61). Yet whatever we should ultimately think about the existence of possibilities and numbers (I leave that question aside), there are crucial disanalogies between them and reasons. Reasons are among the things that can be merely possible or that instead can, well, actually exist. This point Parfit acknowledges (II, 745–747), insisting nonetheless that reasons exist "not only in the wide sense, but also in a narrow *non-ontological* sense," the latter puzzling phrase receiving, however, no other apparent explanation than (once again) that reasons are not "part of the spatio-temporal world." As for the comparison with numbers: reasons, unlike numbers, only exist if certain natural facts (those on which they depend) also exist. Why does this dependence not indeed show that reasons and natural things exist in the same sense? Parfit, like Scanlon, his companion in an ontologically muted realism about reasons, and like many other metaphysically disinclined ethical "intuitionists" in the past, seeks to emphasize a parallel between judgments about reasons and mathematical judgments. But as we can see already (for more, see Section 6.7), the two are importantly different.

Indeed, insofar as a reason consists in a relation between one set of natural facts (those that give us that reason) and another set of natural facts (those possible sorts of conduct the first facts count in favor of), how can the relata be said to exist in the "ontological" sense but the relation only in some etiolated, "wide" sense – particularly if, as Parfit insists, reasons are not somehow constructed by us but are something objective to which we respond? Certainly, reasons do not exist *in the same way* as rocks, stars, and human beings do, inasmuch as they do not exist in space. But this does not mean that they exist *in some different sense* of the term "existence." To say, moreover, that reasons exist in the same sense as such other things, only not in space, does not imply that they exist in some Platonic heaven beyond the world here below. Reasons are nothing other than the import that facts in the world have for our possibilities, and they would not exist if there were not these facts or beings like us with possibilities they can take up. As I indicated in Chapter 1 (Section 1.4), I do think this conception may properly be termed "platonistic," in that it regards reasons as constituting, like Plato's Forms, a third, irreducibly normative dimension of reality in addition to the domains of physical and psychological fact. And I do not deny that few philosophers will be inclined to accept this metaphysical conception, at least when stated in so explicit a fashion. Yet it is not, in my view, an irresponsible metaphysics. Nor is it "obscure," as Parfit likes to complain about any attempt to understand reasons realistically. Its defining concern is to take seriously three fundamental things that seem indisputably true about reasons: they are *normative* and *relational* in character, consisting in how facts in the world count in favor of certain of our possibilities; and they are *real*, existing independently of whatever beliefs or attitudes we may have in their regard.

Another concern leading Parfit to his strange views about existence is epistemological. If reasons existed in the same "ontological" sense as rocks and stars, acquiring knowledge of them would likewise have to involve some causal dependence on them (II, 502). Parfit considers it obvious that reasons have no causal powers. In order to protect his cognitivism against naturalist objections that knowledge of normative facts is therefore a misnomer, he denies that the causal theory of knowledge applies to this case any more than to the case of mathematical knowledge: "we can form true mathematical and normative beliefs without being causally affected by what these beliefs are about" (II, 492).

There are a number of problems with this strategy, as I shall detail later (Section 6.8). For now, I will note several key points. One is that much is to be said for the general validity of a causal theory of knowledge. To know that *p* is not simply to have the true belief that *p* (which could be but luck), but to have that true belief *in virtue of* the fact that *p* is the case. This was no doubt the assumption of the Eleatic Stranger in Plato's *Sophist* who claimed that a mark of what is real, of what can be an object of knowledge, is that it be able to play a causal role.[17] A second point is that Parfit conceives of rationality as a matter of responding to reasons since reasons are objective or fact-given. Yet how can we respond to reasons without thereby being causally dependent on them? He suggests that God or evolution might have given us brains with which we can arrive at truths about reasons without any causal contact with them, just as computers can be designed to produce true answers to mathematical questions without being causally affected by numbers (II, 493–499). But having beliefs that *correspond* to reasons (which is all these two hypotheses could capture) is scarcely the same as having beliefs that *respond* to them. Nor will it do for him to explain, as he sometimes does (I, 32, 47; II, 493, 515), responding to reasons as an awareness of the facts giving us those reasons that causes us to do what we thus have reason to do. This way of talking, as Simon Blackburn made plain in a review of Parfit's book, is perfectly acceptable to an expressivist such as himself who holds that taking ourselves to have a reason to do X means responding to the natural facts that – in the light of our desires and attitudes, he insists – appear to give us that reason.[18] For an objectivist such as Parfit, it must be reasons themselves, not merely the facts that give them to us, to which we respond.

Third, it is far from obvious that reasons cannot really be causes. In everyday life, we certainly suppose that they can be. Often, when judging people's moral character, we try to determine, not only whether they did the right act because of their belief in its rightness, but also whether they believed that it was right, not because of social pressure, say, but *because of the reasons* that made it the right act to do. So too, when we deliberate about what to think or do, we want our conclusions to be *shaped*, not simply by our beliefs about what there is reason to think or do, but ultimately by what are the reasons themselves to think or do some thing. It is true that it can appear difficult to understand how precisely reasons can act as causes, since ordinarily we assume that cause and effect have spatial locations. More on this difficulty later (Section 6.8). But for now it should be clear that if naturalism is to be rejected, some account needs to be given of how responding to reasons involves their playing a causal role in what we think and do. As I said, only a metaphysics can replace a metaphysics. Unless, that is, we take refuge in the sort of "quietism" that urges philosophy to steer clear of grand theories (but that in reality only keeps quiet about its own underlying assumptions). Surely Parfit must feel no sympathy for this way of thinking.

[17] Plato, *Sophist* 247e.

[18] Simon Blackburn, "Morality Tale," *Financial Times*, August 6, 2011.

Thus he struggles – without success, I believe – to explain how he can at the same time assert that reasons exist and yet maintain that they form no part of reality. It is not surprising that when he comes to grapple with Gibbard's quasi-realism in volume III of *On What Matters*, he is obliged to admit that there seems no significant disagreement between their views (III, 224). For Gibbard's later view also has its way of allowing that normative judgments are true or false while denying that reasons exist really, that is, independently of whatever attitudes we may have toward them. Parfit overlooks the naturalistic framework that fuels this account, a sign of how inadequately, despite his intention, he has himself managed to break with that framework.

A final point is that the idea of rationality as responding to reasons, an idea Parfit endorses but to which he is imperfectly loyal, points to a problem in his formulation of his Triple Theory. The Kantian Contractualist Formula on which that theory rests – "everyone ought to follow the principles whose universal acceptance everyone could rationally will or choose" – contains an expression he must regard as incomplete. What people can rationally will or choose needs to be explained in terms of what they have reason to will or choose. (A similar point can be made about the Scanlonian component of the Triple Theory, which relies on the concept of what people can "reasonably reject"). Attributing to the notion of rational willing or choosing a central place in the foundations of morality is a residue of that Kantian doctrine of the self-legislation of reason, which Parfit rightly rejects. In reality, the Kantian Contractualist Formula ought to be replaced by what we might call the Rationalist Formula: "everyone ought to follow the principles for whose universal acceptance everyone has objective reasons." Now recall that the principles in question are not maxims in the Kantian sense of policies, but rather the morally relevant descriptions of acts we might do. The Rationalist Formula could therefore be more limpidly stated (without the detour through "principles") as: "everyone ought to do those actions which everyone has objective reasons to think that everyone should do." This proposition is not trivial. It does not state simply that everyone ought to do what they have objective reasons to do. So the Triple Theory does not come to naught. But the Kantian basis of that theory now looks a lot less substantial than it initially did.

On What Matters is so long a book because of Parfit's ambition to put an end to the deep disagreements in moral philosophy. That ambition has not been achieved. As I have argued, he fails to take seriously the metaphysical task before him, if he is indeed to overthrow the naturalism he deplores. In this regard, I am tempted to say the book is not long enough! But as is shown by most of the critical essays in Peter Singer's recent collection mentioned at the beginning, there are many other points on which his views remain disputed. I think, moreover, that the aim of settling definitively philosophical disagreements is misconceived. The very nature of philosophy makes this goal unachievable. Philosophical problems are fundamental in character, ramifying through different areas of our experience, with many disparate considerations relevant to their solution; they are also cohesive, so that our judgment about how well any particular aspect has been handled often turns on our conception of the problem as a whole. The solution that recommends itself when certain elements are regarded as crucial can therefore easily look mistaken when the problem is approached from another angle, where different considerations are central. Whence what I have called in the Introduction "the law of conservation of trouble" in philosophy.[19] It is like when, in trying to lay a rug, we keep finding that various parts will lie flat only if there is a wrinkle in some other part. In philosophy, disagreement is inevitable. Think, after all, of what typically goes on in a philosophy department! Our ambition ought to be to lay out as best we can the view that on balance seems to us best, while recognizing that others are likely to disagree.

6.5 Scanlon on Reasons

The nature of reasons, one of the two principal themes in Parfit's *On What Matters*, forms the subject of T. M. Scanlon's more recent book, *Being Realistic about Reasons*.[20] Though their views on this subject are in many respects similar, Scanlon disagrees with Parfit on the crucial question on which I too have criticized him. It is the question of what is involved in holding that reasons exist. At the same time, Scanlon and I are ourselves at odds on this very matter. For the basis of his disagreement is quite different from the sort of platonistic theory I have proposed. A close examination of Scanlon's account of reasons, detailing what we share but also what divides us, seems then a useful way to explain further my own position. Despite the title of his book, Scanlon appears to me to fall short, just as Parfit does, of being enough of a realist about reasons. From my perspective, their

[19] See also *The Autonomy of Morality*, chapter 3, §5, as well as my analysis of reasonable disagreement in *What Is Political Philosophy?* (Princeton: Princeton University Press, 2020), chapter 3, §2.

[20] T. M. Scanlon, *Being Realistic about Reasons* (Oxford: Oxford University Press, 2014). In this second half of the chapter (Sections 6.5–6.9), all page references will be given in the text as parenthetical citations.

differences, though important, are ultimately of less import than their common failing.

One may miss how similar are their conceptions of the nature of reasons, given the great contrast in size and style their two books present. Scanlon's slim volume, based on his Locke Lectures at Oxford in 2009, numbers a bit more than a hundred pages, in contrast to the more than 1,800 pages of Parfit's magnum opus. True, a lot of *On What Matters* is devoted to questions in moral philosophy, which Scanlon mostly leaves aside, having laid out in detail a theory of the basic structures of morality in his earlier and now classic 1998 book, *What We Owe to Each Other*. Still, the nature of reasons takes up more than half of Parfit's massive three-volume work. The difference in length reflects the two philosophers' different ways of doing philosophy. Scanlon relies on fewer examples and does not put the ones he does use through a series of variations. Nor is he as keen as Parfit to settle every possible disagreement that might arise with regard to the problems with which he is dealing. In that, he is wise. He focuses only on those points of controversy that allow him to define more sharply the views he wishes to defend.

These are differences of form, however. In substance, their conceptions of the nature of reasons coincide to a remarkable extent. Scanlon too holds that reasons are irreducibly normative in character. The property of being a reason cannot be explained in terms of physical and psychological facts alone. It can only be elucidated by reference to equally normative properties such as, in particular, the relation of "counting in favor of." Reasons, we can say, are considerations – generally having to do with physical or psychological facts, but sometimes further reasons may be involved – that count in favor of possibilities a person has. No deeper sort of explanation is possible. Such is the position Scanlon calls "reasons fundamentalism." "Truths about reasons," he claims, "are not reducible to or identifiable with non-normative truths, such as truths about the natural world of physical objects" (2).[21] He should also have said, in case it turns out that the psychological is not reducible to the physical, that truths about reasons are not reducible either to truths about mental events or states or to such truths in combination with physical truths.

[21] Observe that this is not the same as the position sometimes called "reasons first," which Scanlon also appears to hold (see note 23) and according to which other normative concepts such as good and value are to be analyzed in terms of the concept of reasons. One might hold this latter view yet still believe, as some philosophers do, that facts about reasons can themselves be reduced to facts of a strictly naturalistic, physical or psychological, kind.

A reason to do X cannot therefore be equated, as Donald Davidson supposed, with the belief that doing X will contribute to the satisfaction of some desire or ours. Nor can the reason consist in the fact that doing the action will permit us to satisfy this desire, as in the more recent and sophisticated analysis developed by Mark Schroeder, which Scanlon criticizes in detail (4–7, 46–50).[22] For though doing X might serve some desire we have, there is a reason to do X only if, Scanlon rightly insists, there is a reason to satisfy that desire, the mere fact that we have some desire not by itself giving us a reason to aim to satisfy it. True, we cannot, I would add, desire something in the first place unless we see some reason to regard it as desirable, that is, unless we see it as good. This was, in effect, Aristotle's view,[23] a doctrine famously but wrongly rejected by early modern philosophers such as Hobbes and Spinoza (and countless others after them), who claimed that we regard something as good only because we desire it.[24] For no desire is simply a blind impulse. It is always a response to what appears to be some attractive aspect of its object. However, the reason we see to desire some object is not the same as a reason to satisfy that desire. That is why the fact that a certain action would enable us to fulfill that desire does not necessarily give us a reason to do that action. On both these scores, then, any analysis that attempts to reduce facts about reasons to non-normative facts about desires and the actions that would satisfy them is doomed to failure.

Thus, Scanlon, like Parfit, explicitly rejects the naturalist orthodoxy of our age according to which the only facts that truly exist are facts of a physical or psychological character, facts that fall within the scope of the natural sciences (17). I have already noted (Sections 6.1 and 6.4) how much I share this anti-naturalism. In my view too, reasons have an irreducibly normative character.[25] They consist in the way given facts,

[22] See Donald Davidson, "Actions, Reasons, and Causes," in his *Essays on Actions and Events* (Oxford: Oxford University Press, 1980), 3–19; Mark Schroeder, *Slaves of the Passions* (Oxford: Oxford University Press, 2007), 29, 59, 193.

[23] See, for example, Aristotle, *Eudemian Ethics*, 1235b25–27, and *De anima*, 433a27–29. Scanlon expresses sympathy (2, 34) with an account of goodness in terms of reasons. As he also indicates (87–88), *What We Owe to Each Other* argued as well that desiring something involves perceiving some reason to regard it as desirable. Schroeder tries to counter this argument by claiming (*Slaves of the Passions*, 156–159) that perceiving such a reason can be analyzed naturalistically as perceiving certain aspects of the object as "salient." Nothing is said, however, about just what "salience" consists in or why perceiving some feature of an object as "salient" does not rest on seeing a reason to think it important in some regard.

[24] Hobbes, *Leviathan*, I.vi.7, and Spinoza, *Ethics* III, prop. 9, scholium.

[25] In one respect, my understanding of their normative character may differ from Scanlon's. I regard (see Chapter 1, Section 1.3, and Chapter 6, Section 6.5) our having a reason to do X as tantamount

generally of a physical or psychological nature, count in favor of certain of our possibilities of thought and action. Reasons are not such facts in themselves. If they were, they would not be essentially normative in character. We can, after all, agree about the facts while disagreeing about whether they provide us a reason to do this or that, and when this happens, the subject of our disagreement is the normative import of the facts, that is, the question of whether they count or not in favor of various options. Sometimes we do say the rainy weather is a reason to take an umbrella. But this is an abbreviated way of speaking: more exactly, the weather gives us such a reason.[26] Facts give us reasons in virtue of standing in a certain relation to our possibilities, the relation of "counting in favor of."

It follows that reasons are not only normative but also, as I noted previously (Section 6.4), relational in nature. This is another idea Scanlon and I share. Reasons, he declares again and again, have a "relational character" (3, 4, 31, 33, 44, 120–121), analyzing the relation of being-a-reason-for as the four-place relation R(*p*, *x*, *c*, *a*), "holding between a fact *p*, an agent *x*, a set of conditions *c*, and an action or attitude *a*" (31). I have proposed basically the same thesis in claiming that reasons consist in the way that given facts count in favor of (constitute a reason for) certain of our possibilities of thought and action – which they do, of course, only under certain conditions. My own characterization has the advantage, I believe, of tying reasons to a person's possibilities, that is, to possibilities he or she can take up, since it thereby makes plain that reasons exist only for beings who are in this sense free, a fact to whose significance I shall return in this chapter (Section 6.7) and the next. I must also distance myself from the misleading sentence that "the relational character of reasons is most likely to seem puzzling if we focus on reasons *themselves*, that is to say the states of affairs, *p*, that stand in this relation to agents and

to it being the case that we *ought* to do X, all else being equal. Scanlon never says anything like this, and espouses, in fact, the contrary view that some reasons – for instance, the reason to listen to some enjoyable music – are essentially "optional" in the sense that they "render an action rationally eligible without making it rationally required in the absence of some countervailing reason" (107). I do not believe that there are reasons that are optional in this sense. Every reason tells us what we ought to do, all else being equal. It may of course be overridden by a stronger reason to do something else. But it can be optional to heed a reason only if there are reasons for some incompatible course that are of the same strength or that are, as sometimes happens (perhaps there is also a reason to go shopping), disparate enough to be "incommensurable," resistant to being ranked with it as better or worse or equal. In both kinds of cases, we ought to choose one of the two courses of action, but which one is left open. For this sort of view, see Joseph Raz, "Explaining Normativity: Reason and the Will," in *Engaging Reason* (Oxford: Oxford University Press, 1999), 90–117.

[26] I already discussed this point in some detail in Chapter 1, Section 1.3.

their actions" (120). This remark is indeed puzzling: How can reasons be relational if they are themselves simply one of the terms in the relation? What the relational character of reasons means is that reasons are not the given facts *p* as such, but rather those facts insofar as they count in favor of certain possibilities of ours. However, this is what Scanlon clearly has in mind when he defines the concept of a reason as "a consideration that 'counts in favor of' something for an agent in certain circumstances" (44).

Another element in Scanlon's account of reasons is also on the mark, namely his insistence that there is such a thing as knowledge of reasons. Whether the facts count in favor of this or that possibility of ours is, he argues (as does Parfit), a fact in its own right, not decided by our opinions on the matter, by our taking those facts to constitute reasons, or by our having an allegiance to particular norms or plans that imply that they do so. Our own opinions, decisions, plans, or norms may fail to match the reasons for belief or action we really have. Thus, he too rejects the expressivist analysis of judgments about reasons put forward by Gibbard and others (56–61).[27] As I noted earlier (Section 6.1), Gibbard's view is that judging that one has a reason to do X is not fundamentally to aim to describe correctly an independent fact, but rather to express one's commitment to a norm that permits or requires doing X. To think, as we often do, that this reason is something objective, that one would have the reason even if one happened not to hold such a commitment, is on this view simply to express one's allegiance to a higher-order norm requiring acceptance of the first-order norm. I explained in Chapter 1 (Section 1.4) why this analysis cannot work. It leads to an infinite regress. Only if one supposed that the higher-norm is not just a norm one accepts but is also correct (an assumption that the expressivist must interpret as expressing allegiance to a yet higher-order norm), could one think that the reason to do X is a reason one would have even if one happened not to believe so. Scanlon himself puts the solution perfectly. We need, he says (61), to "cut off the regress at the start by holding that when one makes a normative judgment one is claiming that this judgment is correct, rather than merely expressing one's acceptance of some attitude that supports it."

Reasons are, then, an object of knowledge, and as much so as empirical matters in their being such as they are independently of our attitudes toward them. Kant-inspired philosophers maintain that reasons can be

[27] He has little to say about Gibbard's quasi-realist turn except to criticize the fact (52, 57–59), correctly in my view, that in its analysis of normative judgments it continues to take attitudes of endorsement as basic, instead of judgings to be true.

truly objective without constituting objects independent of our thinking: facts give us reasons, they claim, in virtue of our rationality requiring us to treat them as doing so. Scanlon rejects this line of thought as well – he conducts a running debate with Christine Korsgaard throughout the book (7–14, 44, 100, 121–123) – and he is right to do so.[28] Such theories of the "autonomy" of reason make no sense, as I argued in Chapter 5. Our reason cannot determine by principles it "legislates" for itself what facts in the world will count as reasons, if only because it would have to see reasons to impose these principles on itself. And if, to avoid this difficulty, reason's fundamental principles are instead held to be, as Korsgaard has come to argue, "constitutive" of being a rational being – not seeking, for instance, to avoid contradictions or to adopt the necessary means in pursuing a given end is failing to think or act coherently at all – reason has still not been shown to be (as she supposes) the source of these principles. All this notion of constitutiveness can mean is that coherent thought and action are impossible without at least an implicit acknowledgment of the independent authority of these principles. Whatever reasons such principles point to will therefore have a validity likewise independent of our authorship.

Kantians argue that reasons can be conceived as having authority for our conduct and thereby (in Korsgaard's phrase) "get a grip" on us only in virtue of our rationality. This is true. But it is so simply because rationality consists at bottom in the capacity to respond to reasons. (See Chapter 5, Section 5.5, as well as Chapter 7, Section 7.1). Scanlon sums up the point well: "the 'grip' that a consideration that is a reason has on a person for whom it is a reason is just being a reason for him or her" (44).

6.6 Ontological Domains

So far, then, Scanlon and I are as one. But now I come to our parting of the ways. The divergence has to do with the question of what can be meant by saying that reasons exist. It will be remembered that this is a question on which I differ with Parfit as well (Section 6.4). Parfit rejects, as I do, naturalism as a false metaphysics, since there are not only physical and psychological facts but also normative facts involving reasons, indicating what we ought to believe or do. Reasons too exist. Yet their existence, he warns in the name of a "non-metaphysical cognitivism," should be understood only in a "wide" and not in an "ontological" sense. This, I complained, will not do. What it can mean to say that something exists,

[28] See also his essay, "How I Am Not a Kantian," in Parfit, *On What Matters*, vol. II, 116–139.

though not in an ontological sense, is, to say the least, rather baffling. Moreover, that Parfit regards as existing in "the ontological sense" only those things that form part of the spatiotemporal world, that is, things of a physical and psychological kind, shows that he has not really broken with the metaphysics of naturalism. Only a metaphysics, I have argued, can replace a metaphysics. We need a better, and that means a more complete, account of what there is if we are to do justice to the idea that reasons exist. After all, truths about reasons do have, contrary to Parfit's odd denial, "ontological" implications in his narrow sense of the term: reasons depend essentially on physical and psychological facts, differing in this regard from numbers, which he equally assigns to the shadowy realm of non-ontological existence. If reasons exist in virtue of natural facts existing, how can we not have to develop a comprehensive conception of what there is that encompasses them both?

Now Scanlon too rejects Parfit's notion that reasons exist in some "non-ontological" sense (24–25). What he wants to put in its place, however, is something very different from what I propose. He does not believe, as I do, that we have need of a more comprehensive ontology than naturalism allows if we are to make sense of there being such things as reasons. Instead, he contends that existence-claims are always internal to a particular domain of inquiry since it is the standards characteristic of that domain that settle whether such claims are true or false (19, 27). The basis for saying that this or that reason exists is thus no different in kind from the basis for saying that this or that material object exists. In both cases, our fundamental ways of talking about these sorts of things provide the relevant ways of establishing whether they exist, the appropriate method being in the one case observation and experiment and in the other, Scanlon says (whether this is adequate I will examine later in Section 6.8), "careful reflection" about what counts in favor of what (102). Viewed in this light, talk about the existence of reasons will cease to be problematic. Empirical reasoning about material objects and normative reasoning about reasons are on the same footing, a parity Scanlon seeks to underscore by showing at length how mathematical reasoning too is the way we determine what it is for mathematical objects such as numbers and sets to exist (19, 72–76). The supposed grounds for demoting reasons, like mathematical objects, to existing only in some "non-ontological" sense or to not "really" existing at all disappear.

On this account, there are not then different senses of "exist," as Parfit supposes. There are different domains, whose own standards suffice to determine whether the sorts of things with which they are concerned exist or not. In Scanlon's view, Parfit is not alone in failing to appreciate this truth. Naturalism itself springs from the desire to formulate a single picture of all that exists. Consequently, my contention that the metaphysics of naturalism needs to be replaced by a more comprehensive metaphysics would surely seem to him to be a surrender to the same temptation. A general, domain-transcendent conception of reality has no purpose. The "important and interesting metaphysical or ontological questions," he asserts, ". . . are domain-specific – questions about the metaphysics *of* some particular domain or domains" (25).

Scanlon ascribes his inspiration for this approach to a long-standing interest in the views about ontology that Rudolf Carnap laid out in a famous essay of 1950, "Empiricism, Semantics, and Ontology" (vii).[29] According to Carnap, our statements about some particular kind of entities, about what they are like and which ones exist, always presuppose a more or less systematic "framework" of rules governing which such statements are meaningful and what methods (logical or empirical) serve to establish whether they are true or false. Questions that can be settled by these rules count as "internal" questions. As for the "external" question whether such entities really exist, independently of what the rules of the framework happen to entail, Carnap maintained that this is not a meaningful question at all. "To be real in the scientific sense means to be an element of the system; hence this concept cannot be meaningfully applied to the system itself."[30] External questions are at best the confused attempt to raise not a theoretical but a practical concern, namely whether it is useful to adopt the framework in question.

One obvious difficulty for Carnap's position is that it can be very much a theoretical question whether the entities some scientific theory deals with really exist. Think of the debates about phlogiston or about the electromagnetic ether. Carnap assumed there to be a sharp distinction between theories and the far broader conceptual schemes he called "frameworks," in which competing theories can arise. He offered as examples of such frameworks the languages in which we talk about physical objects, numbers, or sense data. Yet is the distinction between them not instead just a difference in degree of generality? A purely practical, nontheoretical question – a matter of mere convenience – would be, for example, whether one should measure distance in miles or kilometers, since the results would be

[29] The essay is reprinted, slightly revised, in Carnap's *Meaning and Necessity* (Chicago: University of Chicago Press, 1956), 205–221.

[30] Ibid., 207.

factually identical. Insofar as alternative conceptual frameworks involve, however, more than just the use of different conventions, insofar as they are not simply different ways of saying the same thing, the question of which of them (if any) is true, capturing the way things really are, cannot be dismissed.

Doubts of this sort about whether one can clearly demarcate internal from external questions formed part of W. V. O. Quine's famous critique of the "analytic" and "synthetic" distinction, and Carnap mentioned Quine's criticisms in this very essay.[31] Similar doubts arise, I believe, about the use Scanlon makes of Carnap's views about ontology.

6.7 Reasons and the One World There Is

Following Carnap's example (19, 23), then, Scanlon holds that existence claims get their sense only within the particular domain of inquiry in which they are established. Fundamentally, we determine whether something exists by means of the standards appropriate to the kind of thinking in which we are engaged, and thus the significance of our conclusion lies in the role it plays in that domain. Seeking a comprehensive conception of the world understood as the totality of all that exists is, he claims, a metaphysically idle endeavor. "Genuine ontological questions are all domain-specific" (24). As a result, Scanlon rejects Quine's principle that it is our entire body of beliefs, taken as a whole, that defines our conception of what exists (23). For Quine, our ontological commitments consist in the things whose existence we find we must assume, the things we must quantify over, when we translate the entirety of our beliefs into the language of first-order logic.[32] Scanlon does not deny that we can, if we like, form such a "general idea of existence that applies to everything we are committed to quantifying over in a range of particular domains" (23). But this general idea of existence is "empty," he charges, since it serves no function: it does not provide us with any "domain-independent conditions of existence" for evaluating particular claims about what there is (25). Yet is this idea really empty? And can Scanlon himself really make do without it?

To see that he cannot, consider the important point on which Scanlon departs from Carnap's views about ontology. Carnap was wrong, he

[31] Ibid., 215n.

[32] W. V. O. Quine, "On What There Is," in his *From a Logical Point of View* (Cambridge, MA: Harvard University Press, 1961), 1–19.

argues, in maintaining that "the standards of a domain always have the last word on questions about the existence of objects that are quantified over in that domain" (19). Sometimes these standards are insufficient, and we have to bring in considerations from the outside. (This fact may be part of why he prefers his idea of a "domain" to the more exclusionary-sounding notion of a "framework.") Carnap believed that "external" questions about whether the objects satisfying a framework's standards really exist are misconceived: they wrongly suppose there could be some other basis for verifying whether those objects exist and should instead be reformulated as practical questions about the utility of the framework being employed. Scanlon's position is more complex. Claims made in one domain about what exists may have, he observes, presuppositions or implications concerning things said to exist in another domain. In such cases we must look beyond the standards internal to the one domain to ascertain whether the existential claims they license are compatible with those made in the other (19n, 27).

This eventuality seems indeed inescapable in the case of claims about reasons, since statements about reasons describe the normative significance of natural, that is, physical or psychological, facts. For example, the statement

(i) There is good reason not to pursue a certain social policy because it will lead to some very bad consequences.

is true only if we are right, not only about the way that consequences determine what we have reason to do, but also about the empirical fact that the implementation of the policy will have these results. In general, we cannot settle what reasons for belief or action there are by relying solely on the standards internal to the normative domain. We must ascertain by empirical means the facts on which the existence of such reasons depends.

Statements such as (i) Scanlon calls "mixed" normative statements, distinguishing them from "pure" normative claims, which do not, he declares, turn on claims about natural, non-normative facts (20, 36–41). Yet what he means by a pure normative statement does not conflict with the point I am making, namely that since reasons always depend on natural facts, what reasons there are can never be a question internal to the normative domain alone. Consider an example similar to one that Scanlon himself uses. The statement

(ii) Finding himself in a burning building, Jones has a reason to leave as quickly as possible.

counts as a mixed normative statement, since it combines the attribution to Jones of a reason with the assertion that Jones happens to find himself in a certain physical situation, claiming that the first is true because the second is so. Take, however, the statement

(iii) If Jones finds himself in a burning building and remaining there would result in pain or even death, then he has a reason to leave as quickly as possible.

or the generalized statement

(iv) If anyone finds himself in a burning building and remaining there would result in pain or even death, then that person has a reason to leave as quickly as possible.

These, according to Scanlon, are pure normative statements, since their truth does not depend on the existence of any natural, that is, physical or psychological facts.

Presumably, Scanlon considers such statements to be normative in character because they are about reasons. Yet if they are about reasons, it is not in virtue of asserting the existence of any reasons, for they do not do so, any more than they assert the existence of any natural facts. One might indeed think that since they are therefore as much – in the same subjunctivized sense – about natural facts as they are about reasons, it is misleading to characterize them as "pure normative" statements, even though they manifestly differ in their existential implications from a "mixed" normative statement such as (ii). In any case, it should be clear that such statements still represent reasons as being dependent on natural facts, for they assert that *if* certain natural facts exist, *then* certain reasons obtain. Even if, in other words, there may be normative truths – if statements like (iii) and (iv) really deserve that title – that do not depend on truths about natural facts, it remains true that reasons themselves, when they exist, depend on the way things are, physically and psychologically speaking. And that means what reasons there are can never be a question to be settled by the standards of the normative domain alone. It always involves external considerations about whether certain empirical facts also happen to exist.

Not all domains of inquiry are like the normative domain in making essential reference to other domains. As Scanlon observes (21), reasoning in pure mathematics does not concern itself with the mathematical significance of empirical facts, as reasoning about reasons deals with their normative significance. Yet one should remember that the distinction between pure and applied mathematics was not well established until relatively late in the history of mathematics; until the nineteenth century and the development of non-Euclidean theories, for instance, the abstract spatial relations with which geometry deals were usually understood as at the same time characteristic of physical space. That the truth of mathematical statements is not in any way bound up with truths about the physical world is something we have learned about mathematics.[33] In general we cannot assume in advance, without specific knowledge to this effect, that the standards internal to a domain of inquiry are by themselves sufficient to justify the sorts of conclusions with which the domain is concerned. Whether and to what extent a domain of inquiry is autonomous has to be decided case by case.

Now if this is so, then there appear after all to be, contrary to Scanlon, "domain-independent conditions of existence" that the existential claims made in any domain, however well they satisfy its own standards, must also meet. They stand under the general requirement of having to cohere with the existential claims made in every other relevant domain of inquiry. When there is conflict, revision may sometimes prove necessary on both sides. The result is therefore not very different from Quine's view that our ontological commitments are to be reckoned by considering our body of beliefs as a whole, mutually or "holistically" (as he would say) adjusted to one another. Quine may have favored an ontology geared to the makeup of the physical world alone, but the naturalist assumption that empirical science is the measure of all things forms no necessary part of his notion of ontological commitment. Its essential idea is instead that questions about what there is cannot as a rule be settled from within the ambit of any particular domain of inquiry. In order to make plausible his domain-specific kind of realism about reasons, Scanlon tries to push as far as possible a parallel between mathematical and normative statements (23, 26, 28, 70). But with regard to ontological matters, this parallel quickly shows its limits. The existence of mathematical objects is, as we now know, decided by mathematical reasoning alone. But in the case of normative reasoning, a general, domain-transcendent idea of existence, encompassing both empirical facts and facts about reasons, plays an indispensable role in determining what reasons there can be said to be.

33 On the relatively recent appearance of the distinction between pure and applied mathematics, see Morris Kline, *The Loss of Certainty* (Oxford: Oxford University Press, 1982), 87–88, 278–282, and also Ian Hacking, *Why Is There Philosophy of Mathematics at All?* (Cambridge: Cambridge University Press, 2014), 144–164.

From this conclusion it follows that if we understand by "the world" the totality of what exists, the question of how the world can contain both empirical facts and facts about reasons is, contrary to Scanlon (23f.), a significant and inescapable question. What it means to say that reasons exist cannot be explained solely in terms of the methods of normative reasoning. The explanation must also show how they connect more broadly with various aspects of physical and psychological reality. In two respects, this should be easy to see. First, reasons depend for their existence on empirical facts. They consist, as I have said, in the way that physical or psychological facts count in favor of certain of our possibilities of thought or action. But the need for an overall conception of the world to make sense of the existence of reasons does not stop there. As this formulation also indicates, there can be reasons only if there exist beings like us who have, not simply possibilities (as do rocks and trees, which can also be otherwise than they are), but possibilities they can choose. In other words, reasons exist only insofar as there exist beings who are free, able to take up certain ways of being, certain lines of thought or action, in preference to others. In a world without any free beings, or in the actual world conceived apart from the free beings it happens to contain, there would be no such things as reasons. What I have called their relational character – their connecting given facts to the possibilities of self-determining beings – shows by itself that the nature of reasons cannot be understood without seeing how they fit into the world as a whole.

Certainly more needs to be said about each of these points. Can, for instance, empirical facts give rise to reasons on their own or only in conjunction with underlying principles of thought or action? And are the reasons for belief or action we can be assumed to have at a given time limited, as Bernard Williams famously held, to possibilities we could then take up by deliberating soundly on the basis of our existing beliefs and interests? Or may they extend as well to possibilities we would only be able to grasp and choose were we to undergo fundamental changes in our thinking by means other than deliberation, for instance by training? I will not pursue these questions here.[34] Instead, I want to call attention to a further, less obvious way in which understanding what it is for there to be such things as reasons involves placing them within a general

[34] In *What Is Political Philosophy?*, chapter 1, §7, I argue that reasons do not necessarily rest on underlying principles. And for criticism of Williams's claim that the only reasons that exist are "internal" (in the sense indicated), see Chapter 1, Section 1.3.

conception of the world. It has to do with explaining how it is that that we can have knowledge of reasons.

6.8 Being Moved by Reasons

In the case of empirical claims, some sort of causal theory of knowledge appears in order: we can be said to know some fact only if that fact plays a causal role in our coming to know it. For instance, something observed (say, the length of a flagpole's shadow) can count as evidence for a belief (concerning the height of the flagpole itself) only if it depends causally on what the belief holds to be true. Both the facts known and our knowledge of them have thus their place in the universal causal order. If knowledge of facts about reasons fits the same pattern, then understanding the nature of reasons requires placing them too within this general conception of the world. Now to many – both naturalist philosophers and opponents of naturalism such as Scanlon – this sort of conclusion seems to pose an insuperable metaphysical problem: How can we interact causally with things such as reasons that, being normative, have no spatial location? It makes no sense to suppose that reasons occupy some place in space, as we believe that physical and psychological entities or processes must do if they are to act causally on other things.[35] This difficulty encourages in turn the adoption of various subjectivist views (such as expressivism) according to which reasons are not, properly speaking, objects of knowledge at all – views that, at least in Scanlon's eyes (as in mine), are also difficult to endorse.

It is in order to break this "cycle," as he puts it (71), that Scanlon is keen to recommend the virtues of his domain-specific idea of existence. We come to know facts about reasons, he argues, simply by thinking about them "in the right way" (70), that is, by reasoning in accord with the appropriate standards for ascertaining what beliefs or actions certain facts count in favor of and then making sure that our conclusions are compatible with our thinking in other domains. We have no need to suppose that our conclusions depend causally on the reasons they are about, a conviction he shares with Parfit.[36] Here, therefore, a causal theory of knowledge does not apply, as it does in the domain of empirical reasoning (22, 70, 83, 85). Some reasons we discover by deriving them from other reasons we

[35] As I noted earlier (Section 6.4), there would appear to be no difficulty in ascribing to reasons location in time, for we talk of reasons as applying at a certain time or as applying at all times.

[36] Parfit, *On What Matters*, II, 488–503.

assume we have, as when we realize we should adopt a certain course of action because it is the best means to achieving some end we believe we should pursue (101). Other reasons are basic or "non-derivative," yet these too, Scanlon claims, are known by way of reasoning, that is, "by thinking carefully about what seem to us to be reasons, considering what general principles about reasons would explain them, what implications these would have, and considering the plausibility of the implications of these principles" (102). Overall, he says, "careful reflection is the only way we have of arriving at conclusions about reasons for action" (102). Presumably, he would say the same about reasons for belief.

There are two important and related weaknesses in this account of normative knowledge. The first is its over-intellectualized picture of how reasons for belief or action can be grasped. When we are stopped at a traffic light and it turns green, we normally take this right off as a reason to go, without having to engage in any reasoning other than that most elementary sort which consists in just seeing something (such as a light change) as a reason to do this or that. To be sure, we can check our reaction by the step-by-step sort of reasoning that Scanlon describes. So too, we must sometimes pause before acting and reflect about what there is reason to do in a given situation, and then as well we reason in the ways he mentions. And when confronted with the philosophical question of why we should suppose that reasons can be an object of knowledge, we certainly consider which of our various judgments about reasons are really sound and what general principles could plausibly account for them, reasoning back and forth between judgments and principles in order to remove discrepancies and to bring them, as he says (71, 76ff), into "reflective equilibrium." But when in most cases we see a reason to think or act in some way, we do so without much reasoning and without reflecting at all. We simply respond to the situation at hand.[37] I believe that Scanlon was led to his distorted picture by likening so closely the grasping of reasons to mathematical judgments, and in particular, as he repeatedly does, to those in a systematic discipline such as set theory.

Now if often we see we have a reason to do something by simply responding to the situation before us, how is this sort of knowledge of reasons to be explained? Naturally, we ourselves have to have had the sort of experience and training that enable us to react appropriately. But if it is a case of knowledge, if we are indeed responding to the reason the situation gives us to react in that way, then the situation's really giving us that reason must also play a part. In

[37] I say a bit more about this point in note 24 of Chapter 7.

general, what we respond to figures among the causes of our response. Moreover, my point is not merely a result of my choice of vocabulary. It would equally hold if, instead of talking about "responding" to reasons, I spoke, for instance, less vividly of "recognizing" reasons. We cannot count as recognizing something unless its actually being there plays a part in accounting for – that is, in bringing about – our recognition of it. Otherwise, it is only a case of imagining, hallucinating, or projecting that the thing is there. How then can this quasi-perceptual knowledge of reasons be understood if not by supposing that, just as in the case of empirical knowledge, the facts known – in this case the reasons we grasp – play a causal role in our coming to know them? Does this not mean that reasons can be causes and have therefore their place in the causal order of the world?

A second weakness in Scanlon's account, concerning now the reflective knowledge of reasons itself, points in the same direction. This knowledge too is ultimately intelligible only on the assumption that reasons play a causal role in its acquisition. According to Scanlon, we come to know we have a reason to think or do something by reasoning correctly on the basis of the appropriate standards for determining what count as reasons for belief or action. But this explanation does not go deeply enough. The question remains of what it is to come to know this fact by way of such reasoning, and the answer has to be that we do so in response to the reasons it refers to. For if we conclude correctly on the basis of those standards that we have good reason to think or do something, our conclusion, if rational, must be shaped, not merely by an argument that happens to be sound, but by the very soundness of that argument. We cannot, of course, be moved by its soundness unless we perceive it to be sound. But our perceiving it to be sound has to be due to its actually being so, if we are to count as grasping its soundness and thus as knowing its conclusion to be true, namely that we have a reason to do a certain thing. Just thinking that the argument – that is, the application of the relevant standards – is sound, without its soundness being what impels us to think so (if, for instance, we take it to be sound because someone important tells us it is), does not suffice, even if the argument happens to be sound. Now to say that we are impelled by the soundness of the argument to accept its conclusion is as much as to say that the reasons the argument adduces (for why we have a reason to do this or that) and thus that reason itself move us to accept the conclusion that we should do the thing in question.[38] So in

[38] Ralph Wedgwood develops this point nicely in *The Nature of Normativity* (Oxford: Oxford University Press, 2007), 184–192. Earlier, in Chapter 4, Section 4.2, I made the same point

those cases too in which we determine by reflection that we have reason to do something, cases that Scanlon wrongly takes for the whole, reasons have to be understood as able to play a causal role in the formation of belief.

In general, rationality would be an illusion if we could not be moved by reasons themselves. For being rational consists fundamentally in being able to be guided by reasons that count in favor of possibilities we have.[39] Many of the most important activities we engage in – deliberation, conversation, and self-analysis – require us to conceive of ourselves explicitly as rational beings in just this basic sense, that is, as beings whose beliefs and desires can be shaped, not merely by what we regard as reasons, but by the actual reasons that favor one thing rather than another. When, for instance, we deliberate about what we should think or do, we do not appeal to our beliefs as such about why we should choose this or that possibility. (Why should our simply believing something carry any weight at all?) We appeal to what these beliefs are about, namely to the reasons themselves that justify a certain conclusion, for it is by them that we want our decision to be determined. So too in a genuine conversation, where the subject under discussion is what matters. We want the exchange to be governed, not by the mere voicing of opinions nor by the craving to win an argument and certainly not by the hankering to make an impression, but rather by the participants providing one another good reasons to hold this or that view about the subject.

Finally, when we are trying to get clear about our motivations in acting as we did, we certainly want to know, if we suppose we acted rightly, whether we did the right action because we believed it was right and not for some other motive. But we also want to know whether we believed it to be right, not because we were patterning ourselves on the opinions of others, which happened to be correct, but because of the very reasons that made it the right thing to do. "The greatest treason," we may think (with T. S. Eliot's Thomas Becket), would be "to do the right deed for the wrong reason."[40] The same point holds for our moral evaluation of others. We need to determine whether they acted correctly. But we also want to know

against Ronald Dworkin's attempt to maintain that moral knowledge rests on sound arguments without their soundness, and thus without moral reasons ("morons," as he ridiculed them), having to be causally responsible for this knowledge.

[39] In *The Domain of Reasons* (Oxford: Oxford University Press, 2010), chapters 16–17, John Skorupski appears to deny this point, holding that our normative knowledge involves no element of "receptivity" to reasons themselves, which therefore do not form part of reality. Yet how this "cognitivist irrealism" can nonetheless maintain that we have knowledge of "mind-independent truths about moral obligations and rational requirements" (487) is a mystery.

[40] T. S. Eliot, *Murder in the Cathedral*, lines 667–668.

whether they did the right action, not simply because they believed it was right (their belief due perhaps to social pressure), but for the reason itself that made it the right action. Nothing could be further from the truth than to think, as Russ Shafer-Landau has written, that "moral facts" – that is, facts involving moral reasons – "don't have an ineliminable role to play in the explanation of empirical events."[41]

Talk of being moved by reasons, not simply by our beliefs about them, to think this or to do that forms an essential part of everyday discourse. Scanlon himself used the phrase, quite naturally, in his earlier book on *What We Owe to Each Other*: "A rational creature is, first of all, a reasoning creature – one that has the capacity to recognize, assess, and be moved by reasons."[42] But as the examples just mentioned illustrate, such talk is not purely metaphorical. Our ordinary self-understanding turns on the possibility that what we think and do can really be shaped by the relevant reasons and thus on the idea that reasons can be causes. Despite the title of his later book, Scanlon does not seem to me to be realistic enough about reasons.[43]

6.9 A Better Metaphysics

It appears therefore that a causal theory of knowledge, the idea that knowledge involves a causal dependence on the fact known, is not so ill-suited to the domain of reasons as Scanlon supposes.[44] The preceding remarks also underscore, more broadly, how making sense of what reasons are requires understanding their place within the world as a whole and in particular within its causal order. However, this conclusion forces us to face the difficult metaphysical problem I mentioned earlier: How can reasons act as causes? To appreciate the problem, it is important to keep in mind the difference between reasons and our ideas of them. There is no

[41] Shafer-Landau, *Moral Realism*, 115. In this book he holds that the explanatory role of moral facts is limited to determining the moral status of actions or events in the empirical world.

[42] Scanlon, *What We Owe to Each Other* (Cambridge, MA: Harvard University Press, 1998), 23. See also 156, 159.

[43] I have a similar view of the "robust realism" about reasons presented in David Enoch's *Taking Morality Seriously* (Oxford: Oxford University Press, 2011), despite his admirable determination to pursue, without the compromises of philosophers such as Parfit and Scanlon, the non-naturalistic metaphysics involved in holding that reasons exist independently of our attitudes or desires (4). For he too declines to allow that reasons can act as causes (7), even though recognizing that in our thought and action we can respond, not just to our beliefs about reasons, but to reasons themselves (220, 236). His robust realism does not, therefore, seem to me robust enough.

[44] I leave aside the question whether the same conclusion holds for mathematical knowledge, though I suspect that it does.

special difficulty in explaining how our ideas of reasons, being psychological in character, can move us to think and act in particular ways. They do so in the same way that all our beliefs do. Reasons themselves, though, are not beliefs, but rather the possible objects of beliefs. They are neither psychological nor physical in nature, even if they consist in how psychological or physical states of affairs count in favor of certain of our possibilities. Reasons are normative, pointing to what we ought to think or do, all else being equal. It makes no sense to imagine them having some spatial location, something that forms an essential precondition for physical and psychological entities and processes to have the causal efficacy they do. How then can reasons be said to have a causal effect on us, to move us to think and act in the appropriate ways? I have argued that our ordinary self-understanding assumes that they do. Yet is that self-understanding really intelligible?

I believe it is. In Chapter 7 (Section 7.6), I present a detailed justification. Here, in conclusion, I want just to sketch in broad strokes how it is that reasons can be causes. The key lies in the very nature of reasons: although irreducibly normative in character, they depend essentially on the physical and psychological facts in whose relevance for our possibilities of thought and action they consist. If reasons can move us to think and act, it is in virtue of the (far less problematic) way the natural facts that underlie them affect what we do. This does not mean that we are then impelled by the natural facts alone to think and act as we do (see Section 6.4). On the contrary, they exercise their influence only through our conception of the reasons they give us. And if they indeed give us the reasons we believe they do, then they thereby enable these reasons themselves to determine what we do. Without their agency, reasons would remain without any impact on our conduct. It is therefore not only the existence but also the capacity of reasons to move us that depend on our relation to natural facts in the world.

It may be felt that this account of the causality of reasons solves the difficulty only in part. I have been arguing that reasons move us insofar as the natural facts that give rise to them, through our correctly understanding that they do so, play a causal role in shaping what we think and do. Yet surely – so the objection – it does not suffice, if the reasons are to count as moving us, that we just happen to have a correct conception of what they are. Our conception of them must also depend on there being such reasons. That is, it must not merely correspond to what they are like; it has to be due to what they are like, as I was myself at pains to underscore earlier (Section 6.8), and this sort of causal dependence remains to be explained.

I think the objection misses its mark. If correctly grasping that the facts constitute reasons does not simply accompany the way the facts influence our thought and action, but forms instead part of this very way, then our understanding of the reasons is not merely correct. Its correctness is shaped by what makes it correct, namely those facts *insofar as* they give us the reasons in question. An example formulated without explicit reference to reasons may help to make the point more tangible. If you understand that my turning on the light would be a signal to come and you then come when you see me turn on the light, my giving you the signal counts as a cause of your coming. As this example makes plain, there does lie a general assumption behind the argument I am making. I am assuming that if a fact leads us to do something because of the significance we rightly recognize it to have, then its having that significance is a cause of what we do. I do not pretend that this assumption does not call for further philosophical exploration. I am offering here only a sketch. But it does form an essential ingredient of our everyday explanation of human action, and against its backdrop the way that reasons can act as causes becomes intelligible.

In sum, I do not believe, as Scanlon does, that we can understand how there can be such things as reasons without situating them in the totality of what exists. Nor do I believe that we can make sense of how we come to acquire knowledge of reasons except by understanding their place in the causal order of the world. I join with Scanlon in rejecting the metaphysics of naturalism. But, I repeat again, only a better metaphysics, and one that also aims to be comprehensive, can replace it. To take this truth seriously is, in my view, what it means to be truly realistic about reasons. More of this better metaphysics is developed in the following chapter.

CHAPTER 7

The Conditions of Human Freedom

In his *Fourth Meditation*, Descartes defines the essence of human freedom in terms that, somewhat modified, could serve as the motto for this chapter. "In order to be free," Descartes writes,

> there is no need for me to be capable of going in each of two alternative directions *(in utramque partem)* [i.e., to do or not to do a certain thing]. On the contrary, the more I incline in one direction – either because I clearly understand the reason why it is true and good (*rationem veri et boni in ea evidenter intelligo*) or because God so disposes my inmost thoughts (*intima cogitationis meae ita disponit*) – the more freely I choose that path (*tanto liberius illam eligo*).[1]

A first thing to modify is the idea of God possibly affecting the operations of the human mind, an eventuality that I believe we, in contrast to Descartes and his contemporaries, can leave aside. We can replace, however, this idea with a somewhat similar one that is of present-day relevance, namely the idea that our grasping the reason why one of the options is true or better is shaped by the causal order of nature, that is, by the system of antecedent physical and psychological causes. And if, to modify Descartes' formulation in a second regard, this eventuality is understood, not as contrary to our normal way of grasping such a reason, but instead as part of its very explanation, then there results the conception of human freedom I intend to defend in the following reflections. In order to be free, there is no need for us, in a given situation, to be able to choose each of two alternative possibilities – to do or not to do a certain thing – or indeed each of a range of various alternatives. We need only to clearly see a reason to think that one of these possibilities is true or better, even if our thinking this is itself shaped by the causal order of nature.[2]

[1] René Descartes, *Œuvres complètes*, ed. C. Adam und A. Tannery, Paris 1897–1913, VII, 57–58.

[2] This conception is, in many respects, similar to the "actual sequence" view of responsibility or freedom presented by John Martin Fischer in *The Metaphysics of Free Will* (Oxford: Blackwell, 1994) and developed further in his later writings as well as by Carolina Sartorio in *Causation and Free Will*

This conception of freedom has therefore two components. First, it is *rationalistic*. Our thought and action are free insofar as we are exercising our reason and in particular are following our best understanding of the reasons relevant to the situation at hand. And second, it is *compatibilistic*. We are no less free if our thought and action also have their place in the causal order of nature, where by "nature" I mean here (as elsewhere) the totality of all physical and psychological facts, which constitute the domain of the natural (and explanatory social) sciences. Each of these components, however attractive it may be, faces, to be sure, some well-known difficulties. However, an even greater difficulty – since I believe the others are more easily handled – appears to me to lie in whether they can be combined, given what reasons are actually like. How can our thought and action be free in responding to the reasons there are and yet at the same time be shaped by the causal order of nature? The answer I propose to this question is what I consider the most important contribution of the present chapter. Among other things, it underscores the importance of the problem of how reasons can themselves be causes that I discussed at the end of the preceding chapter, and it will enable me to develop further the solution I sketched there.

There are thus two main aims I will pursue. I begin by elaborating (Sections 7.1–7.5) each of the two component theses – the rationalism and the compatibilism – in order then to explain (Section 7.6), as my ultimate objective, how human freedom can and must be anchored in both reason and nature. In the course of this argument, I will have occasion to connect the relation between reason and freedom with an equally intimate relation between reason and subjectivity, which I have developed in other writings, including the subsequent chapter of this book.[3] This means that the connection between freedom and subjectivity will also be a concern, especially in the last section (Section 7.7), where I discuss the role of particular "identities" or self-conceptions in our lives as free beings.

Before proceeding further, one preliminary remark. In speaking here of freedom and particularly of freedom of action, I do not mean the absence of obstacles that in the form of other human beings or external circumstances stand in the way of our doing what we would otherwise be able to do. The kind of freedom at issue has instead to do with our ability to

(Oxford: Oxford University Press, 2016). Both hold that free action is compatible with causal determination since its hallmark lies in being responsive to reasons and not in the ability to have done otherwise. I will have occasion to note, as I go on, some points of difference, however.

[3] See my two books in German, *Vernunft und Subjektivität* (Berlin: Suhrkamp, 2012) and *Das Selbst in seinem Verhältnis zu sich und zu anderen* (Frankfurt: Klostermann, 2017).

determine ourselves how we wish to act, that is, with what the philosophical tradition has often called freedom of the will. For the will, to give this often obscure concept a somewhat clearer meaning, is the capacity to choose between given possibilities of action, and it counts as free – speaking quite generally (the devil is in the details!) – to the extent that we ourselves determine when and how we exercise this capacity, in choosing what to do.[4]

7.1 Reason and the Reality of Reasons

In order to explore the connection between freedom and reason, I must begin by saying how I think reason itself should be conceived. As I have already suggested here and discussed before (Chapter 1, Section 1.3, and Chapter 6, Section 6.3), reason in my view consists in the capacity to be responsive to reasons. (I regard as quite significant the etymological tie between "reason" and "reasons," the Latin root "*ratio*" itself having both meanings, in contrast, for instance, to German's use of the unrelated terms "*Vernunft*" and "*Gründe*"). This conception of reason, as so far described, already differs from some well-known views, and the difference will only appear greater as I go over once again what in my view reasons are. It is, moreover, the essential character of reasons that, as I have also suggested, forms the real difficulty – far more serious than the difficulties usually raised – facing a compatibilist conception of freedom and nature. So our point of departure must be a closer examination of what reason itself is.

Reason, I have said, consists at bottom in the capacity to guide ourselves by reasons in whatever we think and do. Reason as responsiveness to reasons is therefore not to be conceived as one mental faculty among others, opposed to desire or (as in the German Idealist tradition) to the understanding. It is rather the foundation of all the operations of the mind, since our beliefs, desires, and feelings are essentially defined by how they are shaped and oriented by reasons, even if in characteristically different ways, and prove to be, to the extent these reasons actually exist and are

[4] One meets frequently with a distinction between freedom of action, understood as the freedom to *do* what one wants, and freedom of the will, as the freedom to *want* what one wants, that is, to have the desires one desires to have. However, this simple distinction is too simple to be viable. First, our freedom of action is reduced when others make it impossible for us to do what we would otherwise be able to do, whether we want in fact to do it or not. And second, it is also reduced when our will is unfree in virtue of our ability to choose being inhibited by some addiction, obsession, or other sort of inner compulsion. Freedom of the will as I understand it is thus one part of freedom of action in the broadest sense of the term. See Section 7.2.

relevant, more or less rational. I go through this foundational role of reason in some detail in the last section (Section 7.7) as well as in the next chapter. One remark to make here, though, is that it does not suffice, as often assumed, to define reason as our capacity to think and act in accord with general principles. For how do we determine which principles to accept, for which domains they are appropriate, and how we should then apply them in particular circumstances, if not by seeing reasons to answer these questions? More basic to the nature of reason than thinking and acting in accord with principles is the capacity to grasp and heed reasons. Principles invoke a specific kind of reason, namely standing reasons to think and act in one way rather than another that are sufficiently weighty to override competing considerations.

What I mean by a reason thus calls for explanation as well. Most of the previous chapters have already said a fair amount on this score. But it will be helpful if I rehearse the cardinal points. A reason consists in the way certain facts in the world – physical or psychological in kind – count in favor of one of our possibilities of thought or action. Reasons, therefore, in contrast to the facts that give them to us, have a normative character. If I have a reason to do something, this means that I *ought* to do it, if nothing else counts against it.[5] As the last clause indicates, a reason as such holds only *pro tanto*. It is not necessarily decisive, since, in light of other considerations, I may have a reason to believe or do something else. Only insofar as the fact that it is raining and that I normally prefer to remain dry is in question do I have a reason to take an umbrella, and the additional fact that my hands are already full may count against bringing one with me. This shows clearly how much reasons depend on the facts that give rise to them. All the same, they cannot be equated with these physical or psychological facts. The reason to carry an umbrella is not identical with the rain or the desire to remain dry or with their combination, since it consists in the way these circumstances justify that action or, as I say, count in favor of it.

Here is the point where this account of reasons comes into conflict with a ruling assumption of contemporary thought. For if reasons have an irreducibly normative character and if – as we ought to agree – our

[5] Sometimes a reason to do something may be sufficient without being so decisive that it would be right to say we *ought* to do the thing in question. But as I remarked in Chapter 6 (note 25), this is because there are several options all equally justified or too disparate ("incommensurable") to be ranked against one another. In such cases, we ought to choose one of the options, without there being a reason to prefer one to the others.

beliefs about the reasons we have are true or false, depending on whether these reasons actually obtain, then the world itself, as the totality of all that exists, must be understood as having a normative dimension. This means we must reject the prevailing naturalistic conception of the world, according to which nature – that is, the sum total of everything that is physical or psychological in character – is all that really exists. To many today, naturalism in this sense appears self-evident. (I leave aside the views of those who believe in the existence of immortal souls, spirits, and gods, since these things are not what is at issue.) It is nonetheless false. If we think through to the end the implications of our ordinary way of thinking, we will have to acknowledge that the world is not normatively mute, as this dominant world-picture supposes. Reasons form part of reality itself.

There have been a number of ways of resisting this conclusion. One is a strategy I canvassed in the preceding chapter. It is to admit that reasons have an essentially normative character and that they can be an object of knowledge, but to insist at the same time that they do not exist in a "full ontological" sense or that they do not belong to the same world as rocks and stars. Such is the view advanced in different ways by Derek Parfit and T. M. Scanlon – as well as by Ronald Dworkin (see Chapter 4). As typically happens with halfway positions, it wobbles and proves untenable. Reasons consist in the way that empirical facts count in favor of our possibilities of thought and action, and since knowledge of reasons means responding to the reasons there are and thus to the empirical facts that give rise to them, how can these reasons not exist as part of the same world as the underlying empirical facts?

The more common ways of rejecting a realism about reasons come from various versions of what remain the two main currents of modern philosophy, deriving from the paradigmatic figures of Kant and Hume. Subscribing to a naturalistic picture of the world, they each maintain, if in different ways, that we ourselves determine which circumstances in the empirical world are to be regarded as reasons for thought or action. In previous chapters I detailed why these two approaches as well cannot succeed.

Philosophers drawing inspiration from the Kantian tradition hold, in one form or another, that only in virtue of the "autonomy" of our reason do empirical facts in the world take on the status of reasons. Reason establishes what weight the facts of our experience shall have for our conduct on the basis of the fundamental principles of thought and action that it gives itself and of whose authority it is therefore, as Kant declared, the author (*Urheberin*).[6] If, however, we accept the principles we do because, as I have observed, we see reasons to do so, then clearly we are not in a position to prescribe, through the self-imposition of principles, what reasons there are. It is, moreover, the authority of these reasons that founds the authority of the principles they justify, so that it can hardly be said that our own reason is the author of those principles' authority. The authority of reasons and principles is normally something our reason must simply acknowledge. For it is solely in limited, circumscribed cases that we impose on ourselves, or "self-legislate" as Kant says, principles that otherwise would have no authority for our conduct.[7] And then we can do so only because we recognize the antecedent authority of even more deep-seated principles and reasons. I gave an example in Chapter 1 (Section 1.3): if I impose on myself the rule never to borrow, by which I would not otherwise be bound, I do so because I regard myself as subject to the principle that debts are to be repaid and because, given my unfortunate tendency to borrow beyond my means, I see good reason to counter this tendency by impressing on myself just such a rule. The Kantian idea of autonomy is unable to provide a comprehensive account of the nature and authority of principles and reasons.

Sometimes problematic talk of self-legislation is discarded in favor of another way of claiming that we are as rational beings the authors of our fundamental principles of thought and action. They are said to draw their authority from their being "constitutive" of any kind of coherent thought or action we may choose to do: we are not thinking or doing anything at all if we do not do so in accord with such elementary principles as avoiding contradiction and choosing what seem the most efficient means to given ends.[8] As I explained in Chapter 5 (Section 5.5), however, this Kantian strategy for salvaging the idea of autonomy also fails. Principles can be constitutive in the sense indicated without it following that our reason is in any sense the author or source of their authority. On the contrary, the fact

[6] Kant, *Grundlegung zur Metaphysik der Sitten*, Akademie-Ausgabe (Berlin: Königlich Preußische Akademie der Wissenschaften, 1902-), IV, 448. Henceforth most references to Kant's writings will be given in the text, citing the Akademie-Ausgabe (AA), as parenthetical citations. The one exception will be references to the *Critique of Pure Reason*, which will be to the original editions of 1781 (A) and 1787 (B).

[7] Kant, *Grundlegung*, AA, IV, 431: "The will is not merely subject to the [moral] law but subject to it in such a way that it must be viewed as also giving the law to itself [*als selbstgesetzgebend*] and just because of this *as first subject to the law* (of which it can regard itself as the author [*Urheber*]." I have followed, while modifying, the translation by Mary Gregor, *Groundwork of the Metaphysics of Morals* (Cambridge: Cambridge University Press, 1998).

[8] See, for instance, Christine Korsgaard, *Self-Constitution* (Oxford: Oxford University Press, 2009), 32, 67, 81, and *The Sources of Normativity* (Cambridge: Cambridge University Press, 1996), 235f.

that we are thinking nothing intelligible if we assent to a contradiction simply means that the principle of avoiding contradiction has a validity we must respect if we are to be able to think coherently at all. Constitutive principles are principles whose antecedent and unconditional authority constitutes the possibility of all coherent thought and action.

Philosophers in the Humean tradition also maintain that reasons form no part of reality itself but consist simply in a particular way we have of regarding the physical and psychological facts that alone really exist. In their view, however, our projection of reasons onto the world does not stem from principles that we, as rational beings, supposedly impose on ourselves. It has instead its source in more affective elements of the mind – in desires and feelings (as in Hume himself) or more generally in evaluative attitudes to which we are then giving expression. According to contemporary expressivists such as Allan Gibbard and Simon Blackburn, who advocate this latter version, normative judgments of the form "in light of circumstances C, anyone has a reason to φ" do not serve to describe reasons there really are, but instead express one's endorsement of a norm or preference to the effect that everyone, oneself included, ought to act in this way in response to C, even if they may happen not to want to.[9] Yet why, as I have also argued in previous chapters,[10] would one endorse this sort of norm or preference, and indeed as holding independently of whether one wants to or not, unless one believed one had a reason to endorse it thus? Here too, therefore, the foundational role of reasons has been overlooked. Bestowing supposedly the status of being a reason on normatively mute or value-neutral facts – be it through the endorsement of norms, the adoption of preferences, or the self-imposition of principles – would make no sense unless we saw reasons, already understood as valid, to do so.

What different, non-naturalistic picture of the world should we then adopt if we take seriously the idea that reasons form part of reality? Beginning in Chapter 1 (Section 1.4), I have spoken of a kind of *platonism*. We need to recognize that the world, as the totality of all that exists, contains not only physical and psychological facts but also normative facts about reasons, which, in their irreducibility to things of a physical or psychological nature, resemble Plato's Forms (which were also normative in character). No doubt, the term "platonism" will alarm many. And many

[9] Gibbard, *Wise Choices, Apt Feelings* (Cambridge, MA: Harvard University Press, 1990), 164–166; Simon Blackburn, *Ruling Passions* (Oxford: Oxford University Press, 1998), 67.

[10] See Chapter 1 (Sections 1.3–1.4) and Chapter 6 (Section 6.5). In the latter of these passages I discussed the "quasi-realist" efforts of expressivists to show how their account of normative judgments can be made to mimic, without really taking seriously, the idea that reasons exist.

will find it difficult to countenance the rejection of a naturalist conception of the world, Yet the platonism at issue does not seem to me extravagant. It draws on three elementary, indeed everyday truths we should not hesitate to affirm about reasons for thought and action. First, of course, reasons are irreducibly *normative*. But second, they are *real* in the sense that they exist independently of whatever attitudes we may have toward them. Our beliefs about the reasons we have are, like all our beliefs, true or false, agreeing or not with how they claim that things are. Third, however, reasons are *relational*: they consist, as I have said, in the way that empirical facts of a physical or psychological nature count in favor of certain of our possibilities of thought or action. They do not therefore dwell in some realm of their own, apart from the world of stars and stones, since they depend essentially on empirical facts being as they are.

Nor would they exist if there did not also exist beings like us, who have possibilities such facts can favor and who are thus capable of responding to reasons. In abstraction from the existence of beings with this capacity – and as I indicated in Chapter 1 (Section 1.1), the higher animals are included as well – the world would not contain any reasons. That is obvious. But once such beings exist, the world ceases to be normatively mute and contains a normative dimension, consisting in the relevance of various physical and psychological facts to the possibilities of such beings. Normative distinctions – between right and wrong, good and bad, justified and unjustified – do not come into existence by our doing, as though we were their authors. They come into existence simply in virtue of the fact that we exist.

7.2 Reason and Freedom

In thus spelling out the nature of reason and its implications for how we must understand the nature of the world, I have of course assumed that such a thing as reason exists. I will not seek to defend this assumption except to note that any attempt to challenge it, if presenting reasons why it should be rejected, contradicts itself. I turn now to the relation between reason and freedom and, after that, to the question of the compatibility of human freedom and nature. Only with these various pieces in place can we tackle the truly difficult question, which is how our freedom can be shaped at the same time by both the reality of reasons and the causal order of nature.

The intimate relation between reason and freedom is immediately evident when we recall that reasons consist in the relevance of certain phenomena in the natural world for our possibilities. For as I noted Chapter 6 (Section 6.7), the kind of possibilities involved is one whose possession makes us free beings. We are not the sole things in the world with possibilities. A stone or a tree, too, could be other than it actually is. But a stone cannot have a reason to change its place, and a tree cannot have one either, even though a change of location would be for the tree, in contrast to the stone, not merely possible but also good. Something can have reasons only if the possibilities (including those that would be good for it) that these reasons favor are possibilities it can take up – only if it is in this sense a free being. Naturally, there is the question of how accessible a certain possibility must be in order for it to make sense to say that someone has a reason to think or act accordingly. Must the person already be able to think or act in this way? Or does it suffice if the individual would become able to embrace the possibility as a result of new experience, or training, or even a change in way of life? I will largely skirt this important question. The exception is when, in arguing later (Section 7.5) for the compatibility of human freedom with the causal order of nature, I discuss the relationship between *ought* and *can*. For now, the key point is to see that beings capable of reason must be free beings, in that they must have possibilities that they can take up.

It is necessary to go a step further, however. If beings with reason are free in virtue of having possibilities they can see reasons to take up, then they must obviously possess the capacity to guide themselves by reasons in whatever they think or do. This kind of self-determination, to which I will return in Section 7.7, lies therefore at the heart of their freedom. For in the end it is up to us whether we let ourselves be governed by the reasons we may perceive. We cannot be moved by reasons without guiding ourselves by them. Heeding reasons is not anything merely passive, and whether we have acquired the necessary responsiveness depends on our having acquired forms of thought and action that we must also have seen reasons to adopt. Indeed, as I have already suggested, we guide ourselves by what we hold to be reasons in everything we think and do. In this elementary regard, we are, at root, free beings. This is so even if, as will shortly be made clear, our freedom is greater, the better our understanding of the relevant reasons.

Yet what about the inverse relation? Does freedom depend necessarily on the exercise of reason, that is, on our guiding ourselves by reasons? That it does – as I suggested at the outset in reference to Descartes – is straightaway clear if we reflect on how acting freely differs from compulsion. The contrast cannot lie in free actions being uncaused, as though they were purely chance events. They too have their causes, but their immediate causes – whether in the world or in our own mind – are mediated through reasons. Our actions are free insofar as we react to such circumstances in accord with our best understanding of the reasons we have for doing so, and that means that these circumstances are perceived as counting in favor of our actions and only thereby function as causes. Think of the simple difference between moving (freely) out of someone's way and being shoved (through compulsion) out of her path. Or consider a more complicated example, namely actions that are a mix of compulsion and freedom – for instance, those we perform as the result of a threat. To the extent that the threat makes us do something we would not in such a situation have otherwise seen any reason to do, our action is compelled; but our reaction to the compulsion represented by the threat counts nonetheless as free insofar as we could always have refused to comply, yet decided instead to heed the reasons to give in.

It is often said that we act freely when we do what we want to do. This common definition is inadequate, since our will itself, as in an addiction or neurosis, may be constrained by some inner compulsion that keeps us from acting freely by diminishing our receptivity to reasons or to the whole range of reasons that are relevant. Yet even then, our actions are not altogether lacking in freedom. An addict or a neurotic, however driven by his illness he may be, still must decide how to satisfy his compulsive urge. Insofar as he does so for reasons he sees as favoring one or another possibility, he is acting freely.

This fact points to a general truth. Not only is the extent to which we can do what we may want to do a variable matter, given circumstances being more or less favorable to our purposes, but our actions themselves are normally more free or less free. For even if we are not subject to some external or internal compulsion, our action is often not so free as it could be. When a false view or faulty inference leads us to see a reason for the action that does not really exist, or when such errors or simply our inattention prevent us from seeing stronger reasons for the same action or for a different one, these failures keep us from thinking and acting as we should – as we ourselves would admit if only we were aware of them. They keep us therefore from being as free as we could be. Our actions are fully free when they are determined by the reasons that are indeed most relevant in the situation. That was precisely the sort of case that Descartes was imagining in the passage from the *Fourth Meditation* cited at the beginning. I would add that our actions are also not fully free unless we would have acted differently, had better reasons existed for doing so.[11] We seldom act so freely as to satisfy these two conditions. This does not prevent us, however, from being in most cases responsible for our actions and from being appropriately praised or blamed. Responsibility in this sense is a social category, which requires that we act, so to speak, "freely enough." What that term means more exactly is a complicated question, depending on a variety of contextual factors. I will not go into it here. The important point is that acting freely is a matter of degree. Often we are inclined to say (and I will generally follow this practice) that someone has acted freely when she has acted in accord with her *best understanding* of the relevant reasons.

These remarks about the relation between acting freely and the exercise of reason can easily be applied, *mutatis mutandis*, to the question of what constitutes thinking freely. I consequently proceed to the next step in my argument. It concerns the relation between human freedom and the causal order of nature.

7.3 Freedom and Causal Determination

Kant's views on why actions, insofar as they are free, cannot be part of the causal order of nature will stand at the center of my discussion. (Contemporary views will be mentioned largely in the notes). That is because his writings contain some of the strongest and most frequent arguments that have been advanced in favor of the incompatibilism I reject. Focusing on Kant has the advantage of bringing out the connections between these arguments and thus the characteristic logic of the incompatibilist position generally. For he is by no means alone in holding that in order to be truly regarded as free beings we must possess a freedom that enables us, independently of all empirical conditions, to initiate through acting a series of events all on our own. Not only other "libertarian" thinkers hold that position but also so-called "hard determinists" who on just this basis deny the reality of human freedom. The analysis of Kant's paradigmatic arguments will make clear, however, that the real difficulty facing a compatibilist conception of freedom and nature does not lie where he and others suppose. The problem does not lie in the idea that our free actions are causally determined, but rather in the fact that, in order to be

11 Note that this is not the same as being able to act otherwise in the given situation while, recognizing the same reasons, a supposed ability that neither Descartes nor I consider to be essential to freedom.

free, they must be guided by reasons, for reasons themselves (Section 7.1) do not form part of nature.

In the *Critique of Pure Reason*, Kant remarks that there exists a kind of freedom that "can be proved through experience" (A802/B830). It is what he calls "practical freedom" or "free choice" (*freie Willkür*). "We know ... through experience," Kant writes there, that we have the capacity to resist sensory impulses, however powerful they may be, by relying on our idea of what is "useful or injurious in a more remote way" or also, as he would naturally add, of what is morally right. Formulated more generally, this freedom consists precisely in acting in accord with our best understanding of the relevant reasons, and Kant is surely correct: we each know, on the basis of our own experience, that we can act on the basis of reasons, be it through reflection, out of habit, or with a sense of the given situation.

This "practical" concept of freedom, however, is held by Kant to be inadequate since there remains the question whether the exercise of free choice is not itself causally conditioned. When we resist the force of sensory impulses, or whatever the options are like, and act as we think we are most justified in doing, our assessment of the relevant reasons and thus our decision may still depend on further factors that do not lie within our control. How can our action really be free if the way we judge the reasons for so acting is shaped by our character, our upbringing, and our social and historical context? Whence the concern, as Kant puts it, "whether reason itself, in the actions through which it prescribes laws, is not in turn determined by ulterior influences and whether that which with respect to sensory impulses is called freedom may not in turn, with regard to higher and more remote efficient causes, be nature" (A803/B831).[12] The only solution, he maintains, is to postulate a "transcendental" freedom through which we are able, independently of all empirical conditions, to begin a series of occurrences by ourselves (*von selbst*) (A553f/B581f) or more exactly "*all by ourselves* (*ganz von selbst*)," spontaneously (A534/B562; see also A445/B473, A448/B476, A533/B561).

Clearly Kant is assuming that freedom – our capacity to determine for ourselves how we want to act – and nature – the totality of all causally connected events and conditions, even in the domain of human history – stand in opposition to one another. He does ultimately intend to show how to "unite nature and freedom with each other" (A537/B565; also A558/B586), namely by assigning actions, insofar as they are free, to an

[12] In quoting from the *Critique of Pure Reason*, I have often relied on, while modifying, the translation by Paul Guyer and Allen Wood (Cambridge: Cambridge University Press, 1999),

"intelligible world" and, insofar as they are causally conditioned, to a "world of appearances." (Fortunately, I need not go into the complications or indeed incoherencies of this doctrine, since I see no reason to introduce an "intelligible" or transcendental notion of freedom in the first place.) Nonetheless, Kant must count as an incompatibilist. That is because he is convinced that our actions, insofar as they are truly free, cannot belong to the causal order of nature. At first glance, he may appear to be right. For normally we assume that an action is free when the person herself decides to do it and that it is on the contrary unfree when she is compelled by something outside of her to act in this way. How can an action be deemed an expression of our freedom if it is also a causally conditioned part of nature?

This question is often called the problem of "freedom and determinism." However, a couple of clarifications are in order. First, I do not mean the debate, sometimes placed under that heading, about whether our everyday "mentalistic" vocabulary of decision, deliberation, reasons, and freedom can or should be completely replaced by a neuroscientific theory of the brain if we are to understand the way things really are. That idea is, in my view, simply self-contradictory. After all, the scientific theories to which it appeals are presumably held, not because one supposes we are physiologically compelled to accept them, but because one believes they are supported by good reasons to think them true – a distinction that is dissolved by this sort of reductionism. It will not do to object that inquiry may proceed on the basis of an assumption (in this case, that accepting a belief as true depends on having what one regards as good reasons) that it ends up showing is actually false. For in aiming to show by argument anything at all, so even this, one has to assume that it offers good reasons to accept the conclusion. This is an assumption no argument, no philosophical theory, can coherently reject.

I mean, then, instead the problem whether our actions can still be regarded as free if the decisions we make on the basis of our best understanding of the relevant reasons depend, as Kant wrote, on "higher and more remote efficient causes." Consequently – and this is the second clarification – it does not matter for this question whether the causal order of nature, of which our actions may be a part, has a deterministic structure in which every event and state of affairs is a necessary consequence of antecedent causes. Even if certain causal relations (as in, for instance, the quantum mechanical conception of nature) are not deterministic, no one ought to identify freedom with causal gaps. For that must lead to equating freedom with chance, as though being free consisted in acting capriciously or erratically.[13] The key idea is not so much that nature is deterministic as that it is governed by a universal principle of causality according to which everything in nature occurs in virtue of antecedent causes, be they necessitating or not. For the question is whether we are then free when our decisions are causally shaped or conditioned by factors that lie outside our control. If I sometimes refer to the idea of our decisions and actions being "determined" by external causes, I shall not therefore be assuming that they must be determined deterministically.

Does the supposed problem really exist, however? Even if man, as Spinoza wrote, is not a "dominion within a dominion" (*imperium in imperio*),[14] why should nature not be conceived as the *support* of human freedom? Are the external influences that have shaped our capacity to act on the basis of reasons conditions by which we are then *compelled* so to act? Or are they not better understood as conditions that often *enable* us to act as rational beings, serving to develop and enhance our capacity to be responsive to reasons? If the latter is true, then there would appear to be no conflict. Let me formulate the point more precisely. If we are free to the extent that we are able to exercise control over ourselves and our environment, and if the abilities that enable us to exercise this control themselves depend in large part on conditions that do not lie under our control, then is not this sort of dependence, far from canceling the reality of our control or freedom, instead to be regarded as its presupposition?[15] Why should we suppose that, in order to be really free, we must be so free as to be some kind of *causa sui*? Even Spinoza, who begins his *Ethics* with just such a definition of freedom, applicable therefore solely to God, thought it appropriate toward the end of his book to introduce a more modest conception of freedom better suited to the human condition, a conception according to which the freedom of which we are capable is both causally shaped by external factors yet also responsive to reasons.[16]

Yet the opposite viewpoint underlies the efforts of many anti-compatibilist philosophers either to explain the possibility of freedom or

[13] Despite this well-known implication, some philosophers continue to identify freedom with causal gaps, as though they saw no other alternative. John Searle does so explicitly in *Rationality in Action* (Cambridge, MA: Harvard University Press, 2001), chapter 3. This is chiefly because he fails to recognize that freedom consists in being moved by reasons. See note 33.

[14] Spinoza, *Ethics*, Part Three, Preface.

[15] The kind of control in question, which consists in being guided by reasons, is what John Martin Fischer calls "guidance control" and is to be distinguished from what he calls "regulative control," which is the ability to act otherwise than one does and which, he and I agree, is not necessary for freedom. See Fischer, *The Metaphysics of Free Will*, 132f.

[16] Cf Spinoza, *Ethics*, Part One, Definition 7, and Part Four, Proposition 66, scholium.

instead to deny it. This is evident in two of the most familiar arguments that are commonly advanced in this context and that Kant himself often deployed. According to the "consequence argument" of Peter van Inwagen (who belongs to the first group of philosophers), our actions do not lie within our control if they are the consequence of past events and laws of nature that do not themselves lie within our control.[17] And according to the "basic argument" of Galen Strawson (who belongs to the second group), we can be responsible for our action only if we are responsible for the features of our character on the basis of which we act, so that we could only be free if we indeed had the nature of a *causa sui*.[18] Fundamentally speaking, the two arguments are not very different. Their common core appears already in Kant, when he writes in the *Critique of Practical Reason*:

> The necessity in the causal relation can in no way be united with freedom; instead they are opposed to one another as contradictory. For from the first it follows that every event, and consequently every action that takes place at a point of time, is necessary under the condition of what was in the preceding time. Now since past time is no longer within my control (*Gewalt*), every action I perform must be necessary in virtue of determining grounds *that are not within my control*, that is, I am never free at the point in time in which I act.[19]

To formulate the shared form even more abstractly: both arguments presuppose that if X does not lie within our control and Y is a necessary (or at least a causal) consequence of X, then Y, as well as what follows from Y, must likewise fail to lie within our control.[20]

This assumption may at first appear obvious. But when Y is precisely our ability to exercise control over ourselves and over our environment, namely by acting on the basis of reasons, both arguments lose their plausibility. The fact that certain things lie in our power is not compromised if the conditions for this control are not similarly in our power.

[17] Peter van Inwagen, *An Essay on Free Will* (Oxford: Oxford University Press, 1983), v, 16, 56. There exist in fact various versions of this argument, and I am presenting what I consider its most plausible form.

[18] Galen Strawson, *Freedom and Belief* (Oxford: Oxford University Press, 2nd edition, 2010), 24f, 291.

[19] Kant, *Kritik der praktischen Vernunft*, AA V, 94 (see too V, 96f). I have followed, while modifying, the translation by Mary Gregor in Kant, *Practical Philosophy* (Cambridge: Cambridge University Press, 1996).

[20] On the shared assumption of the two arguments, see Marcus Willaschek, "Inkompatibilismus und die absolutistische Konzeption der Vernunft," *Philosophisches Jahrbuch der Görres-Gesellschaft* 115 (2008), 397–417. The assumption is what John Martin Fischer calls the "Principle of the Transfer of Powerlessness" in *The Metaphysics of Free Will*, 8.

It would seem indeed a virtue of Kant's "practical" concept, for which freedom consists in acting in accord with our best understanding of the relevant reasons, that it allows for this ability to be causally conditioned in both its development and its exercise. For it thereby fits with our ordinary view that freedom is variable in its extent, depending on how much control we have become able to exercise over ourselves and the things around us. Kant, however, famously rejected a "comparative" concept of freedom in favor of a transcendental freedom that is obviously a matter, not of more or less, but of all or nothing (AA V, 96). This idea of a free being that, as Kant declares (but he is not alone in this thought), can initiate a series of occurrences all by itself, without having to rely on conditions that are not under its control, is nothing other than the fantasy of a pure self-mover that somehow – in any case, freely – generates its own freedom.[21] There is no reason to make such a fantasy, if it is even coherent, the cornerstone of a theory of freedom.

7.4 Acting and Knowing

To defend his incompatibilist conception of freedom, however, Kant also appeals, and indeed more extensively, to two further arguments, which are similarly representative. The first appears often in Kant's writings and is commonly considered, in fact, to be the basis of his account of freedom. It turns on his distinction between the *two standpoints* of action and knowledge. Already in the *Critique of Pure Reason* (A550/B578), without speaking explicitly of two standpoints, and then at greater length in the third section of the *Groundwork of the Metaphysics of Morals* (AA IV, 448, 450ff), Kant asserts that when we as agents deliberate and decide how to act, we cannot avoid proceeding "under the idea of freedom." We have to regard ourselves as free beings who themselves determine how they want to act. When we take up, however, the standpoint of knowledge – that is, the standpoint of theoretical instead of practical reason – we have to conceive of ourselves as part of the world of experience and, viewing then our actions, like everything else, as explicable in terms of their causal

[21] In modern times Roderick Chisholm, following Kant, turned this idea of a pure self-mover into the explicit basis of his theory of human freedom. According to his concept of "agent causation," we as agents are supposedly able to cause certain events without ourselves being dependent on the causal influence of antecedent events. See Chisholm, *Human Freedom and the Self* (Lawrence: University of Kansas Press, 1964), §11. However, the concept of agent causation, which has been defended by others as well, makes no sense, since it cannot explain why someone decides to act at one point in time and not at another.

connection with other empirical events, we can therefore no longer regard them as free. Even today the two standpoints doctrine, if sometimes under different names (for instance, the distinction between participant and observer perspectives), is often cited as grounds for being skeptical about compatibilist accounts of freedom and causation.[22]

The doctrine in question sets out from the correct observation that as agents we must act under the idea of freedom. When we deliberate about how we should act, we must assume that it is not yet settled how we shall act and that it is up to us to decide which of the possible actions we will do. The possibilities we see before us and among which we must decide have to be possibilities that in our view are left open by the given circumstances. For no one deliberates about what they regard as already determined.

In this case, however, as Kant admits, we need as agents to rely on no other idea of our freedom than that of free choice (*freie Willkür*), that is, of the capacity to act on the basis of our understanding of the best reasons that he calls "practical" freedom and whose existence is attested by our experience. Although he considers that concept of freedom to be inadequate, since the question arises "whether reason itself, in the actions through which it prescribes laws, is not in turn determined by ulterior influences" (A803/B831), this passage immediately adds:

> In the practical sphere (*im Praktischen*) this does not concern us, since in the first instance we ask of reason only a precept (*Vorschrift*) of conduct; it is rather a merely speculative question, which we can set aside (*bei Seite setzen*) as long as our aim is directed to action or omission.

Why then should this question subsequently turn out to be inescapable and impel us to adopt a deeper, transcendental conception of freedom according to which being free means, independently of the totality of empirical conditions, "initiating a series of occurrences *all by ourselves*" (A534/B562)? Why are we thus obliged to recognize that "it is this transcendental idea of freedom on which the practical concept of freedom is grounded" (A533/B561)?

According to Kant, this "speculative" question forces itself on us precisely when we switch from the standpoint we occupy as agents in the world to the standpoint from which we pursue knowledge of the world.

[22] An example is Jürgen Habermas, "Freiheit und Determinismus" in his *Zwischen Naturalismus und Religion* (Frankfurt, 2005), 155–186, and "Das Sprachspiel verantwortlicher Urheberschaft und das Problem der Willensfreiheit" (2006) in his *Philosophische Texte* (Frankfurt, 2009), V, 271–341. See also note 36.

For in seeking to know why we act as we do, we seem to discover that our exercise of reason, like any other empirical phenomenon, is in fact subject to "ulterior influences" and that our decisions and actions are determined by other events in the causal order of the world. The problem thus lies in how we can continue to assume that we are free beings when, taking up the standpoint of knowledge, we come to see how much we are a causally conditioned part of the world. As agents we proceed as though it is not yet settled what we will do, since it is up to us to choose which of the possibilities before us we will take up. How is that perspective consistent with what we learn about our actions in the effort to understand why we have acted as we did, recognizing that the course of our deliberation has been shaped by our experience and character and sometimes so much so that the conclusion at which we arrived is the only one we could have adopted under these circumstances? How can we believe at the same time that we have many possibilities and yet ultimately only one? In order to continue to think that we are free, we must attribute to ourselves, so Kant argues, a transcendental capacity of freedom that enables us to act independently of all empirical preconditions.

This argument involves a number of mistakes, however. One hitch is that the two standpoints of action and knowledge cannot be sharply separated from one another. On the one hand, the agent – and precisely as an agent – has to regard his actions as part of the causal order of nature. In order to evaluate the advantages and disadvantages of the possible courses of action open to him, he has to establish, among other things, their causal presuppositions and consequences. And when it is a matter of carrying out a more or less complicated action (writing a sentence on the blackboard as opposed to simply raising one's arm), he has to make sure to do each step in the process in such a way as to make the next step causally possible. Why then should understanding ourselves and our actions to be causally conditioned shake our conviction that we are free, if this kind of understanding belongs to the very standpoint that we as agents must adopt? On the other hand, the standpoint we assume in pursuing knowledge presupposes the same sort of "practical" freedom that Kant regards as integral to the standpoint of acting. Anyone who seeks to know how things really are assumes that it is not already settled what conclusion she will arrive at, since it is up to her to form her judgments on the basis of the evidence available. After all, making knowledge-claims figures among the actions that we do. How then can viewing our actions from the standpoint needed to know what they are like undermine our self-understanding as free beings?

However, the main weakness, which I must analyze in more detail, is this. The fact that our way of judging what we have reason to do is shaped causally by our experience and character does not entail that our actions are any less free. For it remains true that we are acting on the basis of our understanding of the reasons there are. Why is this "practical" freedom not all that freedom essentially means? If someone deliberating about which of his possible actions he should choose were to reflect at the same time that his way of deliberating is shaped by his experience and character, even to such an extent that the conclusion to which he sees himself coming is under the circumstances the only one he could arrive at, he would not be in conflict with himself. For it is not as though he could then cease deliberating and simply predict his choice by reference to these antecedent factors. No, he would still have to deliberate, since in his case experience and character exert their influence on his conclusion precisely through shaping the course of his deliberation. Naturally, he might also integrate his knowledge of them into his very deliberation, thereby altering his deliberative situation, and he would then no doubt deliberate differently and might even arrive at a different conclusion. Yet in this case, too, he would not need to be disturbed by the thought that this very way of proceeding was also a result of his character and experience.

It is also not true that such a person, as he deliberates and at the same time recognizes the determining influence of various causal factors on his deliberation, would have to say to himself, inconsistently, that he has several possibilities and yet only one. When he thinks he has several possibilities, he means that in advance of deliberating he is not compelled to carry out any particular one of these options. But when he thinks he has but one possibility, he means something different and compatible with the first thought: namely, that his deliberation, as it has been shaped by his experience and character, can lead him ultimately to choose only one of the available alternatives. If he is convinced that these factors, however much they determine the way he deliberates, nonetheless allow him to perceive the good reasons to act as he does and would – if there existed better reasons to act differently – steer him in their direction, what kind of freedom could he still wish he had? What else, as I argued before (Section 7.2), can it mean for our actions to be "fully free"? Should he lament that his will is determined by reasons at all and by what enables him to perceive them? Would not a will that was not so determined be, as Peter Bieri aptly says, "a nightmare, since this would mean that our will goes its own capricious way, whatever we may think"?[23] Or should he imagine that he would be still more free if, like a god, he did not have to rely on experience and character in order to grasp the reasons for belief and action there are?[24]

From this it follows that the typical thought of someone who believes her action is free – "I could act otherwise than I am" – is likewise compatible with her decision being causally determined. She means by this thought that she could act otherwise if she saw some reason to do so,[25] and her ability to grasp this reason, like her grasping the reasons for which she in fact acts, may well be dependent on her experience and character. What she does not or should not mean is that under precisely the same conditions – that is, without seeing any further reason to act differently – she could indeed act differently. For an arbitrary act of this sort would be purely random, a senseless movement that, far from being an expression of her freedom, would scarcely deserve to be called an action. A conception of freedom relying on this kind of being able to do otherwise (often termed an "alternative possibilities" conception) is just not plausible. We can of course decide, in a spirit of rebellion, to do the exact opposite of what we perceive good reasons to do. However, we are then acting in this way only because we see some reason or other to engage in a bit of self-assertion.[26]

[23] Bieri, *Das Handwerk der Freiheit* (München: Hanser, 2001), 81. In many respects my views about the essence of human freedom coincide with Bieri's as presented in his magnificent book.

[24] In order to bring out the point clearly, I have formulated the preceding argument by considering the case of someone who is deliberating. But it should be plain that the same point holds when, as we more frequently do, we respond to reasons, not by reflecting, but instead out of habit or through an immediate sense of the situation (see Section 7.3). That our habits of mind or powers of intuition are shaped by our past experience and other aspects of our character does not prevent them from being responsive to the reasons there are. It does not then make our actions any less free.

[25] I am thus adopting something like the so-called conditional analysis by which philosophers such as Schopenhauer (*Preisschrift über die Freiheit des Willens*, II) and G. E. Moore, *Ethics*, (Oxford: Oxford University Press, 1912, chapter 6) have explained "could act otherwise" as meaning "would act otherwise if one decided to do so." But I have formulated it more carefully than usual. Not only should the condition adduced consist ("rationalistically") in a perception of reasons rather than in merely a decision; also, the consequent of the conditional should be "could act otherwise" and not "would act otherwise," since the object of the analysis is an ability. The thesis is that being able to do otherwise, which the agent has in mind, is an ability that is solely conditional and not absolute: it is not, in other words, an ability compatible with everything in the given situation remaining the same (thus, with the same reasons being in place). When critics of the conditional analysis (such as Roderick Chisholm in *Human Freedom and the Self*, §3) object that the conditional "X could act otherwise if he ___" would also be true in cases where X is not able to satisfy the condition "if he ___" but where "X could act otherwise" is false, they are presupposing an absolute conception of being able to act otherwise, for only in this sense would the latter sentence then have to be false. That is, X could still have the conditional ability even if the condition is not satisfied.

[26] This is how Descartes analyzed the phenomenon in his two letters to the Père Mesland of May 2, 1644 and February 9, 1645 (*Oeuvres complètes*, IV, 111–120, 173–175).

Rarely are our actions *fully* free in the sense I have indicated. Often we fail to see, because of inattention or inexperience, the decisive reasons that obtain in the given situation, and even when we act on the basis of a correct understanding of the relevant reasons, we may have been unable to perceive better reasons for a different action, had they been available. As I have emphasized (Section 7.2), freedom is a matter of degree: we are more free or less free.[27] Yet to whatever extent our action may count as free, its freedom is not put into doubt if our understanding of the reasons for which we act is shaped by our experience and character. Nor is it true that an action, once it is viewed as an object of empirical knowledge, must lose any appearance of freedom it may first have possessed. To think otherwise simply presupposes that causal determination and freedom are essentially incompatible, and this assumption, contrary to adherents to the two standpoints argument, is in no way obvious.

7.5 Ought and Can

We come finally to the third of Kant's main arguments for the need for a transcendental conception of freedom, an argument that likewise belongs to the standard repertoire of incompatibilism.[28] It too appeals to an essential feature of the realm of action, though not to the prospective standpoint from which we act, but rather to the retrospective standpoint from which we judge the actions of others (or our own). Consider the passage in the *Groundwork of the Metaphysics of Morals* in which Kant clarifies why freedom is not really a concept derived from experience (*kein Erfahrungsbegriff*):

> All human beings think of themselves as having free will (*dem Willen nach als frei).* From this come all judgments to the effect that certain actions *ought to have been* done even though they *were not done.* (AA IV, 455)

The same line of reasoning occurs in several passages of the *Critique of Pure Reason*, as when Kant declares that "the abolition of transcendental

[27] In *The Metaphysics of Free Will*, 164ff, John Martin Fischer distinguishes between "strong" reasons-responsiveness, where a person would have acted otherwise than they did if better reasons to do so had presented themselves, and "weak" reasons-responsiveness, where this is not so, and he holds that only the latter is necessary for responsibility or acting freely. I prefer to say that freedom is a matter of degree and that someone who acts with strong reasons-responsiveness acts more freely, is more responsible for their action, than someone who is only weakly reasons-responsive.

[28] See, for instance, Peter van Inwagen, *An Essay on Free Will*, 161ff, and Geert Keil, *Willensfreiheit* (Berlin: de Gruyter, 2007), 10, 136–153.

freedom would at the same time eliminate all practical freedom." For, he continues,

> the latter presupposes that although something has not happened, it nevertheless *ought* to have happened, and its cause in appearance was thus not so determining that there does not lie a causality in our power of choice (*Willkür*) such that, independently of those natural causes and even contrary to their power and influence, it can bring something about . . . and thus begin a series of occurrences *all by itself*" (A534/B562; s. also A547f./B575f., A550/B578, und A555/B583)

Basically, the argument is as follows. Whenever we blame someone for an immoral action, even though their bad behavior can be causally explained by their circumstances and character, we are supposing that they were still able to act differently and to do what they should have done. In other words, we are supposing that they possessed the freedom to do what is right even under those empirical conditions. This argument, like the preceding one, rests on the assumption that in seeking to explain a person's action, we inevitably come to realize how much the action was determined by a whole series of antecedent causal factors. It relies on this assumption, however, only in conjunction with the decisive premise, which is the familiar principle of "*ought* implies *can*": that someone ought morally to do or to have done something presupposes that they can do or could have done it.

Now one can hardly dispute that *ought* depends on *can* in some way. It would make no sense to say, for instance, that someone ought to do something if the action in question – running a mile in less than three minutes – is physically impossible. However, an action may be *physically* possible without being, for a given agent, *motivationally* possible: she might not have it in her, in virtue of the beliefs and desires her present state of mind permits – so in virtue of the motives she could presently muster – to be moved to do the action. It is the relation between *ought* and the motivational *can* that is really at issue in this third incompatibilist argument. Kant and other adherents of the argument have an especially narrow conception of this relation. They hold that if a person ought, at some particular time, to act in some way, then she must at that very time be able, both physically and motivationally, to do the action in question. That is just what the principle "*ought* implies *can*" asserts. The freedom so to act that the person is presumed to have must be a capacity she already has, not one she could acquire. The import of this conception becomes evident when we consider cases (as Kant himself certainly was) where we believe people ought categorically to act in certain ways. If everyone ought unconditionally to keep their promises or respect the bodily integrity of others, whether they happen to want to or not, so whatever may have been their experience or whatever their character, then they must, so the argument concludes, have a freedom or capacity to choose to comply with these fundamental moral requirements that is itself independent of all empirical conditions.

This interpretation of the relation between *ought* and *can* departs, however, quite a bit from our usual ways of thinking. When, for instance, we bring up our children to act rightly, we assume that they do not yet have the motivational capacity to behave as they nonetheless – so we continually repeat to them – ought to be doing. For it is this capacity that we seek to instill as we impress on them the importance of certain distinctions. That they are not yet able to do what they ought to do is shown by the part of this learning process that consists in rebukes of the form, "you ought not to have done what you just did." Naturally, we would not say that they ought to act in the way we demand if they could not acquire the capacity to act well. But we do not assume that they already possess this capacity in some inborn, "transcendental" sense. It is a freedom to resist the force of one's immediate inclinations for the sake of what is right that can only be acquired through experience and training. Similarly, we also believe that people can lose the capacity to act rightly, without it then ceasing to be true that they ought to act in this way. This is particularly so if the individual is responsible for losing the capacity. If someone who was once able to do the right thing acquires through a dissolute way of life such bad habits that it is no longer possible for him to take any interest in what is right, we still do not hesitate to condemn his conduct when he acts wrongly.[29]

As these two scenarios demonstrate, our common understanding of the *ought* and *can* relation is not at all like Kant's understanding of it. In saying that someone ought to comply with some moral requirement, we do not presuppose that he must then necessarily have it in him, motivationally, to comply. Perhaps his experience and character are such that he is unable to take any interest in so acting. Yet we still maintain that he ought to act as he should if he is himself to blame for this total disinterest or if he could be taught, by a process that includes precisely the insistence that acting rightly is what he ought to be doing, to acquire – or perhaps to acquire again – the capacity to be moved by moral considerations. In other words, the relation

[29] This is essentially Aristotle's view of the matter. See the *Nicomachean Ethics*, 1114a3–21.

we suppose there to be between *ought* and *can* is one in which the *can* designates a causally conditioned freedom or capacity to act rightly. The circumstances in question highlight a fact I mentioned earlier (Section 7.2): a person may have a reason to do something even if the course of action the reason recommends is not one she is able at the time to take up, but can become accessible to her only under certain conditions. The rationale for this ordinary conception of the relation between *ought* and *can* is, moreover, not difficult to grasp. Morality is understood as an ongoing system of universally binding demands that normal adults with a proper sort of upbringing should be able to comply with and that other human beings – notably children or those who have become corrupt – have to be given the ability to appreciate through training and socialization.

I see nothing that counts against this ordinary conception, while all our experience speaks in favor of it. The well-known principle "*ought* implies *can*," which Kant exploits to argue for his incompatibilist notion of freedom, is therefore false.[30] It does not hold across the board. The *can* of motivational capacity is certainly related to the concept of *ought*. But the relation is not one of implication.

In sum, Kant along with many others is wrong to think that either the various features of the realm of action or the kind of knowledge we pursue about human actions gives us any reason to suppose that in order to be truly free beings, we must be able, independently of all empirical causes, to "initiate a series of occurrences all by ourselves." The so-called practical conception of freedom, which Kant seeks to leave behind and which (as I formulate it) holds that being free consists in acting on the basis of our best understanding of the relevant reasons, however much this capacity may be determined by our experience and character, is perfectly adequate. According to this conception, we are indeed able as agents to begin a series of occurrences by ourselves – though not entirely by ourselves. This is what we do whenever we bring about a change in the world that otherwise, had we not acted, would not have occurred. More than this is not needed for us to count as free.

[30] Others have endorsed the principle for different purposes, yet it is still false. David Estlund, who endorses the principle explicitly though with no interest in a Kantian notion of freedom, is a good example. Estlund has argued that people are not released from moral demands just because they find themselves unable to will to comply with them. I agree. But the reason is not, as he supposes, that they really can comply, but rather that *ought* does not imply *can*. It seems to me that Estlund fails to appreciate how motivational incapacity is a real inability. See his *Utopophobia: On the Limits (if any) of Political Philosophy* (Princeton: Princeton University Press), 28, 93.

7.6 Reasons as Causes

In response to my effort to demonstrate the compatibility of freedom and causal determination, one may be tempted to repeat what Kant wrote in a famous passage of the *Critique of Practical Reason*. To think that we act freely because our actions rest on our decisions, when these decisions are themselves causally shaped by antecedent conditions such as experience and character, means resorting, he says (AA V, 96–97), to a "wretched subterfuge" and offering "nothing better than the freedom of a turnspit." In Kant's eyes, any such conception reduces our decisions, even though they lie in our own thinking and not outside us, and hence our actions as well, to merely another set of events among all the events that make up the universal chain of cause and effect.

This conception is not, however, reductionistic. For a decision to act one way rather than another represents a *qualitative difference* in the chain of cause and effect, even if it does not constitute an exception. However much our ability to weigh and evaluate reasons may be causally shaped by our character and our experience, it is nonetheless responsible for our actions being due, not simply to antecedent events and circumstances, but to such events and circumstances insofar as they give us, in our view, good reasons to act as we do. The things to which we react and which therefore – along with the factors that have shaped our ability to respond to reasons – figure among the causes of our action are indeed causes only by way of acting on us in the form of reasons. After all, is not the crucial point on which freedom differs from compulsion the fact (see Section 7.2) that in acting freely we are not compelled by mere causes, but rather impelled by reasons?

This idea of a qualitative difference in the chain of cause and effect brings us, however, to the real difficulty facing a compatibilist conception of freedom and nature. As I have tried to show, it does not lie where one usually imagines, namely in the supposed opposition between freedom and causal determination. Instead, the problem consists in the fact that our actions, however causally shaped they may be by our experience and character, count as free insofar as they are responsive to reasons, which as such do not, as I explained earlier (Section 7.1), themselves form part of nature. It is in this regard that freedom requires more than nature alone. Before explaining more particularly why this gives rise to a significant problem, I want first to point out some of the merits of the idea that free actions constitute a qualitative difference in the causal order of nature in which they nonetheless have their place. I have arrived at that idea by way of two largely independent arguments – the one against naturalism, the other in favor of compatibilism – and it will be useful if I first lay out the attraction of the position as a whole.

One advantage is that it avoids the dilemma into which philosophical discussions of human freedom all too frequently fall. Either our actions, in accordance with a universal determinism, are the necessary consequence of antecedent causes like any other natural phenomenon – and then this kind of necessitation hardly corresponds to our experience as agents – or their causes are "indeterministic" (in something like the quantum-mechanical sense)[31] – and then it becomes difficult to see how our actions, to the extent that antecedent causes do not suffice to explain them, will not be simply random, erratic, and thus anything but free. The dilemma disappears once it is realized that in the case of free action the relation between cause and effect is of a special kind. Insofar as the events and circumstances prompting our action do so by way of giving us reasons to act as we do, the causal relation is also a relation of justification. Even if our action happens to be completely determined by these causes (as I indicated in Section 7.3, it does not matter for my purposes whether the causal order of nature is always deterministic), it is so in virtue of being motivated by them in the form of reasons. It is not necessitated by them in the purely causal way in which one physical state or event follows automatically upon another.

A second advantage is that it becomes intelligible how our actions, determined though they may be by the overall causal order of the world, can also at times embody something new and unexpected. This kind of originality, which constitutes the very epitome of human freedom, is possible precisely because free action represents a qualitative difference in the chain of cause and effect. For not only do things in the world then act on us in the form of reasons that justify the action we do. In addition, the reasons involved, however much our ability to grasp them is shaped by our experience and character, may recommend a line of conduct that goes well beyond a routine response to the causes of our action taken by themselves.

[31] Such is indeed the approach taken by Robert Kane, *The Significance of Free Will* (Oxford: Oxford University Press, 1996). Quantum indeterminism is the neurobiological basis of those "self-forming actions," he claims, in which we form our very characters by choosing at certain moments between incommensurable ways of life. The latter embody different sets of fundamental values each supported with reasons for preferring it to others, but for which there are no more basic reasons to favor the one kind of reasons over the others. All our various actions are free, Kane maintains, to the extent that they derive from such undetermined self-forming choices. Yet precisely because these constitutive choices between different kinds of reasons do not, it is assumed, rest on any deeper reasons, they cannot but be arbitrary, and thus the actions they are held to give rise to scarcely look free but instead ultimately capricious.

A person's discreetly helping me in some way may give me, for instance, a reason to show my gratitude, not with a predictable thank-you, but instead by some gesture that is similarly discreet. Possessing a sense for the particularities of concrete situations may be the result of typical processes of habituation. Nonetheless, the insights this capacity makes possible, the reasons it allows us to grasp, can be unanticipated and even surprising.

Even when this happens not to be so, there exists an inner tension in the way we as free beings form part of the causal order of nature. True, our actions are causally shaped by the world, both through the external circumstances to which we respond as well as through the past experience that determines how we perceive and judge the reasons these circumstances give us. Yet every action, instead of letting things take their course, aims at changing the world to some degree, if only to make sure that it continues to go on its present way. No agent wants, insofar as she acts, to remain in the bosom of nature. She seeks instead to shape things herself in accord with her ideas of how they should be. Her freedom does not cease then to be causally conditioned. Still, every action in its aim sets itself at least partly in opposition to the sequence of cause and effect to which it in other regards belongs. Compatibilism should not be understood – in contrast perhaps to the connotation of the term, but certainly counter to many of its usual formulations – as holding there to be a seamless union of freedom and nature.

Precisely this inner tension, nonetheless, brings us back again to the problem I described at the beginning of this section. For the tension stems from the fact that our actions have their place in the chain of cause and effect in virtue of responding, insofar as they are free, to reasons that are not themselves part of nature. The problem is that not only our ideas about the reasons there are but reasons themselves, if they are indeed to motivate what we think and do, have to be able to have a causal efficacy. After all, without the possibility of being moved by reasons and not just by our ideas of them, which can always be false or only true by luck – that is, true without being due to their object – rationality would be an illusion. Yet how reasons can act as causes appears difficult to understand, given that reasons are of a completely different, normative character than the phenomena of nature. According to the standard conception of causal relations, cause and effect must occupy positions, indeed correlative positions, in space and time. Yet reasons have no spatial location; one reason cannot be three centimeters distant from another. (They may have temporal position, in that a reason may obtain at one time but not at another). To perceive the problem, it is essential therefore to keep in mind the difference between reasons themselves and our ideas of them, for the latter clearly have a location, namely in our minds.

So let me state the problem once again. There are no good grounds, I have argued, to deny that all our actions, to whatever degree they may be free, are causally determined in at least two regards – not only by our experience and character, which enable us to perceive reasons for what we do, but also by the events and circumstances in the world to which we respond because of the reasons they give us to act as we do. The real difficulty in understanding how freedom is possible does not then lie, as so often supposed, in the causal determination of our actions. The latter should be obvious. It lies instead in how reasons themselves, when our ideas of the reasons for which we act are true and we hold them because of these very reasons, can figure as well among the causes of our actions. How can the normative act? The question of how reasons can be causes is an essentially *ontological* question. And since it focuses on the ultimate structure of reality, beyond what the empirical sciences can tell us, it has a *metaphysical* character.

In pointing out this problem near the end of Chapter 6 (Section 6.9), I emphasized how much our ordinary thinking presumes that reasons can indeed be causes. Before tackling the problem head on, it will be useful to review the three everyday kinds of experience I mentioned there to illustrate this point, and I will then add a fourth. First, *deliberation.* When we deliberate about what we should think or do, we do not appeal simply to what we believe are the reasons to draw one conclusion or another, for why should our beliefs as such carry any weight? What matters is the object of those beliefs, namely the reasons themselves, since it is by them that we intend for our decision to be determined. Second, there is *conversation* – that is, genuine conversation – in which people care about exploring together the topic at hand and not (as all too often) about merely voicing their opinions, winning an argument, or making an impression. They want the course of the discussion to be steered by the good reasons for the views that are being exchanged.[32] Third, there is the *analysis of motives.* Besides wanting to know whether someone (another or even ourselves) who acted rightly did so because they believed the action was right, we also want to know, if that is so, whether they believed it was right because of the reasons that made it right or were instead merely following

[32] This, I believe, is what Jürgen Habermas is getting at with his famous phrase about "the unforced force of the better argument" (*der zwanglose Zwang des besseren Arguments*). For references and an analysis, see chapter 5 of my book, *Das Selbst in seinem Verhältnis zu sich und zu anderen.*

the opinions of others that just happened to be correct. This kind of psychological analysis can be difficult and sometimes inconclusive, but the possibility of true virtue rests on the distinctions involved.

Finally, let me add what we ordinarily believe is involved in *inference*. When we draw a conclusion from given facts, we want our inference to be guided, not merely by those facts themselves, but by the reasons we presume they give us for that conclusion. I may look in the backyard and, seeing pig tracks in the snow, be prompted to exclaim, "There has been a pig in our yard!" But my wife, who knows well the habits of our neighbor, may correct me, saying, "You've been misled by what you see. I too see the pig tracks, all right, but they don't offer a good reason to conclude a pig has been around, since the butcher next door likes to play with pig knuckles in the snow."

So much, then, for the pervasive role that the idea of reasons acting as causes plays in our everyday thought. There are also general considerations that count in favor of this idea. If the way things are in the world causes us as free beings to act as we do because of the reasons it gives us, then surely these reasons themselves, and not just the way things are, must be able to move us. Although reasons can move us to do something only if we grasp them, our grasping of them is itself a response to the existence of such reasons. If we can claim to know that we have a reason to think or do something, a causal theory of knowledge would appear to apply here as elsewhere: to know that *p* is not simply to have the true belief that *p* (which could be simply luck), but to have that true belief *because of* the fact that *p* is the case. (See Chapter 6, Sections 6.4 and 6.8). It will not do, moreover, to object that there is a gap between our grasping certain reasons and our acting, at the appropriate time, in accord with them – that we first have to decide whether to comply with these reasons.[33] Insofar as we are rational, there will be no such gap. Our freedom as rational beings consists in being responsive to the reasons there are to think or act in a certain way. Any gap between grasping and responding is a defect in our rationality, the expression perhaps of some weakness of will, and to that extent we are less than fully free.

Yet I have still offered no account of precisely how it is that reasons can indeed be causes. It is hard, in fact, to think of earlier accounts one could

[33] In *Rationality in Action*, John Searle defends such a view as part of his overall incompatibilist thesis (see note 13) that freedom consists in gaps in the causal order of nature. His arguments for this view are rather weak, however. Mainly he appeals to cases where we have to decide between different reasons for the same action (65f). Yet action in such situations that is rational and thus free, instead of being capricious, is action in which we are moved by knowledge of further reasons to prefer one of the given reasons to the others.

lean on. The problem has rarely been so much as acknowledged.[34] Either the nature of reasons has been misunderstood, or people have balked at thinking through its actual consequences.

Thus, there have been some contemporary philosophers who agree that reasons exist independently of our attitudes toward them. Derek Parfit and T. M. Scanlon are notable examples. Yet as I recounted in the preceding chapter, they deny, out of an inordinate fear of "metaphysics," that reasons play any causal role, though without then explaining or even mentioning the sorts of everyday experiences I have just run through. Other philosophers, following the lead of Donald Davidson, readily grant that reasons can act as causes, but only because they equate reasons with psychological states, whose causal influence on our behavior is obvious. Davidson conceived of reasons as combinations of beliefs and desires, the reason to take an umbrella being understood as the belief that it is raining combined with the desire to remain dry.[35] I have already indicated (Section 7.1) what is wrong with this conception of reasons. Not only does the reason to take an umbrella depend on the fact, not on the belief, that it is raining, and not only does it not depend necessarily on a desire to remain dry – one may have such a reason whether one wants to remain dry or not, because one ought to stay dry – but reasons are in any case not psychological, but rather normative in character. The problem is how something normative can have a causal influence. Finally, some philosophers have dismissed this problem by claiming that the rational explanation of actions and the causal explanation of events in nature are two quite different though equally indispensable concerns we have. One need not worry, they believe, about how the things the two perspectives deal with hang together in reality itself.[36] This kind of insouciance is ill-conceived, however. If we act freely

[34] Much as I agree with the "actual sequence" conception of freedom developed by John Martin Fischer and Carolina Sartorio, which aims to show how free action as responsive to reasons is compatible with causal determination (see note 2), neither ever confronts the problem, since both decline to enter into a discussion of the nature of reasons. See Martin Fischer and Mark Ravizza, *Responsibility and Control* (Cambridge: Cambridge University Press, 1998), 68n11, and Sartorio, *Causation and Free Will*, 111.

[35] Davidson, "Actions, Reasons, and Causes" (1963), reprinted in his collection *Actions and Events* (Oxford: Clarendon Press, 1980), 3–19.

[36] A recent example of this sort of view seems to be the position of Jürgen Habermas in his essay "Das Sprachspiel verantwortlicher Urheberschaft," especially 278–279, 326–341. Despite talk at the end about an encompassing framework of evolutionary "natural history," his insistence in the name of a "transcendental pragmatism" on the unbridgeable distinction between these two perspectives (not unconnected with his similar insistence on the distinction between participant and observer standpoints; see note 22) leads him to reject the need for any "ontological" account of how they work together (332–333).

when things in the world move us to act in virtue of the reasons they give us to act as we do, then these reasons must also be able to move us to act and precisely as part of that very process. The problem is thus to explain how the causal structure of one and the same world can include both empirical facts and reasons together. Without such an essentially ontological (and metaphysical) account, any compatibilist conception of nature and freedom must be radically defective.

How, then, to proceed? Though the problem has largely gone unrecognized, a solution is not, I believe, hard to find. As outlined already at the end of the preceding chapter, it rests on a basic point I have made throughout this book. Reasons, irreducibly normative though they are, still depend on the empirical, physical or psychological, facts in whose relevance for our possibilities of thought and action they consist. The idea, then, is that when reasons act as causes, it is by means of the (far less problematic) way that the empirical facts underlying them act causally on us. Viewed in this light, the difficulty in understanding how the normative, which is not as such spatially located, can play a causal role disappears. For the empirical phenomena on which reasons rest do naturally exist in space and time. This does not mean, I emphasize, that the empirical facts alone move us to think and act as we do. For they determine what we do only in virtue of our conception of the reasons they give us, and when this conception is correct, then only in virtue of those reasons themselves. But it also does not mean that the empirical facts do not figure among the causes of what we do. The idea is rather that they shape how we think and act by giving us the reasons for which we do so. Their causal influence is, as it were, the vehicle for the causal force of the reasons involved. Thus, not just the existence of reasons but also their ability to move us to think and act depend on empirical facts. Freedom depends on nature, even if it cannot be reduced to it.

A couple of examples may make the idea clearer. When, for instance, I hurry quickly to the train platform because I am late, I recognize this reason for haste (given my wish to catch a particular train) in virtue of seeing on the station clock what time it is. The reason to run only impels me to run because the time shown on the clock and my desire not to miss the train, which I understand give me that reason, together do so. Or – a somewhat more complicated example – the good reasons that lead me to believe that Caesar crossed the Rubicon in 49 BC do not have to do with my observing the crossing myself, but with my having read various texts whose reports about the event, so I assume, are reliably connected with its actual occurrence. It is in becoming acquainted with the historical documents that the reasons these documents give to believe in the event can have an effect on my thinking.

One may perhaps object that the problem has been solved only in part. Does there not remain the question of what exactly is the process by which reasons, however much their causal force is due to the causal influence of the empirical facts underlying them, are able to have an effect on our thinking? This objection stems, I suspect, from a lingering reluctance to accept either the reality or the causality of reasons. For one could equally well ask what exactly is the process by which physical phenomena can have a causal effect on the mind so as to move us to think as we do. This question is notoriously controversial and unresolved. Yet almost all sides to the dispute agree that there exists this causal dependence of the mental on the physical, whatever may be more fundamentally the process on which it rests. The same attitude is appropriate in the present case. Many aspects of our everyday experience only make sense if we suppose that reasons themselves can shape what we think and do. What I have tried to show is how this can be so by removing an important impediment to its acceptance. Reasons may not themselves have any spatial location. Yet they can still act as causes. For reasons can move us when the empirical facts on which they depend move us to think and act in certain ways and do so by virtue of giving us those reasons. I do not claim that this account offers a full explanation of how reasons can be causes. But it does provide the framework in which their causality becomes intelligible.

7.7 Self-Formation

With this, the long argument is complete by which I have wanted to show how freedom involves at the same time responding to reasons and belonging to the causal order of nature, even though reasons are not themselves part of nature. I have not yet come to the end, however. This account needs to be fleshed out a bit, so that it begins to do justice to the full measure of what we understand as freedom. Up until now, I have focused on individual episodes of thought and action. Yet we are not free simply insofar as we guide ourselves by reasons. Our freedom also includes our ability to develop conceptions of the self that we are and want to be – that is, "identities" – which regulate over the long term how we exercise our responsiveness to reasons in order thus to expand our freedom. These self-conceptions – we may think of ourselves as a parent, a Christian, a journalist, or more abstractly as someone who helps others or who intends to go their own way in the world – designate certain kinds of reasons as more important for us than others or as being relevant in certain situations while not in others. In general, they represent therefore an ideal of a life lived well, serving to organize our various interests, activities, and social roles so that we can ourselves determine the direction and course our lives will take. Our freedom does not consist solely in the relation we have to the world in responding to the reasons events and circumstances give us. It also consists more far-reachingly in the ability to make this relation an object of reflection and thus to shape our lives as a whole.[37]

One might perhaps feel that only now, with this turn to the idea of self-determination, has the essence of freedom really come into view. So far, I have repeatedly claimed that in thinking and acting as we do we always find ourselves determined from without in two respects – on the one hand by the causal order of nature, in that our experience and character shape the way in which we judge how we should think and act, and on the other hand by the circumstances in the world to which we are reacting and that means, insofar as we are being rational, by the reasons they give us. Yet if we are so thoroughly determined from without, what sense can the idea of freedom really make? Are we not free insofar as we can be, if not pure self-movers, then at least partly self-determining and not solely determined by outside factors?

However, I explained early on (Section 7.2) why such an objection is mistaken. In the two respects in which as free beings we are determined from without, this external determination takes place only because we are at the same time self-determining in a fundamental way. Though our thought and action are shaped by the circumstances in the world to which we are reacting as well as by our own past experience and character, we think and act as we do by guiding ourselves by the reasons that then appear to us relevant. This elementary form of self-determination, in which we adopt one or another of our possibilities, forms the very basis of our freedom. We are free beings insofar as we have not only possibilities – as everything does – but possibilities we can take up, and we take them up by aligning ourselves on reasons we see as counting in their favor. It is essential to keep in mind, however, that this self-determination does not consist in endowing these reasons with the authority they have for what we do. On the contrary, it requires acknowledging the authority they possess

[37] Another question that arises, when we go beyond the level of individual episodes of thought and action, is what constitutes the continuity of the self over time. This question concerns our "identity" in a different sense. For a discussion in connection with the concept of the self presented later in this section and in the next chapter, see my book *Les pratiques du moi* (Paris: PUF, 2004; English translation: *The Practices of the Self*, Chicago: University of Chicago Press, 2010), chapter 7, §1.

in themselves. To be sure, there would be no such thing as reasons unless there existed beings like us, with possibilities they can choose. But as I also explained at the beginning in Section 7.1, this does not mean that we are the authors of their claims on our conduct. Even in the case of principles that are so fundamental to all our thought and action as to define what it is to think and act coherently, we are dependent on an order of reasons that are not of our own making. If responding to reasons is self-determination, it is so only insofar as we are letting ourselves be determined.[38]

This kind of inseparability of self-determination and letting oneself be determined forms indeed the very nature of subjectivity. I lay out this thesis in greater detail in Chapter 8 (Sections 8.2–8.3). Here a brief summary is in order before I go on to explain how our particular self-conceptions can serve to expand our freedom.

As should be evident, self-determination and letting oneself be determined form the two relations involved in the characterization I have proposed of our basic rationality, namely guiding oneself by reasons. It consists in both a relation to reasons (or to what one takes to be reasons) and in a relation to oneself. Now this relation to oneself constitutes, I believe, the very relation we bear to ourselves by which each of us is a subject or a self. It is what I meant at the outset of this chapter by an intimate connection between rationality and subjectivity.[39] I prefer, though, using the term "self" rather than "subject," since the reflexive pronoun makes the self-relatedness manifest and it also carries far less philosophical freight. Yet if it is a near-truism that each of us is a self in virtue of an essential relation we bear to ourselves, it has not been so clear what the nature of this self-relation is. In modern philosophy ever since Descartes, it has mostly been understood as a relation of self-knowledge. Either we are essentially aware of ourselves – of our own thoughts and mental states – through reflection. Or, since this approach appears circular (as the object of reflection, the self or subject would already have to exist), we are held to be aware of ourselves through some pre-reflective kind of self-acquaintance that precedes any distinction between subject and object, knower and known. Yet this ploy has the disadvantage of substituting for a paradox a complete mystery.

The impasse can be overcome by abandoning the assumption that the constitutive relation of the self to itself is some kind of knowledge-relation.

[38] A similar perspective is developed in the excellent book by Martin Seel, *Sich bestimmen lassen* (Frankfurt: Suhrkamp, 2002).

[39] This is the theme of my book *Vernunft und Subjektivität*.

Such is precisely my aim in claiming that the defining relation of the self to itself consists in guiding ourselves by reasons. For this relation to ourselves has instead a *practical* character, one in which we *commit ourselves* to think and act as we see reason to do. Its constitutive role is evident in the very nature of such basic elements of our mental life as belief and desire. We cannot believe something without holding it to be true and that means without supposing (rightly or wrongly) we have reasons to think it true; at the same time, belief is a disposition, not only to affirm what is believed, but also to think and act in accord with its presumed truth and that means in accord with the reasons its being true would give us. So too with desire. Every desire represents its object as something desirable and thus as something there are reasons to have or pursue; at the same time, it tends to move us, unless we keep it in check, to think and act as the apparent desirability of its object gives us reason to do. In both cases, therefore, both the formation and the function of these two mental states lie in the way we guide ourselves by reasons. This is so, moreover, in advance of any kind of knowledge we may have of our beliefs and desires. When we do become aware of them, it is normally by way of reflection, and the object of our reflection is then the belief or desire in its particular manner of being responsive to reasons and thus as already part of our self. There is no need to suppose we must be equipped with some pre-reflective, inevitably mysterious kind of self-knowledge or self-acquaintance.

Up to this section, I discussed guiding ourselves by reasons chiefly in regard to the idea of freedom. But as I observed earlier (Section 7.2), all our thought and action are minimally free insofar as they are responsive to what we take to be reasons – and the better our understanding of the relevant reasons, the freer we become. Thus, the relation to ourselves in virtue of which each of us is a self is none other than the fundamental kind of self-determination that makes us at our core free beings.

To return now to the role of self-conceptions: we can reflect not only on this or that belief or desire but also on the whole way we happen to respond to reasons, how we rank for instance certain sorts of reasons over others in determining what to think or do. In this case, reflection aims at developing a conception of the kind of self we are as well as of the kind we want to be. For when we are seeking to figure out what we are actually like, our aim is never solely factual. Reflection, in general, is not an activity we exercise for its own sake, contemplatively as it were, but always in order to solve some problem (see Chapter 1, Section 1.2). At the very least, reflecting on the overall way we think and act is motivated by a desire to achieve a greater clarity about what we are doing. Usually, however, the intended revision is more substantial. We want to devise a better way of judging and complying with what we have reason to do. Either way, we are engaged in working out with what self-conception we ought to live our lives. Each of us is thus not only a self but also a being for whom the kind of self we are is an object of concern. As Heidegger remarked, we are beings for whom our very being is an issue.[40]

Now, not every self is capable of developing this sort of reflective relation to itself. A self, as the reader will perhaps have noticed, is, according to the view I have presented, any being with beliefs and desires. This means that the higher animals too must count as selves or "subjects." I see nothing problematic in this implication. Philosophical preconceptions alone – such as the notion that only a being that can say "I" is a self or that only a being that can speak has concepts – stand in the way of the obvious truth that a dog, a cat, or an ape can see reasons to act one way or another and thus has its own perspective on the world. They can also reflect about whether in a given situation they have reason to act in some way. Sometimes I see my dog Hardy clearly pondering whether he can succeed in making off with someone's glove. However, human beings differ from the other animals in having the reflective capacity to make the general way they have of responding to reasons into an object of their attention and judgment. In order to mark this difference, I will reserve the concept of a *person* for beings such as us, who can be concerned for the kind of self they are and should be. A self is not necessarily a person, and we human beings are (perhaps) the only persons there are.

As persons, we can thus develop various ideas of a life lived well, seeking to regulate the kinds of reasons for thought and action we should concern ourselves with. None of us in fact lives without some such conception, however vague or conventional it may be. In specifying what sort of possibilities of thought and action we should care about, both in relation to others and in regard to our own good, it enables us to shape our lives as a whole. Our aim is to lead our lives, not to let them simply happen to us. For even if we accept a conception requiring us to live with piety or reverence as part of a larger whole, we have to choose and arrange our various activities so that they proceed in accord with that ideal. Whatever their character, the self-conceptions or "identities" that define for us the meaning of our lives are an expression of our fundamental interest in determining ourselves how we will live.

40 Martin Heidegger, *Sein und Zeit* (Tübingen: Niemeyer, 1967), 191: "Das Dasein ist Seiendes, dem es in seinem Sein um dieses selbst geht." Also 12.

By itself, having some idea of what is overall important to us serves to expand our freedom. For without one, we would be reduced to stumbling from one situation to the next. Failing to take account of the interlockings and long-term costs and benefits of our various possibilities, we would be constantly confronted with the unwelcome consequences of a string of unconnected decisions. Each of us has then a reason to take the course of our lives in hand and embrace some overarching conception of the self we want to be, a conception of how to rank and respond to the reasons that appear to speak in favor of this or that possibility. To be sure, self-conceptions also regularly show us the significance of new classes of reasons. If I were a Christian (or more exactly a certain kind of Christian), I might see a deeper, not solely moral, reason to consider generosity to others as more important than the pursuit of my personal interests. But in any case, not only does in general our freedom consist in responding to reasons, but heeding the imperative reason to develop and refine a conception of how to live our lives as a whole vastly increases our freedom, making us more intelligent in choosing what possibilities to pursue.

How much freer our self-conceptions make us depends, however, on their content. To the extent they rest on self-deception or false beliefs, but more particularly to the extent they fail to reflect our long-term interests, abilities, and circumstances, we are less free than we could have been, since then we are kept from grasping the reasons there are to shape our lives differently and for the better. In fact, our real interests, our capacities, and the actual circumstances of the world we find ourselves in are the three basic factors to which any conception of the self we want to be has to seek to do justice. Depending on how well we succeed in respecting these factors, we are more free or less – though we should also recognize that they can change over time, and sometimes unpredictably, so that our self-conception, however reasonable it may be at the time, can always strike us later as woefully inadequate.[41]

It should also be clear, however, that the comprehensive kind of self-determination involved is at the same time a letting oneself be determined, and in the same way that is true of our individual thoughts, beliefs, desires, and actions. When we consider what direction we want to give our lives as a whole, we likewise have to guide ourselves by reasons that appear to favor

[41] On the consequences of this fact for the nature of one's individual good and especially on the inevitable role of chance and the unexpected, see chapter 10, "The Idea of a Life Plan," in my book *The Autonomy of Morality* (Cambridge: Cambridge University Press, 2008).

one possibility over others. And in this case too, the way we judge the reasons for this or that self-conception is causally shaped by our experience and character, just as when we determine what to believe or do in particular situations. For how else would we have the materials to devise, much less to evaluate, a conception of the kind of individual we want to be? That our self-conceptions are in these two regards always conditioned is vividly confirmed by the familiar experience of thinking back on a past understanding of our ultimate purposes that we have long left behind and of finding that it seems now to have been the work of somebody else. We look with astonishment at how deeply this conception was determined by what happened to be our interests, ways of thinking, and circumstances at the time, and often to an extent of which we then had little if any inkling. And so we can infer that our present views about the way we want in general to live our lives, however much they may appear to be the result of careful deliberation, are likewise determined from without in manifold ways, without our being fully aware of them.

To be sure, we are normally inclined to think, if nothing in the world compels us to act against our conscience or our aims, that we are, all by ourselves, the authors of what we do, free from the operation of external forces. That is an illusion, however. As Charlotte so beautifully and aptly puts it in Goethe's *Die Wahlverwandtschaften* (*Elective Affinities*), a novel devoted to exploring the limits to which we can be in charge of our lives,

> As life sweeps us along, we believe that we are acting on our own, that we are choosing our activities and pleasures. But actually, if we consider things closely, it is only the plans and desires of the time that we too are impelled to carry out.[42]

We ought not to harbor false expectations about the greater freedom we can achieve in looking beyond our individual decisions to develop a conception of the self we want to be, exercising systematic control over how we respond to the various reasons we may see to think or do this or that. None of us can thereby become the author of ourselves. At whatever level, self-determination is possible only through being determined, and precisely in the two regards I have been emphasizing.

Even when we determine on the basis of some self-conception what sort of reasons we will take seriously in choosing among our possibilities, we do

[42] Goethe, *Die Wahlverwandtschaften*, Part Two, chapter 8: "Indem uns das Leben fortzieht, glauben wir aus uns selbst zu handeln, unsere Tätigkeit, unsere Vergnügungen zu wählen; aber freilich, wenn wir es genau ansehen, so sind es nur die Pläne, die Neigungen der Zeit, die wir mit auszuführen genötigt sind."

so, first of all, only because of heeding the deeper reasons that appear to favor that very conception and thus because of the events and circumstances in the world that give these reasons to us. No self-conception can produce anything like a *self-constitution* of the self. It can only contribute to our *self-formation*, since each of us is constituted as a self only through our relation to an independent order of reasons that cannot be our own creation (Section 7.1).[43] And second, even if such a conception does succeed in giving a shape to our lives as a whole, it does so only in virtue of a dependence on our experience and character that make us able to grasp the reasons for this conception. The self-determination that we as persons can achieve is still part of the causal order of nature, though it does represent like all our free actions a qualitative difference in the chain of cause and effect, consisting as it does in being moved by reasons.

We are free only insofar as we are at the same time conditioned. Dissolving the apparent contradiction this proposition may seem to express is itself one of the most important achievements of a true freedom of mind, since it reconciles our reason, the basis of our freedom, with the conditions for its exercise. This was also Goethe's conviction, to which he likewise gave voice in the *Wahlverwandtschaften*, this time in Ottilie's diary:

> Should someone declare that he is free, he will feel the next moment the conditions to which he is subject. Let him venture to declare that he is conditioned and then he will feel that he is free.[44]

In this chapter, the relation between reason and freedom, along with their conditions of possibility, has been the center of attention. In the next, I turn to the relation, already touched on in this final section, between reason, reasons, and subjectivity. There the focus will be on what it is to be a self and on the ways in which self-knowledge is possible.

[43] According to Christine Korsgaard, our self-conceptions or "practical identities" serve to constitute us as selves, since they are the source of all reasons for action that we have. See Korsgaard, *The Sources of Normativity*, 101f, and *Self-Constitution*, 20–26. This claim is false, however, in two regards. Not only do such identities really function by enabling us to perceive and rank reasons that already exist, but they have become ours because we have seen reasons to adopt them. Korsgaard denies, of course, that there exist reasons we must simply acknowledge because she holds that we must regard ourselves as the authors of the reasons we have. See note 8 above, as well as my critique of Korsgaard on this score in Chapter 5, Section 5.5.

[44] Goethe, *Die Wahlverwandtschaften*, Part Two, chapter 5: "Es darf sich einer nur für frei erklären, so fühlt er sich den Augenblick als bedingt. Wagt er es sich für bedingt zu erklären, so fühlt er sich frei."

CHAPTER 8

Self-Knowledge and Commitment

8.1 Why Does Self-Knowledge Matter?

Self-knowledge is usually held to be something of great value. Yet over the centuries there have been many different conceptions of the sort of self-knowledge it is important to acquire. Among modern philosophers, the dominant view has been that self-knowledge consists paradigmatically in our becoming aware of our own mental states, whatever they may happen to be, by means of reflecting on them as each of us, alone and at will, is able to do. But this has not always been the leading view. So it is worth considering why there have been a variety of different conceptions and why the modern notion has come to hold sway.

When, for instance, Plato's Socrates, taking to heart the Delphic inscription "Know thyself," declared that self-knowledge is the knowledge we ought to acquire before every other kind,[1] he did not have in mind anything like the modern conception of self-knowledge I have just sketched. He meant instead grasping the nature of our fundamental capacities and interests, so that we can then determine the character of our true good. The dialogue, *Alcibiades I*, develops this view explicitly: the goal of the self-knowledge of which the Delphic oracle spoke is the cultivation of the individual. This self-cultivation consists in exercising the right sort of concern for oneself (*ten epimeleian heautou*, 127e), and for this a knowledge of the nature of the self is clearly necessary (129a). For we cannot, Socrates points out, care about ourselves in the appropriate way unless we know what general aspects of our existence make up our true self. And even when we have settled that matter – it is our "soul" (130c), he claims, since our aim is to improve, not our possessions or our body, but ourselves – we must go on to discover what particular possibilities for

[1] See, e.g., Plato, *Phaedrus* 229e-230a: "I am still unable, as the Delphic inscription orders, to know myself; and it really seems to me ridiculous to look into other things before I have understood that."

good and bad the individual self (*auto hekaston*, 130d), that is, our own soul, happens to contain.

That the main difficulty lies precisely here is so obvious that Socrates does not need to point it out, especially as he is engaged in a conversation with the notoriously corrupt Alcibiades. For if the self we must seek to know consists ultimately in the particular capacities and interests whose cultivation will enable us to live our life well, then we may find it difficult to distinguish these elements from other, less valuable parts of our soul, since it is we ourselves, with all our deficiencies and defects, who are carrying out the inquiry. This is why, according to Socrates, self-knowledge (*to gnonai heauton*) is no easy matter: no simpleton inscribed those words on the temple wall at Delphi (129a). The best way to proceed, he claims, is to understand "know thyself" as "see thyself" (*ide sauton*, 132d). That is, just as the eye can only see itself in a mirror, so it is necessary to perceive the self that we wish to know, but that we at the same time are, in something that reflects it back to us. The needed mirror can only be another self, which already better knows its way around in these matters and which can elicit from us in a conversation, as Socrates is trying to do with Alcibiades, a recognition of our best possibilities (132d–133b).

Although the authenticity of this dialogue has often been challenged in recent times, what should be undisputed is that the *Alcibiades*, if not composed by Plato himself, was written by someone in his milieu and that it explains perfectly why the dialogue form belongs to the heart of Plato's philosophy. Only indirectly, in conversation with others, Plato believed, is the self-knowledge to be secured that is of philosophical importance – namely a knowledge of our own best capacities and interests. It is therefore a conception that is quite removed from the modern notion of self-knowledge I mentioned earlier, a knowledge that can supposedly be acquired directly through reflection on our own mental states.

Augustine offers another example of the fact that the self-knowledge held to be of philosophical moment has been differently conceived by different philosophers. When Augustine turned inward in his *Confessions* to explore his own soul, his object was not the capacities and interests whose development leads to human flourishing, but also not the peculiarities of his individual thinking or the essential features of human consciousness as such. His concern lay with those memories and experiences that reveal his relation to God, since only by this sort of turn inward can the most important kind of truth about himself be grasped. Only thus, he expressly claimed, can the Delphic demand, "Know thyself," be satisfied. Human beings, according to Augustine, are always curious to learn about the lives of others, but when it comes to themselves, they are naturally inclined to self-deception, so that we can only be sure we have reached our true self when we hear in ourselves the confirming voice of God: "To hear from you what one is is to know oneself."[2] According to Augustine too, therefore, the voice of an other is necessary for achieving the kind of self-knowledge we require. Yet this is not by way of a conversation, as in Plato, since the other is God, and the object of this self-knowledge is not so much man himself as man in his relation of dependence on God.

As the examples of Plato and Augustine show, conceptions of self-knowledge typically focus on certain things we can know about ourselves while leaving others entirely out of account – such as whether we are strong enough to run an ultramarathon or how long we are likely to live – which we might in fact want very much to know. They take shape, therefore, with an eye to what they regard as the defining aspects of the sort of beings we are, whether it be our ability to live our life well or our relation to God. This means, in turn, that they draw on certain underlying philosophical concerns. Whence the many different conceptions of self-knowledge there have been. As such deeper concerns change, so too do conceptions of what it is to know ourselves.

If, then, self-knowledge since early modern times has come to signify principally a reflective knowledge of whatever beliefs and desires, thoughts and feelings, happen to make up our mental life, it needs to be asked what sorts of preoccupations have made so boundless and miscellaneous a set of facts about ourselves seem so important a domain of truths to possess. One concern finds exemplary expression in Montaigne: when man's place in an overarching natural and divine order of ends becomes difficult to discern, we can seek satisfaction in surveying and relishing the variety of our experience for its own sake, without appeal to any higher authority. "I am myself the subject of my book," Montaigne wrote in his preface to the reader, for as he explained in one of his essays (II.10), "Whoever is looking for knowledge, let him fish for it where it lies; there is nothing I profess less. These are my fancies, by which I seek, not to know things, but only myself."[3]

[2] Augustine, *Confessiones* X.3: "Quid est enim a te audire de se nisi cognoscere se?" See too X.5: "Quod de me scio, te mihi lucente scio, et quod de me nescio, tam diu nescio, donec fiant tenebrae meae sicut meridies in vulto tuo" ("What I know of myself, I know only through your light, and what I do not know of myself, I do not know until my darkness becomes like midday in your visage").

[3] Montaigne, *Les Essais*, edited by P. Villey (Paris: PUF, 1999), 3 ("Je suis moi-mesmes la matiere de mon livre") and 407 ("Qui sera en cherche de science, si la pesche où elle se loge; il n'est rien de quoy

However, a different motivation, far more influential for subsequent philosophy, makes its appearance with Descartes: knowledge of our own mental life is thought to possess an exceptional kind of certainty, an immediacy and indubitability,[4] that not only in times of intellectual disarray and upheaval makes it the secure foundation for acquiring every other kind of knowledge and thus for all our dealings with the world as a whole. Clearly, self-knowledge in this sense is very different from the conceptions to be found in Plato or Augustine. Which capacities and interests serve to define the human good, which thoughts and feelings bring us closer to God, are not immediately accessible or certifiable beyond all possible doubt, as the knowledge of our own mental states supposedly is according to Descartes and so many other modern philosophers. Self-knowledge in the Cartesian sense also differs clearly from the sort of self-description practiced by Montaigne, which makes no claims to certainty and is not intended to lead to any knowledge of the world.

We today may no longer believe that the project of founding knowledge on unshakable foundations is feasible or even makes sense. But that does not mean we have ceased to think, like Descartes and others after him, that the immediate knowledge of the contents of our own mind, whatever they may be, is the kind of self-knowledge that matters crucially. It is not denied, of course, that we can come to a knowledge of our minds by other, indirect (inferential) means and that particular aspects of our being – for example, unconscious states or general traits of character – may not be ascertainable in any other way. But, so the idea goes, the beliefs and desires, the thoughts and feelings, of which we *are* conscious are as a rule the object of an immediate self-knowledge. Such a view is so widely shared and so well known that I do not need to cite any of its adherents; there are some, no doubt, among my present readers. For this kind of self-knowledge, on account of its immediacy and thus alleged immunity to the forms of error to which all our other knowledge is exposed, is assumed to draw upon the intimate, pre-reflective acquaintance with ourselves that makes us the thinking and acting beings that we are.[5] Indeed, insofar as to

je face moins de profession. Ce sont icy mes fantaisies, par lesquelles je ne tasche point à connoistre les choses, mais moy").

4 See, for example, Descartes, *Second Replies* (AT VII, 160): "*Cogitationis nomine complector illud omne quod sic in nobis est, ut ejus immediate conscii simus. Ita omnes voluntatis, intellectûs, imaginationis & sensuum operationes sunt cogitationes*" ("I include under the term of thought everything that is in us in such a way that we are immediately conscious of it. Thus all the operations of the will, the intellect, the imagination and the senses are thoughts").

5 Descartes refers to this intimate, pre-reflective self-acquaintance explicitly when in the *Sixth Replies* (AT VII, 422) he writes of "*cognitione illa interna, quae reflexam semper antecedit*" ("that internal

be a self is to be constituted by a fundamental relation one has to oneself, we are held to be selves on this view precisely in virtue of having an intimate acquaintance with our own thinking. Without it, we could not, for instance, act on the basis of our beliefs. Suppose, for instance, we have the belief that there is a door across the room. If we were not intimately acquainted with the fact that we have this belief, or at least with the fact that we have inferred that we have it, the belief would not be available to us as we figure out how to go about satisfying our desire – another fact about ourselves with which we would have to be intimately acquainted – to leave the room. Only because, it is presumed, we are in this way largely transparent to ourselves, can beliefs and desires we happen to have not merely *cause* us to act in certain ways (behind our backs, as it were), but serve to *guide* us in our conduct – conduct for which we can thus count as responsible. Only thus are we able to be centers of thought and action.

This, then, is the heart of the motivation underlying the modern, Cartesian conception of self-knowledge, giving it the prominence it enjoys and displacing older conceptions such as those propounded by Plato or Augustine. The apparent motley of things this conception considers the crucial objects of self-knowledge – all the various beliefs and desires, thoughts and feelings, that happen to make up our mental life – is in reality tied together by a single underlying concern with what it is to be a self, responsible for what we think and do.

In fact, the idea of the mind's self-transparency has played a central role as well in the primacy that modern philosophy, beginning too with Descartes, has generally accorded to epistemology among its other parts. Insofar as we are thought to be intimately acquainted, not only with the contents of our own thinking, but also with our basic faculties of mind, we will be able to take up questions such as "what is knowledge?" and "how is knowledge possible?" so as to determine the conditions under which knowledge-claims may be raised and validated, without having to rely on some prior understanding of the world itself and thus before tackling problems in any other domain.[6] This perspective stands in contrast, for instance, to what is to be found in Plato and Aristotle. For them,

awareness that always precedes reflective knowledge"). The notion shapes much of modern philosophy, often equally explicitly, the most famous case being Fichte's concept of the I's "intellectual intuition" of itself.

6 Descartes made the point explicitly in one of his very first writings. See his *Regulae ad directionem ingenii* VIII (*Œuvres*, ed. by Adam and Tannery, X, 395): "*Nihil prius cognosci posse quam intellectum, quia ab hoc caeterum omnium cognitio dependeat, et non contra*" ("Nothing can be known prior to the intellect, since on it depends the knowledge of everything else, and not vice versa").

epistemological questions possessed no special priority over ethical and metaphysical inquiries. Though the primacy of epistemology has sometimes been said to disappear with the "linguistic turn" in the twentieth century,[7] the situation has not, I believe, basically changed. Not only is it unclear how the meanings of our words can be explained independently of our factual beliefs. The notion that ideally it is possible to get clear about how our language functions apart from some prior view about the way the world is draws on the very same idea that lies at the basis of the primacy of epistemology: it continues to assume that, because we have an intimate acquaintance with the workings of our own mind, we are able to determine in advance, prior to dealing with the world itself, the conditions under which we can, collectively if not individually, make sense of it.

I will not pursue this last theme further. I have done so elsewhere.[8] What should be clear is that the Cartesian revolution in philosophy was profound and pervasive. It goes deeper than the foundationalism and the demand for an exorbitant type of certainty that are usually cited, and its influence is far harder to throw off than commonly supposed. At bottom, it consists in the idea of the mind's essential self-transparency and in the consequences that appear to follow from it. The one that forms the object of this chapter is the conception of self-knowledge that continues to dominate much of philosophical thinking today. It holds that we have an immediate and infallible access – a "privileged" access, as it is often termed – to the contents of our own minds.

Now, I do not think there really exists any self-knowledge of this kind. The conception in question arises from a misunderstanding of the nature of the intimate relation that we do bear to ourselves. Thus, one aim of this chapter is to explain what sort of beings we really are in this regard. What I will be laying out can in fact be considered "a metaphysics of the self." For it will show how this essential relation we have to ourselves involves a relation to a normative order of reasons that, as I have been arguing throughout this book against the naturalist metaphysics also so prevalent today, forms part of the structure of reality as a whole. But there is more. As I indicated at the beginning, different views of self-knowledge are possible. So a further aim is to suggest – contrary to what I am calling the Cartesian conception, but in accord with the lessons of everyday

[7] See, for instance, Michael Dummett, *Origins of Analytical Philosophy* (Cambridge, MA: Harvard University Press, 1996), 127f, 184.

[8] See "Das philosophische Interesse an Selbsterkenntnis," in Oliver Koch (ed.), *Subjekt und Person. Beiträge zu einem Schlüsselthema der klassischen deutschen Philosophie* (Hamburg: Meiner-Verlag, 2019), 23–39.

experience – that the self-knowledge that truly matters is considerably difficult to achieve.[9] Ultimately, in fact, the present chapter may be regarded as presenting an argument, based on a better account of what being a self consists in, for why we should return to something akin to Plato's ethics-centered idea of self-knowledge. That I have overall a complex attitude toward Descartes' thought should thus be clear. In the preceding chapter, his view of the relation between reason and freedom served as a model for my own approach. Yet here my objective is to show why we need to get beyond what I call the Cartesian tradition in our thinking about the self and self-knowledge.

Before proceeding, two clarifications are necessary about my use of the word "the self." First, I believe that what I am calling the self is what other philosophers have had more or less clearly in view when talking about "the subject" or, in the German-speaking world, "the I" (*das Ich*). However, I much prefer the term of "the self" since the reflexive pronoun makes plain that it is a matter of a fundamental relation we bear to ourselves, one that makes each of us a self. A further, incidental reason to prefer the term is that it forms part of ordinary usage as the other two terms certainly do not. Secondly, it should also be apparent that if I speak of each of us as being a self, I am not referring to some entity or mental substance distinct from the human being each of us is. (Talk of our being a "subject" or an "I" can easily create that impression.) Being a self is instead a property of the publicly identifiable human being, a property consisting in their having a fundamental relation to themselves. What I believe the nature of this essential self-relation to be will become clear in Sections 8.2 and 8.3.

8.2 First and Third Person

Let us look then more closely at the Cartesian conception of self-knowledge. Central to it is the idea that we have two distinct ways of acquiring knowledge of our own beliefs, desires, and other mental states. First, we can, if we like, pursue such knowledge in the same way we acquire knowledge of other people's thoughts and feelings, beliefs and desires, namely by drawing inferences from what they do, including from what they may say (sincerely or not) about what they think and feel. This

[9] This aim is much like that of Quassim Cassam in his *Self-Knowledge for Humans* (Oxford: Oxford University Press, 2014), though our ways of pursuing it are in many respects different.

is self-knowledge based on taking up toward ourselves the same sort of *third-person perspective* to which we are condemned when seeking knowledge of other people. Just as – so this conception assumes – we cannot get into their minds so as to be there, as it were, in the way in which they are already and essentially there, but must observe them from the outside and draw conclusions from their behavior (in the broad sense indicated), so we can decide to regard ourselves too from the outside, as though we were simply one more person among others, describable in third-person terms, and infer what it is we believe and want from our observations of what we do and say. Self-knowledge acquired in this fashion is no different in kind from our knowledge of the minds of others and possesses therefore no special sort of certainty.

But, so the view goes, we have another route to knowledge of our own minds that is more natural, more immediate, and endowed with far greater certainty. This is self-knowledge from the *first-person perspective*, which we acquire not by observing ourselves from the outside, but instead by looking inward, discovering by reflection what we believe and desire in virtue of an intimate, pre-reflective acquaintance with our own mental life that we alone enjoy, though everyone has a similar acquaintance with their own. Self-knowledge of this kind, it is claimed, possesses a certainty to which knowledge acquired from the third-person perspective, either of others or of ourselves, cannot aspire. This is held to be so in two respects. For although when we reflect and say, for instance, "I believe it is going to rain", we can certainly have gotten it wrong about what the weather will be like (the belief itself may be false), we cannot, it seems, be making any mistake either about who it is to whom we are attributing the belief or about the fact that this is what we believe. Both sorts of error – misidentification and misattribution – are always possible in the case of our claims about what other people believe or desire. Not so, however, in our own case, at least when we rely upon first-person reflection. Even if there is more to our mental life than that of which we are reflectively aware, what we do perceive, when we look within our own minds, we cannot but perceive correctly.

As I have said, I do not think there really exists self-knowledge of this first-person sort. The questionable metaphor of "inner" and "outer," the idea that reflecting about our thinking as opposed to thinking about the world itself consists in directing our attention toward what is going on "inside" our mind and not toward an "external" world that lies outside, has often seemed indispensable in articulating this view. That by itself is grounds for skepticism, though as we shall see (Section 8.4), the metaphor can be rejected and the view still maintained.

However, it is for systematic reasons that the notion of first-person self-knowledge seems to me a mistake. All the knowledge we can have of our own minds is knowledge acquired from the same third-person perspective from which we acquire knowledge of other people's beliefs, feelings, and desires. True, when we straightaway say, without observing ourselves and drawing inferences, that we believe or desire, think or feel something, it seldom makes sense for others to challenge what we say. Yet the special authority, the "first-person authority," that such statements possess and that makes them unchallengeable is not an epistemic certainty, for they are not expressions of self-knowledge: they do not aim to describe or report pre-existing facts. They have instead the character of *avowals*. They serve to express our feelings, beliefs, or desires. In particular, they express the commitment to think and act in accord with the implications of the avowed feeling, the presumed truth of the proposition believed, or the perceived value of the object desired. When I declare, "I hope that he will come soon," I am not describing my hope, but rather expressing it, and in the form of an utterance that announces my intention to think and act accordingly. Utterances of this sort cannot be challenged as false, since, strictly speaking, they are neither true nor false. They are declarations of intent, and if they can be questioned, then on the score that they are insincere and that we are not really committing ourselves to think and act as they entail.

Such avowals do attest to an intimate relation we have to ourselves as thinking and acting beings that we can have to no one else and no one else can have to us. But this constitutive self-relation does not consist, as the Cartesian picture holds, in our being intimately acquainted with the contents of our own minds, a pre-reflective acquaintance with ourselves that gives our reflective claims about what we believe, feel, and desire a certainty our claims about other people's minds cannot possess. The way in which we are intimately related to ourselves has to do with a theme I have pursued throughout this book. We alone, no one else in our place, can commit ourselves to think and act in one way or another, doing so by guiding ourselves by what we regard as relevant reasons. It is this practical, not cognitive, way of relating to ourselves – *guiding ourselves by reasons* – that makes each of us a self or subject. In our avowals, in which we declare what we feel, believe, or desire, this essential relation to ourselves comes then to reflective expression. The idea of the mind's inherent self-transparency is thus to be rejected.

Such is the account of subjectivity, of what it is to be a self, that I have presented in earlier writings.[10] I gave an initial account of it toward the end of Chapter 7 (Section 7.7). Here I want to develop the critique of the idea of first-person self-knowledge that it entails. To begin, I shall review the basic, third-person way in which we come to know what other people believe, desire, and feel. This sketch will serve as the starting point for pursuing the question whether knowledge of our own minds can ever be acquired in an essentially different way.

8.3 Understanding Others

We determine what other people think by interpreting their behavior, including what they say, and this consists in attributing to them beliefs, desires, and other mental states that make their behavior intelligible, that would have shown them, in other words, a reason to act as they did. Thus, one (but certainly not the only) basis we can have for attributing people beliefs is their simply saying they believe certain things, since ordinarily their having such beliefs makes sense of these statements: it forms part of the reason why they have said what they did. The exceptions are cases in which other parts of their behavior, which we interpret by the same method, lead us to think that their reason for saying what they did must be quite different and that these statements were in fact confused or insincere.

That there should be this inherent connection between interpretation and rationalization becomes clear when we consider the nature of these mental states themselves.[11] A belief, for instance, is not some sort of mental event but rather a disposition, and it is more than simply a disposition to assent to the truth of what is believed, for we would not be said to believe something if we assented to its truth but otherwise conducted ourselves in complete indifference to its implications. To

[10] See *Les Pratiques du moi* (Paris: PUF, 2004) (English translation: *Practices of the Self* [Chicago: University of Chicago Press, 2010]), *Vernunft und Subjektivität* (Berlin: Suhrkamp, 2012), and *Das Selbst in seinem Verhältnis zu sich und zu anderen* (Frankfurt: Klostermann, 2017).

[11] In what follows I focus on beliefs and desires for illustrative purposes, since they exemplify clearly the two "directions of fit" by which mental states may relate to the world, aiming either to fit the world (as with beliefs) or to have the world fit them (as with desires). I do not mean to imply allegiance to various theories constructed on the basis of this contrast between belief and desire, such as the idea that beliefs by themselves are unable to motivate or the idea that normative judgments, since they are action-guiding, cannot be understood to be expressive of beliefs. I reject both those views. For details, see *The Autonomy of Morality* (Cambridge: Cambridge University Press, 2008), chapter 5, §8, as well as Chapter 1, Section 1.3 and Chapter 6, Section 6.3, in the present book.

believe that *p* is to be disposed to think and act in accord with the presumed truth of *p*. Or more exactly, as I indicated in Chapter 7 (Section 7.7) as well as in this one when talking about avowals (Section 8.2), it is to be disposed to think and act in this way through being committed to doing so, to heeding the reasons for thought and action which the belief that *p*, in conjunction with other relevant elements of our perspective, points us to. Naturally we may sometimes end up thinking and acting in ways that go contrary to the implications of our beliefs. But when we discover it, we normally feel that we have failed to do what we ought to have done, what we had reason to do.

This, then, is why attributing a belief to someone depends on determining whether her having that belief would have shown her a reason, by her own lights, to act as she was observed to do. However, beliefs do not only point us to reasons. They arise themselves from our heeding reasons. Just as we cannot come to believe something unless we regard it as true, so we cannot regard it as true unless we take there to be reasons to think it is true. (Just try to believe that the number of stars is even rather than odd!) Thus we typically attribute a belief to someone, not simply if his having that belief would make rational sense of his behavior, but only if, given what we can observe of his behavior and what we already know about his situation and perspective, we can infer as well that he could have thought he had reason to hold such a belief. In short, people have the beliefs they do and so we can attribute to them particular beliefs, because they are fundamentally beings who in their thought and action guide themselves by what they regard as reasons. Only thus can they acquire beliefs as well as act on them as they do.

A similar story applies to desires. In both their formation and their function, they too involve guiding ourselves by reasons. A desire is not a mere impulse that happens to us, though that is what some thinkers appear to suggest. We come to desire something by perceiving it to be in some respect desirable or good, which means that we see, or think we see, some reason to want it. True, desiring something is not the same as perceiving that it is good; it involves, as the perception alone does not, feeling impelled to pursue its object. Yet this feeling consists in our being driven to attend to what appears to make the thing attractive, even if at the same time we may judge that it is not really or in all respects good. Moreover, every desire, whether momentary or habitual, disposes us, all else being equal (which of course is often not so), to think and act in accord with the presumed value of its object, that is, to heed the reasons for thought and action it points us to. Desires too embody commitments in this sense, though our better judgment may always overrule them. Consequently, the desires we attribute to people are those that, given what we have observed of their behavior and situation, they could have seen, or thought they saw, reason to conceive and that they could regard as giving them reason to act as in fact they do. As in the case of belief, what they say they desire is an important piece of this behavioral evidence. Generally, the fact that they say they desire X is a good basis for supposing they have this desire, though in rare instances we may conclude, given other aspects of their behavior, that they are confused or really desire something quite different.

The situation is the same with all other mental events or states, such as emotions and feelings, that similarly have some "intentional" content or object-directedness, since in purporting to relate appropriately to their objects they take shape in response to reasons and function in turn by indicating reasons for what we should then do and think. We say of someone that she is in love when her having this emotion would give her reason to act as she does (including saying that she is in love) and the emotion is one that by her lights she could have reason to feel in her circumstances. Attributing to others mental qualities that are not similarly intentional in character – sensations such as an experience (a *quale*) of redness or a pain in the leg – is thus somewhat different. As a rule, we think that someone is in pain, not because the pain would have given her reason to show agony in her face, but simply because her being in pain is the best causal explanation of her facial expression. If, however, we conclude that she is in pain because she says that she is, then we are assuming that her saying this is something she does for reasons, among them the fact that she is actually in pain.[12]

Now the same third-person procedure for knowing someone else's mind by determining what would make rational sense of his behavior is one we can also deploy in seeking to know our own state of mind. If we are puzzled about whether we really believe or desire a certain thing, we can, for instance, consider whether our believing or desiring it would show us a reason to act or talk as we do as well as whether such a belief or desire is one our situation could have given us reason to acquire. In such cases, our conclusions have no more authority, no essentially greater chance of being correct, than the conclusions at which other people may arrive if they are trying to figure out what we believe or desire. Certainly we are likely to have more evidence at our disposal. At the same time, we may well lack the

[12] I have discussed further this difference between intentional and non-intentional mental phenomena in *Dernières nouvelles du moi* (with V. Descombes; Paris: PUF, 2009), 64–68.

objectivity that others are able to exercise and may thus substitute our notions of what we would like to think we believe or desire for the conclusions the evidence actually warrants. That other people, not just friends but even strangers, may prove more insightful than we about what we really think is an all too familiar fact.

Thus, we can say so far, by way of summary, that knowledge from a third-person perspective of another's or of our own mind is knowledge acquired by observation and inference. It consists in making the person's behavior intelligible from their point of view on the basis of evidence that is in principle available to anyone.

Now it will surely be objected that examining ourselves in the same external way we ascertain what others think is not how we usually acquire knowledge of our own minds. Instead of seeking a rationalizing explanation of our observed behavior, we reflect. We ask ourselves whether we believe or desire a certain thing or what our belief is about a certain matter, and the very pondering of these questions is the means by which we arrive at an answer. Settling such questions by reflection instead of by observation and inference is something we alone can do, as the person whose beliefs and desires they are. And that is because, so the objection continues, we are intimately acquainted with them, so that our self-attributions in these cases possess a certainty, a special authority, that third-person self-knowledge can never attain. It would be odd, after all, if someone were asked what it is he thinks about some matter and he replied, "Why ask me? Your opinion is as good as mine." A person who habitually determined what he was thinking simply by observing his behavior and drawing inferences from his observations would seem to be suffering from a pathological condition. Indeed, how could such a person function at all, for how could he know that the person about whom he was gathering all this information was he himself? Only a fundamental self-transparency, only an intimate acquaintance with the beliefs and desires we happen to have, enables us, so it will be argued (see Section 8.1), to think and act on their basis. The way in which reflection forms our primary means of acquiring knowledge of our own thinking appears therefore to vindicate the Cartesian conception of self-knowledge. Contrary to what I have claimed, we seem to have, and centrally so, a first-person immediate access to the contents of our own minds.

It is necessary therefore to examine more closely what such a process of reflection really involves. Before doing so, however, I want to make a parenthetical remark about the underappreciated importance of the third-person relation we can take to ourselves. Philosophers commonly consider first-person thoughts about ourselves as the interesting and crucial phenomenon to be analyzed. In opposition to the view they then often espouse, I have been maintaining that, whatever its other attributes, the first-person perspective is not a vehicle of self-knowledge. But quite apart from this disagreement, I also believe that our capacity to take up a third-person attitude toward ourselves is in itself a remarkable phenomenon. This was a theme of the first two chapters of this book.[13] We are not the only beings that can respond to reasons. The higher animals too have beliefs and desires, and they too can reflect and deliberate (within certain limits) about what they should do in a given situation. But no dog certainly and no ape, I believe, can look at itself from the outside and conceive of itself as simply one dog or ape among others, but always regards everything in the world from its own first-person point of view, or at most, when imitating the behavior of another dog or ape, from the point of view of another that is in some way important to it, or from a shared first-person viewpoint when acting as a member of a group. Our capacity for thinking of ourselves from a completely third-person perspective – that is, impersonally, as but one human being among many – is in fact what enables us, unlike them, to be moral beings. Since, however, I have examined that point at some length in Chapter 1, I leave it aside here and continue with the analysis of reflection as a means of self-knowledge.

8.4 Knowing Our Own Mind

We need, in fact, to clarify just what is understood by the term. Sometimes what is meant by determining by reflection what we believe or desire is consulting our memory, recalling to mind thoughts and actions we suppose may embody mental states of the sort that is in question. Yet reflection in this sense is but another third-person vehicle of self-knowledge. For not only are we then inferring what we now believe or desire from what we believed or desired in the past. We must also interpret the thoughts and actions we recall, if we are to regard them as expressing certain beliefs or desires. For we cannot remember our beliefs or desires as such, but only the past behavior – our having said this or felt or done that – which we consider to be indicative of them. In these cases we are therefore engaged in the third-person enterprise of drawing conclusions from evidence, and in the two respects mentioned. In principle, another

[13] Chapter 1, Section 1.1, and Chapter 2, Section 2.3.

person could proceed identically, employing the same evidence (she cannot remember, of course, our silent thoughts, but we can recount them to her), making similar inferences, and arriving at no less authoritative statements about the contents of our mind than we do. It may not be that often that we ascertain our state of mind by observing our present behavior. But frequently we do rely on this second third-person method, based in memory rather than observation, when we are puzzled about what it is we believe or desire in some regard or we want to make sure we have not made a mistake on that score.

Similar remarks apply to another way we are said to acquire self-knowledge by reflection, commonly called "introspection." Often we take our present thoughts and feelings as indicating what we believe or desire. Yet once again, this is a third-person process involving inference from evidence. We cannot behold our beliefs and desires themselves, but only mental episodes that we interpret as expressing them. The fact that I find myself repeating to myself today will be a better day or imagining how good a steak would taste is certainly good grounds for thinking that I believe today will be better or that I would like to have some steak. But other interpretations are possible. Moreover, although the thoughts and feelings on which I rely are in the first instance available to me alone, I could voice them out loud, and then anyone else could draw the same conclusions as I do and might even see reason to correct my understanding: someone might object that I don't really believe today will be better, but only keep thinking this in order to convince myself it will not be any worse.

If therefore reflection is supposed to be a first-person means of self-knowledge, it has to be a very different sort of activity. It has to consist in determining that we believe or desire a certain thing without basing ourselves on evidence drawn from our past or present actions, talk, or thoughts and feelings. Now our most common way of settling whether we believe or desire a thing does not appear to resort to such evidence. And though it certainly counts as a form of reflection, it does not in fact involve looking inward at all, contrary to the usual way of conceiving the possibility of first-person self-knowledge. If we are asked or ask ourselves whether we believe Mary is a thief or whether we want to eat some blueberries, we normally direct our attention not toward ourselves but toward Mary or blueberries and answer the question by thinking about whether Mary is in fact a thief or whether some blueberries would taste good. As Gareth Evans observed in a now famous passage, we settle the matter not by looking inward, inspecting our minds by way of some mysterious "inner sense," but instead by looking outward at the very things the belief or desire in question would be about.[14] We do then consider evidence, but it does not have to do with ourselves and our own state of mind. It is evidence bearing on whether the belief is true or whether the object is good. When we seek to ascertain whether another person believes that Mary is a thief or wants to eat some blueberries, our focus is very much on that other person's mind (and behavior), and we can generally answer the question without concerning ourselves with Mary or blueberries themselves. But not so in our own case. So while this form of reflection is first-person in nature – only questions about our own mind can we settle in this fashion – it also displays, in Richard Moran's helpful phrase, a striking kind of "transparency": in answering the question about what we think we look, as it were, right through our own thinking and at the world itself.[15]

Clearly, this transparency is very different from the idea of transparency that lies at the basis of the Cartesian conception of self-knowledge. That idea was that the mind is fundamentally transparent to itself, allowing us to have an immediate knowledge of the contents of our own mental life. Here the transparency has to do with the way that reflecting on what it is we believe or desire operates, not by doubling the mind back upon itself, but rather by making it transparent to the world. It will turn out, in fact, that transparency in this sense points to what is essentially wrong in the Cartesian model of self-knowledge.

For why is it that this kind of reflection combines the two properties of first-personness and transparency? Moran is absolutely right, I believe, to say that it is because we have effectively taken up the attitude of *deliberating*, in a practical mode, about what to believe or desire. For in general we deliberate about what we take to be up to us, and we do so by considering the matter itself, in order to figure out what reasons there are to handle it one way rather than another. When, therefore, we determine whether we believe or desire something by focusing, not on our own minds, but on the object of such a belief or desire, we are in fact engaged in making up our minds about whether to believe or desire the thing. As a result, so Moran also rightly claims, the conclusions at which we thus arrive, "I believe that Mary is a thief" or "I would like to eat some blueberries," have the character of *avowals*: in them we are committing ourselves, either for the first time or now explicitly unlike before, to

[14] Gareth Evans, *The Varieties of Reference* (Oxford: Oxford University Press, 1982), 225ff.

[15] Richard Moran, *Authority and Estrangement* (Princeton: Princeton University Press, 2001), 101.

believing or desiring the thing in question.[16] It is because such conclusions do not report the discovery of some fact but instead express an intent that they enjoy that first-person authority which makes them normally immune to challenges concerning their truth. So I have already argued (Section 8.2) and indeed, in all these respects, Moran's views coincide with my own.[17]

True, not every avowal is the avowal of a commitment, as Dorit Bar-On has observed in working out a similar theory of first-person authority in terms of avowals.[18] The exceptions are cases in which what we avow are non-intentional states of mind, as when we say, "I feel pain" or "I am hungry." Yet this is not surprising, since sensations of this sort, as I also indicated earlier (Section 8.3), do not involve responsiveness to reasons or thus embody commitments.

I now come, however, to the point where, despite all this common ground, I differ quite importantly from Evans, Moran, and Bar-On. They continue to hold on to an essential element of the Cartesian edifice, namely the idea that reflection in this first-person mode constitutes a form of self-knowledge. I, on the other hand, believe that avowals, whether they express intentional, object-directed states of mind or instead sensations, do not represent instances of self-knowledge and that all our ways of knowing our own minds are therefore third-person in character.

My reason for denying that avowals represent instances of self-knowledge is, so it seems to me, simple and straightforward. In general, insofar as we are avowing something, our attitude is not that of aiming to describe correctly the state of mind we are in. We are instead involved in expressing a state of mind. We have not become spectators of ourselves, thus introducing within our minds a division between subject and object – in this case, between ourselves as knowers and ourselves as known – of the sort that is characteristic of all knowledge or attempts at knowledge. Instead, we are at one with ourselves inasmuch as the act of avowing consists in simply giving voice to what is avowed.

For this reason, avowals cannot constitute episodes in which we acquire knowledge of our own minds. Yet Evans, for instance, maintains that when we ask ourselves whether we believe a certain thing and, focusing our attention on the subject matter, declare that we indeed believe it, we are precisely thereby coming to know that we have this belief.[19] How can that

[16] Moran, *Authority and Estrangement*, 60ff, 83ff.

[17] See especially chapter 5 of my *Pratiques du moi* (*Practices of the Self*).

[18] Dorit Bar-On, *Speaking My Mind* (Oxford: Oxford University Press, 2004), 137.

[19] Evans, 225: "If a judging subject applies this procedure, then necessarily he will gain knowledge of one of his own mental states."

be? Evans offers no justification of the idea, but he does assume that in such cases we are *ascribing* the belief to ourselves, and this assumption is probably the key. For Bar-On also assumes it, builds the assumption into her account of avowals, and concludes on this basis that avowals embody a special kind of first-person self-knowledge. Here is her reasoning. Avowals, she holds, "self-ascribe the very conditions they express."[20] Insofar as they express states of mind, they do not report or make knowledge-claims, and thus the authority they clearly possess and that makes them immune to challenges concerning their truth is to this extent expressive rather than epistemic in nature. Yet they also ascribe these states of mind to the person making them, and in this regard they typically – the exceptions being such marginal phenomena as insincerity, self-deception, and wishful thinking – count as being true and constitute therefore a "privileged" kind of knowledge, the privilege consisting not in any special epistemic authority, but rather in the fact that the self-knowledge comes from that person avowing her state of mind, which of course only she can do.

Yet why suppose, as Bar-On does, that in acts of avowing we do two things at once, express a state of mind and self-ascribe it? We cannot do the two things in one and the same act, since only if we do the first can we *then* do the second. We do not, after all, avow the mental state as self-ascribed, but rather ascribe it to ourselves as one we have expressed or avowed. Moreover, must we in fact ascribe it to ourselves? Certainly we can do so if we want, as others can too, since it is a general truth (the exceptions were noted above) that someone who avows a mental state is in that state. So in particular someone who avows that she believes something does as a rule commit herself to thinking and acting in the appropriate way and thereby acquires that very belief. Yet we need not in fact ascribe to ourselves some belief when we avow it. We may simply avow it and no more. (We may not even be aware that we have avowed it, as when I keep muttering, "I love her," without realizing I am doing so.) The belief is certainly self-ascribable, but only in actually self-ascribing it do we acquire any self-knowledge. Bar-On regards it as a merit of her account of avowals that it preserves "semantic continuity": avowals appear to function logically like ordinary statements of fact, as when I avow, "I believe Mary is a thief," and you regard that statement as equivalent to "Larmore believes Mary is a thief," or when I declare more broadly, "I believe Mary is a thief and you do as well, so that makes two of us." However, such cases can be

[20] Bar-On, 23. Succinct statements of the various elements of her theory can be found on the following pages: 10–15, 231–232, 263–264, and 336.

readily explained by everyone knowing the general truth I mentioned: avowals are normally conclusive evidence for the existence of the mental states they avow.

Now for just this reason, the self-knowledge we may acquire by way of our avowals is third-person in nature. Only we, it is true, no one else in our place, can avow our state of mind. Our avowal is itself first-person. Yet we come thereby to know that such is our state of mind in the same way that another person would come to know it: we base ourselves on our avowal, regarding it as indicative of our believing, desiring, or feeling what we have avowed. Naturally, our avowals may sometimes be silent. We may not speak them out loud, and in that case no one else will be able to form on their basis a view about our state of mind. But that does not change the fact that we ourselves, if we then think of ourselves as believing, desiring, or feeling a certain thing, have acquired this self-knowledge by inferring it in a third-person way from our unvoiced avowal. For if we had voiced our avowal to ourselves and someone had happened to overhear it, that person could have come to know our state of mind in the same way as we in fact did.

In general, it is imperative to distinguish clearly between an avowal and the self-ascription that may be founded on it. When we are unsure, for instance, whether we do indeed believe something and, turning our mind in the way Evans describes to the subject matter of that possible belief, we then say, aloud or to ourselves, "yes, I do believe Mary is a thief," we consider of course that we have answered the question. But we have done so only because we regard the commitment that avowal expresses as the endorsement of a belief we have had all along. For our aim in this case was not to make up our minds for the first time about Mary, but rather to ascertain what we in fact believe about Mary's honesty, and the self-knowledge we have acquired is therefore knowledge we have inferred from the avowal, in a way that anyone else could do as well. It is not knowledge embodied in the avowal itself. Here, then, is yet another third-person route to knowledge of our own minds, based not on observation, memory, or introspection, but on avowals, and one that is easily mistaken for a first-person mode of self-knowledge since avowals themselves are first-person in character. This mistake lies at the very heart of the Cartesian conception of self-knowledge.

8.5 Overcoming the Cartesian Tradition

As I noted, Richard Moran too, despite explaining much as I do the special authority of avowals in terms of their practical nature as expressing commitments, holds on, unlike me, to a defining element of the Cartesian conception. It is the idea that this form of reflection constitutes a privileged, first-person way of knowing our own minds. Numerous passages in his book develop, as he says, "a picture of self-knowledge as involving the ability to avow one's state of mind and not merely to attribute it to oneself.".[21] The subtitle of his book is precisely "An Essay on Self-Knowledge." Why does he take this tack? Why does he adopt this hybrid view instead of the uncompromising – in his judgment, no doubt far too radical – position that I have taken? One reason, suggested by the sentence I just quoted, may be that in company with Evans and Bar-On he runs together avowing a belief with attributing that belief to oneself. That would be a mistake. For though the latter does involve a claim to self-knowledge, it is not identical with the act of avowing, but rather forms a second act performed on its basis. There is, I have argued, an essential difference in attitude between avowing a belief – in which (as Moran agrees) one takes up the practical stance of committing oneself to what such a belief entails – and holding it to be true that one has that belief, in which one has adopted a basically theoretical stance toward oneself.

I suspect, however, that Moran would resist the idea that self-knowledge derives from a "theoretical" attitude toward oneself. Certainly Elizabeth Anscombe, to whom he acknowledges a philosophical debt, rejected any such equation when she attacked modern philosophy's "incorrigibly contemplative conception of knowledge" and argued that the agent's knowledge of the intention with which she acts – that is, of what she is doing – is a case of "practical knowledge," whose hallmarks are that it is immediate, not based on observation and inference, and that "it is the cause of what it understands."[22] Anscombe's account is cited by Moran as a model for his own view of avowals according to which they embody a practical, not theoretical or spectator-based, knowledge of the beliefs and desires they

[21] Moran, 100. See also in particular the following pages: xxix, xxxi, 3, 90, and 134.

[22] G.E.M. Anscombe, *Intention* (Oxford: Blackwell, 1957/1963), §§ 28–32, 48. Anscombe (§48) claims to be quoting from Aquinas (*Summa theologiae* Ia IIae, Q3, art. 5, obj. 1) the striking phrase that practical knowledge is "the cause of what it understands." This is an inaccurate rendering of the Latin – ". . . *intellectum practicum, qui est causa rerum intellectarum*" – which means simply ". . . the practical intellect, which is the cause of things understood." For Aquinas, the practical intellect is indeed an organ of knowledge, telling us what we should do. But when he goes on in this article to mention the relation of the practical intellect to what it knows (*ad suum cognitum*), he plainly has the following in mind: though the practical intellect puts into practice what it knows – which action is to be done – by moving us to so act, it thereby causes, not what it knows, but rather the result or realization of this knowledge, namely the action done, which conforms to this knowledge. It is, as Aquinas says, the cause of things it *has* understood (*causa rerum intellectarum*). This is a far more banal position than the one Anscombe is defending.

express, a knowledge that, as he insists throughout his book, does not rest on observation or inference.[23] So the purported insights of Anscombe's theory of intentional action are probably another reason he has for considering avowals to be both practical and cognitive.

I do not have a similarly positive opinion of Anscombe's views. Only a magical kind of knowledge could bring its object into being by the very act of knowing it, could be "the cause of what it understands." Knowledge involves getting it right. The idea of rightness disappears if the object of knowledge is supposedly produced by the knowledge itself, as opposed to being what it is independently of our knowing it. When someone acts, it is true, she usually knows far better than anyone else the intention with which she is acting – that is, what exactly she is doing – and this superior knowledge is rooted in her being herself the agent. But the superiority does not lie in her having a special kind of knowledge of her intention. It comes instead from the fact that as the agent she alone can avow, at any point in her action and to herself or to others, her intention in acting as she does, and typically she does so to herself from time to time if her action is somewhat complicated, involving a sequence of steps. As with avowals of belief and desire, she then rehearses to herself the point of her action by attending, not to what is going on in her mind, but to the phenomena in the world that are the object of this attitude, in this case the situation to which she is responding and the changes she is engaged in bringing about in it. However, she can also attend to these avowals themselves and on their basis say to herself or others, in a way now meant to embody a bit of self-knowledge, that she has a certain intention. The knowledge she then has of her intention does not produce her intention, but she and only she can produce the conclusive sort of evidence, the avowals, that yields such knowledge. It makes sense, of course, to say that, even when she is not avowing to herself the intention with which she is acting, she "knows what she is doing." But all this phrase means is that her attention is focused on doing the action – that is, she is not distracted – and not that it is focused as well on the fact that she is doing it, which would indeed amount to an instance of self-knowledge.

I mentioned earlier (Section 8.3) that it would seem odd if someone were asked what it is she thinks about some matter or what she is doing and she replied, "Why ask me? Your opinion is as good as mine." Yet we

[23] Moran, 126 and, e.g., 10–11, respectively. See also his essay, "Anscombe on 'Practical Knowledge'," in J. Hyman and H. Steward (eds.), *Agency and Actions* (Cambridge: Cambridge University Press, 2004), 43–68.

can see now why such a case is not an embarrassment for the view that all our self-knowledge is third-person. For her statement would be odd, not because she has a first-person way of knowing her beliefs or intentions, but because she has the first-person capacity of avowing her present beliefs or intentions (by focusing her attention, for instance, on the matter at hand) and thereby giving herself what is as a rule the best sort of evidence for knowing what she believes or intends. Normally, the person herself is thus the ideal person to ask. Though sometimes we may be so puzzled as to what we believe or intend and so distrustful of what we might avow on the matter that we do reply in despair, "Your opinion is as good as mine."

I have been arguing that knowing our own mind in a third-person way is not so peripheral a phenomenon as often supposed. It does not occur only when we draw conclusions about our beliefs and desires from observing our behavior, which is certainly rather unusual. It also includes the quite common methods of determining what we believe and desire by recalling relevant thoughts and actions in the past, by exercising introspection, or by basing ourselves on what we may avow of our beliefs, desires, and intentions. These four seem to me the only modes of self-knowledge there are (in addition, of course, to relying on other people's opinions about us), and all of them are third-personal in the sense that anyone else could in principle employ them as well as we in determining what we believe or desire, even if the last kind involves relying on evidence we alone can provide. I see no convincing example of truly first-person self-knowledge, nor do I even understand what such a kind of self-knowledge could be like. For knowledge-claims in general, aiming as they do to get it right, are such that others must always be able in principle to confirm or dispute their correctness.[24] Whence the well-known truth, which some philosophers seem to have forgotten, that others often know us better than we ourselves.

At the same time, there is, as I said earlier (Section 8.2), a first-person relation we have to ourselves that is constitutive of the very beings we are. It is, however, a relation that characterizes us not as knowers but as doers, as beings who can and must commit ourselves. To be a self or subject is indeed to have a constitutive relation to ourselves. Yet this self-relation does not, as much of modern philosophy in the wake of Descartes has

[24] Consider in this regard Gilbert Ryle's remark that "to know" is an "achievement word," and that it makes no sense to speak of achievement or success where there is no possibility of failure. See Ryle, *The Concept of Mind* (London: Hutchinson, 1949), 152–153.

held,[25] consist in an intimate acquaintance with ourselves and our own thinking. After all, the idea that our basic relation to ourselves is one of self-knowledge leads either to paradox if it is conceived as a relation of reflection – for the self must already exist if it is to be the object of reflection – or to mystery if it is defined as a pre-reflective acquaintance with ourselves in which there is therefore no distinction between subject and object. The latter seems incomprehensible. Yet just this sort of obscurity must attend any attempt to make real sense of the essential self-transparency the Cartesian conception attributes to the self.

However, the relation to ourselves that makes each of us a self is not a relation of knowledge at all. It is instead, as I have explained (Section 8.3), the relation of guiding ourselves by reasons. Since reasons in turn consist in the relevance of facts in the world to our possibilities of thought and action, the relation to ourselves that is constitutive of our subjectivity cannot (as the Cartesian idea of an intimate self-awareness easily suggests) exist independently of our dealings with the world, much less (as that idea was originally intended) ground all our knowledge of what lies outside our mind. On the contrary, this relation to ourselves is inseparable from our relation to the world. The Cartesian conception has encouraged the notion of the self as a realm of interiority. In reality, being a self is necessarily, as Heidegger could have put it, being-in-the-world.[26]

Thus, although I believe there is no such thing as first-person self-knowledge, I also believe it would be a case of pathological self-estrangement if we related to ourselves only in the third person, as spectators of what we think and do. Absolutely speaking, this is in fact impossible, for we would then cease to be selves altogether. However, the constitutive relation that we have to ourselves and that no one else can assume in our place does not, I repeat, consist in our having a special kind of awareness of our mental states and actions (any knowledge we may have of them others may similarly have), but rather in their embodying commitments that we adopt in guiding ourselves by reasons. Moreover, though

[25] It is interesting to note that Locke is something of an exception in this regard. In his *Essay concerning Human Understanding*, he began by endorsing what is in effect a Cartesian conception of the self: "When we see, hear, smell, taste, feel, meditate, or will any thing, we know that we do so ... And by this every one is to himself, that which he calls *self*." However, he shifted a few pages later to a definition far closer to the practical conception I have proposed: "*Self* is that conscious thinking thing ... which is sensible, or conscious of Pleasure and Pain, capable of Happiness or Misery, and so is concerned for it *self*, as far as that consciousness extends" (II.xxvii. 9 and 17).

[26] The Heidegger of *Being and Time* spurned the terms of "self" and "subject." But as I indicated in note 40 of the preceding chapter, his concept of Dasein is in reality a concept of the self, and a very promising one at that.

one reflective capacity that distinguishes us from the other animals is our ability to take up a third-person perspective on ourselves (see Section 8.3), another such capacity, which is first-person in character, is our ability, also no doubt based in the possession of language, to undertake such commitments reflectively. This is exactly what we are doing when we avow some belief, desire, or intention. For then we are explicitly taking on a certain commitment or explicitly endorsing a commitment we already have in an exercise of what can be called – since it is not an act of self-knowledge – practical rather than cognitive reflection.[27] Avowals thus give emphatic expression to the practical relation to ourselves in virtue of which we are selves at all.

All our self-knowledge is therefore based on evidence and inference, just like the rest of our knowledge. None of it has the special immediacy and authority that so many since Descartes have imagined it possesses. For our minds are not such as to be essentially self-transparent. As with all conceptions of self-knowledge, the Cartesian conception has been fueled and shaped by an underlying philosophical concern. In this case, it has been a concern for what makes us selves responsible for our thought and action: we are able to think and act on the basis of our beliefs and desires only because, it has been assumed, we are intimately acquainted with them. But this is a misunderstanding of the nature of the essential relation in which we stand to ourselves, a mistake that has led to everything else that conception gets wrong. The constitutive relation we have to ourselves is instead one of guiding ourselves by reasons. It forms part of the very nature of our beliefs and desires, whether or not we happen to become aware of them, whether or not they become objects of self-knowledge. They arise in virtue of being responsive to reasons, and they dispose us to think and act in accord with the reasons their presumed truth or the presumed value of their object points us to. It is, consequently, this self-relation of guiding ourselves by reasons that enables us to be responsible for what we think and do. For in heeding reasons, we commit ourselves, as we alone, no one else in our place, can do.

If we take these conclusions to heart, then Plato's conviction that self-knowledge is the most difficult kind of knowledge to achieve can come again to possess the centrality it once enjoyed. We will then recognize that the knowledge of ourselves that truly matters, that is crucial for the sort of

[27] Reflection as discussed in Chapter 1 was largely cognitive in character. For more on the difference between these two kinds of reflection, see *Les pratiques du moi* (*Practices of the Self*), chapter 3, §4, and chapter 5.

beings we are, has to do with the capacities and interests that enable us to live our lives well. For we are selves in virtue of guiding ourselves by reasons, and thus how we should think and act is necessarily a constant, all-pervasive concern. We exist only in and through the ways we go about figuring this out, with whatever degree of success. We cannot therefore avoid asking ourselves, if only implicitly or fragmentarily, what interests to pursue and what capacities to develop. This means, as Plato also saw, that the kind of knowledge of ourselves we must regard as indispensable is fundamentally ethical in character. It concerns how we should live. Such is the conception of self-knowledge we should embrace, if we are to really get beyond the Cartesian framework.

Index

For EU product safety concerns, contact us at Calle de José Abascal, 56–1°, 28003 Madrid, Spain or eugpsr@cambridge.org.

www.ingramcontent.com/pod-product-compliance
Ingram Content Group UK Ltd.
Pitfield, Milton Keynes, MK11 3LW, UK
UKHW020353140625
459647UK00020B/2453